ASK A MATCHMAKER

ASK A MATCHMAKER

MATCHMAKER MARIA'S NO-NONSENSE GUIDE TO FINDING LOVE

MARIA AVGITIDIS

ST. MARTIN'S
ESSENTIALS
NEW YORK

First published in the United States by St. Martin's Essentials, an imprint of St. Martin's Publishing Group

ASK A MATCHMAKER. Copyright © 2025 by Matchmaker Maria LLC. All rights reserved. Printed in the United States of America. For information, address St. Martin's Publishing Group, 120 Broadway, New York, NY 10271.

www.stmartins.com

The Library of Congress Cataloging-in-Publication Data is available upon request.

ISBN 978-1-250-34235-5 (trade paperback)
ISBN 978-1-250-34236-2 (ebook)

Our books may be purchased in bulk for promotional, educational, or business use. Please contact your local bookseller or the Macmillan Corporate and Premium Sales Department at 1-800-221-7945, extension 5442, or by email at MacmillanSpecialMarkets@macmillan.com.

First Edition: 2025

10 9 8 7 6 5 4 3 2 1

To my husband, George.
You are the best thing that has ever happened to me.

To my children, Yianni and Alexandra.
You are the greatest.

CONTENTS

INTRODUCTION

HOW DID I BECOME MATCHMAKER MARIA?

GROWING UP, I WAS TOLD stories about matchmaking. Some stories were about my *yiayia*—or, as non-Greeks would say, "grandmother"—and how she'd make animated faces when matching others. She had secret signals, like rubbing her elbow or stirring her coffee uncomfortably long, that would mean "Great," or "Absolutely not!" These stories that my mother told me always made me laugh. However, my favorite matchmaking stories were the ones that involved both the divine and the unmistakably human.

Each night, my mother would open up a book of Greek mythology given to her by her own mother, and I would learn about the Olympian Circle.[1] I was dazzled by the legends of the Greek gods and goddesses. Fantasies of heroes and mythical creatures, whose powers would mostly complement one another but many times come into conflict, would spin in my mind as I dozed off to sleep.

The stories I loved the most centered around the dichotomy of Zeus. On one hand, he was the mighty ruler of the gods, capable of swinging lightning bolts out of his fist. But on the other, he was someone with a very complicated love life.

I mean, this god really got around.

First we have his wife, Hera, the queen of the gods and the goddess of marriage and family. Their children were Ares, Hebe, Eileithyia, and Hephaestus. Then, Zeus fell in love with the titaness Leto. She bore the twin gods Apollo and Artemis. Then there was the mortal princess Semele, whose demise was orchestrated by the jealous Hera. Zeus still managed to save his unborn child with Semele, the god Dionysus.

Then there was Alcmene. Zeus disguised himself as Alcmene's husband, Amphitryon, to seduce her. Who does that?! Zeus. Zeus did that. This led to the birth of one of the greatest Greek heroes, Hercules. Then there's Io, Europa, and more babies and more women.

If you think that wasn't enough, he had more children with Danaë, Maia (who gave birth to the god Hermes), and Callisto.

Ah, yes, appropriate reading for a seven-year-old!

So we know Zeus was the original Greek Lover™. But what if I told you he was also the original matchmaker, too, scouring his Olympian Circle for matches?

His most famous setup, according to Homer's *Odyssey*,[2] was Aphrodite and Hephaestus, the god of blacksmiths and craftsmen, to prevent the other gods from fighting for her affection. Although this pair had contrasting personalities—she was obsessed with the finer things in life, and he was happiest sweating over a hot anvil—their union was presented as balanced. A worthy, stable match! Whatever one lacked, the other had. Aphrodite was known for her passion and allure, and Hephaestus was more reserved and hardworking. The lesson was that these elements together—beauty and grit—could go hand in hand.

And of course the matchmaking was generational, too!

One day, Eris, daughter of Zeus, was feeling snubbed because she hadn't been invited to a party. So she threw a golden apple into the soiree and said it should be given to the "fairest" of all the attendees. Three goddesses—Hera, Athena, and Aphrodite—claimed the apple. Unable to decide among themselves who deserved to be deemed the most beautiful of them all, they asked Zeus to make the ruling. Zeus, all-powerful as he was, knew there was no good answer, and that picking *anyone* would create discord. Instead, he appointed Paris, the prince of Troy, to decide. Aphrodite offered a bribe to Paris. If he chose her, she promised to grant him Helen, the most beautiful woman in the world. Now Helen was already married to Menelaus, the king of Sparta, but a deal is a deal, right? Paris abducted Helen, married her with Aphrodite's blessing, and took her to Troy. Menelaus was pissed. He gathered an army and they went to Troy to take Helen back, and this led to the most epic of wars in Greek mythology, the Trojan War.

Aphrodite was . . . the worst matchmaker ever. Imagine going to bed in the second grade reeling from the consequences of bad matchmaking.

So, as a child, I felt matchmaking in my bones. It was there, deep in my marrow, years later, when my guidance counselor asked, "What do you want to be when you grow up?" I might not have possessed the right vocabulary to explain my truth, but I knew it all along.

The aptitude tests I took as a kid knew it, too. The result I always got told me to become . . . a guidance counselor. You might be surprised to hear that, but it actually makes sense. At my core, I like sherpa-ing people through the most important decisions of their lives. A guidance counselor would show you a variety of pamphlets on potential universities and majors you could study. A matchmaker kind of does the same. They're just helping you pick a person instead of a course load. And it's way less dramatic than Zeus and Hera and Aphrodite and Paris.

Like Zeus, I have my own circle that represents community and a sense of belonging. And in all my social circles, I always get the same question: "You're a matchmaker? How did that happen?!" I've lived a lot of lives—from study-abroad student to corporate girlie to now, a global matchmaker—and all these steps have simply fit together like a beautiful, unexpected puzzle. I feel like every piece was inevitable!

I think a lot of people believe that I always planned to be a matchmaker. That somehow I majored in matchmaking with a minor in heart-adorned clothing from Love University. But when I was seventeen years old I didn't wake up and say, "I want to set people up on dates." I didn't have a poster of Jane Austen's *Emma*—starring one of fiction's most famous matchmakers—hanging on my wall. However, now that I've lived a little more, I recognize that there were situations in my life that led me to decisively choose this path. I didn't stumble into this profession. There were opportunities, and I followed through on them. That's who I am: someone who gets stuff done, for myself and others.

So let's start from my beginning. Back in the nineties, my parents would send my sister, Chrisoula, and me off to Greece to stay with our extended family for the summer. I have no idea what you think we were watching on TV in my aunt's apartment in the center of Athens at this time, but I'm pretty sure you're not guessing the truth: the American soap *The Bold and the Beautiful*. It's a series—and as of this writing, is still, somehow, miraculously running—that follows the machinations and romances of Los Angeles fashion-mogul family the Forresters. We all l-o-v-e-d, loved *The Bold and the Beautiful*.

At a certain point, one of my grandmothers couldn't read the subtitles anymore, so she tasked me, an eight-year-old, to translate the dialogue from English to Greek for her. I was ready. This was the era before helicopter parents and parental controls on iPads. Parental advisory stickers for album covers and I are the exact same age. And Chrisoula and I had flown to Greece as unaccompanied minors with a stranger smoking a cigarette next to our little heads for nine hours. Telling my *yiayia* about which Forrester cheated on which fashion executive wasn't going to scandalize me. As I translated the drama and passion on-screen, I realized I was using different words and phrases to express love, like *agape* or *eroteumenos* or *pathiazmenos*, to name a few, based on the context of the scene. A seed was planted.

Summers later, I would hang out with my Greek cousins and read their teenybopper magazines like *Super Katerina*, which was like the Greek version of *Tiger Beat*. There was a section where you could read the lyrics from popular songs. I would study them intently, highlighting how the word "love" would contort to a different word or phrase in Greek.

Later, back in New Jersey, I started hanging out at the mall like any good suburban American teen worth their messy eyeliner. We would meet boys from neighboring high schools, and I realized all my time in Greece had actually been my strategizing round. All my knowledge of soaps and love song lyrics was a secret weapon. When my friends came to me for advice, I was their compass. If they were "secretly" dating someone after school, the quick glances of acknowledgment as they passed in the hallway would throw them into an anxious panic, and I'd be talking them down to reality in the cafeteria. Or another dating millennial/Gen X problem: the politics of AIM log-in/log-off behavior and the away messages we'd post. I loved this era of dating because through the lyrics and the italicized fonts, I could pinpoint what level of dating panic my friends were experiencing and knew how to be their *Guiding Light*—to reference another iconic classic soap.

***

Circles have always been a consistent theme in my life. Yes, I love a good hoop earring and a winding Greek folk dance, but I'm really talking about social circles. I first realized how important they are when I was eighteen. At that tender age I moved from suburban Central Jersey (it's real, and I won't hear otherwise) to Athens, Greece, to attend college. Though I had visited Greece every summer for the entirety of my childhood, this was the first time I was there fully alone, living as an adult expat.

In a sea of Athenian students who lived with their parents, I was one of the few without that luxury. So I found myself a reasonably priced apartment by my college, and that became my home. No roommates, no family, just me and my friendly smile. As a result, my living room was always filled with friends. I eventually connected with people from all over: Ethiopia, South Africa, Germany, Hungary. I even met my best friend, Moshoula, who would go on to become the *koumbara* (sort of like a maid of honor) at my wedding, which culturally means she is even closer to me than blood relations. She is chosen family.

Still, I don't want to say my apartment was party central, because it wasn't. Unlike American college culture—which is branded as all red cups and keg stands—Southern European university parties weren't all about getting smashed and making out with the nearest person at the beer pong table. We didn't even have a beer pong table. My friends were on the debate team—*I* was on the debate team. These were wine-and-cheese parties where unexpected people were encouraged by me to get to know one another. I was a nineteen-year-old slinging charcuterie boards and community . . . before charcuterie boards were even trendy.

Although I just thought I was having fun, I was actually building a social muscle that would help me once I made my next move—and eventually to write this book.

***

I moved to Manhattan after graduation. I was planning to go into foreign affairs and had laid out the perfect path to that goal: going to graduate school at NYU's Center of Global Affairs and paying the bills with a big-girl job at a market research firm. The job taught me a lot about people's online buying behaviors. And, even better, it gave me health insurance.

But I started to think about my future—and all the student-loan debt I was accruing. It was time to create another social circle, one that would help me find my career one day. So I started hosting cocktail parties after work every Thursday for the NYC international relations community. I asked some of my classmates to invite people they knew who already worked at the kinds of places I was interested in. Think: the United

Nations and other consulates in New York City. I even had my professors get involved; they are the people best equipped to help match someone with the right hiring manager or leader. Each person invited was tasked to bring a friend. We could help one another build our circles together.

Well, it didn't take long for someone to *meet* someone at one of these. Like, *dating* meet. In hindsight, I realize I was actually hosting singles events. Who else could go for cocktails at 7 P.M. on a Thursday but the unencumbered? It was rare to meet someone who had a spouse or a minivan's worth of kids back at home waiting for them. Everyone was single. The couple quickly got married. They told everyone, "You have to talk to Maria. She knows people!"

I now consider this moment my professional origin story. The day after the couple got married, three men offered me money to set them up. The summer of 2009 quickly became one I would never forget. I emailed all my friends—"Listen, I met these three guys, and they want me to set them up. If you know anyone, introduce us by email. By the way, they hired me! $500!" I wrote, proudly.

I hit the pavement. I parked myself at a French café on the Upper East Side, and I would meet a few women a week for long interviews. If I thought it was a match, I'd connect them. Two of those guys were in relationships by Labor Day. I still had that last guy, though . . . So another email was sent out.

"Hey, friends! Okay, I've got one guy left. I really want to get him in a relationship, especially since he paid me $5,000!"

Did you catch that? I had made a typo in my reminder email. The $500 in my initial email at the beginning of the summer had accidentally been bumped up to an alleged

$5,000 matchmaking fee. With that extra zero, suddenly more people were interested in hiring me. That's the day I learned that you're worth as much as you tell people you are.

Suddenly, Agape Match was born. I named my company Agape because, well, I had one weekend to figure out a name if I wanted people to start writing me checks! Reflecting a bit, I thought, of all the words and phrases Greek people have for love, *agape* is the biggest one. I'll just call it that. *Agape* is the deepest form of love in Greek.

I wasn't only setting up Greek people, but I was young and confident. I was sure that if people learned how to properly say "Gucci," they could also pronounce a five-letter Greek word. And, ultimately, I would be fine if they messed it up a little. I had survived decades of Americans butchering my maiden name (don't even get me started on when it's paired with my married name). Someone saying *"agape"* wrong wouldn't faze me.

Initially, my clientele was mostly made up of New Yorkers. In 2010, I kicked off my singles events. My annual Valentine's Day party was called the Love Lockdown. The women were given locks and the men were given keys. They'd be instructed to find their match to win a raffle ticket for a big prize. Each month, I also hosted a dinner party called Dinner with Strangers. I would invite four guy friends and four girl friends with the instructions to bring a friend. Sixteen people would meet at a restaurant each month to enjoy a meal in one of the Greek restaurants where the manager would give me a deal—for all the business I was bringing in, I could eat for free. In 2013, one of the managers at Jay-Z's 40/40 Club witnessed a Dinner with Strangers party, and asked if I could host their Valentine's Day party. "Maria, we'll give you a free open bar for two hours." Don't twist my arm! You got it. Four hundred people showed up three weeks later.

Circles grew all over the city. And, along with them, relationships blossomed. As the years went on, I became a better matchmaker. I would pore over dating feedback from each first and second date of my clients. I was constantly learning what dating obstacles they were encountering. I found ways to provide constructive yet no-nonsense advice to make them better—better daters and also better partners. I didn't simply want to throw people into any old relationship just so I could cash my check. I wanted to get my clients into healthy, long-lasting partnerships with the loves of their lives.

As I look back on my career, it's so clear how technology has changed the way I do my job. The way I find my clients matches is different, as is how I extend my circle. Back in the day, I used Foursquare, Facebook, and Twitter. Classic millennial marketing. Instagram, for me, was more or less a place where I posted photos of food and weird facial expressions.

In the summer of 2016, Instagram launched Stories. It was a new element of social media where you could post a photo or some other update on your life and it would expire within twenty-four hours. By now, you probably know it well. Maybe you use it to subtly get the attention of your crush. Or your ex (we're going to get you out of that habit by the time you finish this book). In 2016, I rolled my eyes at Stories, as many millennials did back then. Something new I have to learn. Grumble, grumble.

But then, in the summer of 2018, Instagram released a new feature to Stories: Instagram Story questions.

I decided to have a go at it. This new feature gave me something to do during my commute to the office. Did anyone want to ask me a dating question? Tap, tap. Is this mic on?

I remember I received about fifteen questions the first time. The questions revolved around my world: dating and relationships. Oh yes! Hello. I'm a fourth-generation matchmaker. I set people up for a living . . . just like my grandmother. "How can I tell if they're The One?" "What do I talk about on a first date?" "I'm going to a speed dating event. What do I wear?!" Easy questions to answer in my eyes. I knew exactly what to advise.

I was also a new mom. I don't know about other people's experiences, but having a kid made my bullshit meter so sensitive. I didn't have time to coddle people with an answer as if I was writing a recipe for the best waffles with all the fluff about my most recent, life-changing trip to Belgium at the beginning. Instead, it was—*boom. Pow.* Here's your answer. The few friends I had that followed me absolutely loved it. That was on a Wednesday.

I'm someone who loves formalizing a system. So I announced to my small following that I would be back next Wednesday to answer more questions. And I was. "When do I ask her to be my girlfriend?" "My ex finally texted me to apologize five months after we broke up. Why now?" "New guy's texts are all over the place. Do I give him a chance?" I thought, whoa . . . let's go! I quickly wrote my no-nonsense responses. I didn't think when I published them. They were answers of clarity. My sister, Chrisoula—my best friend, my biggest fan, and a fellow matchmaker, too—exclaimed that night to me that I was giving them the advice their friends did not have the courage to. I loved that. I wanted to stay true to that. I didn't have time to waste . . . and neither did my followers. I'd act as the lighthouse to decode modern dating. Ask a Matchmaker Wednesdays were born.

Two months later, I would get a phone call that would completely change my life.

Girls Gotta Eat podcast host Rayna Greenberg invited me on the show after finding me online. I quickly said yes. Rayna and her co-host, Ashley Hesseltine, had just started their podcast earlier that year, and my podcast diet was made up of *This American Life, Savage Lovecast,* and *99% Invisible.* I had no idea what I was getting myself into.

I listened to some episodes as I drove around Boston in circles trying to convince my eleven-month-old to sleep. I loved it! Their chemistry was off the charts. Of course I was elated to join them in the studio a few weeks later to talk about dating.

The episode went live on October 22, 2018, and it flipped a switch I didn't even realize was off. I went from being the New York City matchmaker with a local following to a matchmaker on the national stage. I got thousands of new fans who connected with my message. Suddenly, my circle was so much bigger than I had ever expected it to be, and my mission became clear. I'd spent my career talking to singles, helping them navigate modern dating trends, and matching them into long-term relationships. Yes, they had mostly been in the tri-state area. But that didn't mean those were the only people I could help. I was better than that. Right? Surely I could become the matchmaker *everyone*—far beyond the land of grandma-style pizza slices and fast walking—needed me to be: the no-nonsense advice giver with an instinct for good dating.

Since I started Ask a Matchmaker Wednesdays, I have answered over eight thousand questions.

I've only skipped three Wednesdays, and one of those Wednesdays was *not* the day my daughter was born. I used that specific Ask a Matchmaker Wednesday as a distraction to calm my nerves before heading into my C-section. Am I crazy? Yes! Crazy to help you find clarity and love!

Ask a Matchmaker became a podcast in 2020, and now it's a book! Here we are, me and you, in our own little circle. And I'm going to use this opportunity to give you all my secrets, Matchmaker Maria–isms, and tips and tricks to teach you how to understand the dating landscape, fix your picker, expand your social circle, and have better dating experiences.

I will offer my intuitive insights and advice, honed not only by my professional experience but also by the advantage of being a fourth-generation matchmaker. Every question I've ever been asked during Ask a Matchmaker Wednesdays, from "Where are they?" to "How will I ever recover from this breakup?" has guided the unique perspective I have on dating, and I'm so excited to share all the hope and love stories throughout to help visualize what your future could look like, too. Together we're going to transform the way you connect, form, and maintain relationships. It's going to be a little bit of a look into my work as a matchmaker, a little bit of a memoir, and a lot of dating tips that will help you find a relationship you love *and* like.

And eventually, one day, I hope you'll think of me when you're dancing with your person around a circle of friends at your wedding.

1

FROM COURTING TO CLICKING

HOW DID WE BEGIN SWIPING AWAY OUR SOUL MATES?

SHE LOOKED IMPOSSIBLY CHIC, EVEN with the hangover, sitting across from her three best friends at their favorite diner. And even she was tired of hunting for Mr. Right. "I've been dating since I was fifteen. I'm exhausted. *Where is he?!*" she asked over eggs and coffee. You probably know her, too, since she's Charlotte York, the preppiest member of *Sex and the City*'s fab foursome.

Charlotte's plea for her white knight bubbled up in the season-three premiere of *Sex and the City*, which aired on a temperate summer night in June 2000. She'd hit the end of her rope before smartphones were invented . . . before dating apps . . . before male podcast hosts told their eager listeners to `ask women for their "body counts" or wannabe TikTok influencers instructed them on attracting "high-value men"—and how to be a "high-value woman" in return.

Charlotte was fed up with her romantic woes before everything you've ever experienced in dating had likely ever happened. Yes, this is a TV show. And yet . . . it's a question I, a professional matchmaker, hear every single day: "Where are they?"

Some of the answers I have heard, from others, are abysmal: "He'll be here when you least expect it." "You just have to stop looking." "You're too pretty to be single." How obnoxious do you have to be to tell someone deep in the dating trenches any of *that*.

And then I think about the perspectives of the people offering up those empty platitudes. They likely never had to date after 2012. They've probably never even had to figure out the difference between swiping right and swiping left. In fact, if you said the word "hinge," half of them might think you're sharing a shopping list for a home improvement project, and then they may even tell you . . . "Go to Home Depot! Just look confused! There are lots of eligible singles there that will want to help you!"

That's why, more and more, I've started to get the "Where are they?" question. And every time I hear that question, the person asking sounds demoralized. Exhausted. Just like Charlotte.

I was five years old the first time someone begged me to help them unravel the mysteries of the heart.

My first "match" was in kindergarten. Boy likes girl, girl likes boy, and me, an extroverted child, running to and from each person to make sure they know what I know. They dated for a long time, which mostly meant that they sat next to each other on our school field trips. Eventually we became teenagers, and like the plot of an after-school special, they broke up at our prom, but they had twelve happy years together. I've aimed for longevity in my matches since before I could tie my own shoes.

My entire adolescence is littered with such stories. Me, meddling. Someone else, falling in love. A few years later, at my first (and only) corporate job, I set up my coworker Ryan Allison with a woman named Allison Ryan. I found her on Facebook by simply searching his name in reverse. I found the pairing so hilarious, and he was such a good sport. They both were. It wasn't a match, but I learned a lot about Ryan in the process. Less than a year later, Ryan and I would go to a comedy club with my cubicle mate, Janice. I could feel the chemistry between them, so I left the show early. I knew when to (Cupid's) *bow* out. Two years later, they married.

Over fifteen years later, I don't go a day without explaining the "whys" of romance. Once, I was just a part-time graduate student and corporate girl helping friends meet (and maybe make out) over some cheese fries and watered-down cocktails. Now I'm Matchmaker Maria, the CEO of Agape Match and a dating professional who has set up over five thousand first dates. My days are spent answering questions like "Why can't I find someone?" and "Why is my picker broken?" At the heart of every discussion is a single theme: "Why is dating simply a *nightmare?*" That essential question is probably what brought you to this book. Thankfully I'm here to tell you that dating isn't a punishment—it's a privilege. And we're going to strategize your way into finding, or keeping, the love of your life.

After years of swiping, messaging, and sitting at the same dimly lit bar, such lofty goals might seem impossible. But finding partnership didn't always feel like unearthing a trustworthy dick pic from a haystack filled with commitmentphobes and time thieves. To understand why relationships seem so complicated right now, we have to understand how dating culture evolved to where it is today. After all, nothing affects the future quite like the past.

Throughout this book, I will guide you through the layers of influence that shape our dating experiences, providing you with the tools and insights needed to identify and attract the right person for you—and hopefully enjoy a lifetime of happiness with them. My goal is to empower you with the knowledge and hope that, amid the ever-changing process of dating, love is always within reach if you remain open and true to yourself.

PEOPLE USED TO COURT. NOW THEY DATE. WHAT'S THE BIG DEAL?

For so much of Western heterosexual human history, dating wasn't dating. It was courting. Which is when two people spend time together for the express purpose of deciding whether they want to get married. The key word there is "married." This was not a process meant to establish a long-term relationship that *could* result in a walk down the aisle at some indeterminate point. There was no "Hopefully he'll text me back in three days and set up a date." There was intention and speed, particularly since people usually courted within their established cultural communities and social circles. Not only could individuals vouch for everyone involved, but parents probably knew parents, and maybe even grandparents. The whole family was in on the operation. A couple could be married within weeks.

People married so quickly back then largely because societal norms demanded it (as did their parents). The culture at the time didn't always see love and marriage as the same thing.[3] Marriage was an economic, familial, and oftentimes religious necessity. Love was more of a bonus rather than a requirement. And as there were limited opportunities for higher education and careers, young women (even teenagers) were encouraged to marry as their primary path to social and economic stability. Societal expectations and cultural values placed a huge emphasis on starting families and adhering to traditional gender roles.[4]

Dating, on the other hand, is a rather new concept.[5] Unlike courting, dating is a process where we meet each other likely without being attached to the outcome. People date for the experience and the high of meeting someone new. They can meet someone different that their usual "type", even for just an evening of fun and take time to learn what kind of person fits their lifestyle. Sometimes, through the process of dating, we'll meet someone who feels so necessary we can't live without them. So we keep dating them, and maybe, we marry them, too.

WHAT THE HELL DOES A BICYCLE HAVE TO DO WITH DATING?

The seismic shift in dating, and really many aspects of society, begins with the bicycle.[6] I'm not talking about that old-timey bicycle you're probably imagining. You know, the one with the big wheel in front and the tiny wheel in the back. That was impossible for women to ride. Their long skirts and restrictive garments made *that* vehicle more of a death sentence than a ticket to freedom. I'm talking about the bike that was invented in the 1880s, where the wheels were finally equal . . . perhaps foreshadowing what was to come.

Access to a bicycle provided women with the opportunity to traverse an entirely new world, both figuratively and literally. For those who could afford such a luxury item, a bicycle offered unchaperoned independence. As women biked from town to town, the claustrophobic echo chamber of their microcommunities expanded. In exchange, they were offered more social interactions and participation in public life. Women were able to broaden their social circles for friendships. Their opportunities for romantic connections exploded.

The suffragettes, who were at the forefront of the women's rights movement, utilized this mobility to organize, campaign, and challenge societal norms.[7] The bicycle was their symbol of women's emancipation and progress. This newfound physical independence—which led to economic and political independence—gave women the power to pedal their own path. They could make personal decisions about whom to date and marry without the pressure to wed for financial security. They started enrolling in college en masse and those numbers continue to rise today. Women were no longer just daughters waiting to be wed. They could date within their cultural and religious communities, but also on campus or at their workplace. Sports clubs, fraternity houses, lecture halls, and more all became locations where singles could mingle. Eligible singles could interact based on mutual interests and intellectual compatibility rather than solely on economic or social expectations. This period marked the beginning of relationships based on shared goals and personal compatibility.

Pop culture further influenced the evolution of dating in

the twentieth century, reflecting and shaping societal attitudes with movies like *Beach Party*. The 1963 teen rom-com
follows an anthropologist who is so shocked by the romantic culture of the kids that he heads to the sunny beaches
of California to study the relaxed lifestyle of surfer youths.
The topic was such a hit—and source of fascination—that six
more *Beach Party* films were made in just three years.[8] This
was what I like to call the first wave of modern dating, pun
not intended!

In 1965, television shows like *The Dating Game* brought a
never-before-seen approach to the dating landscape. They introduced the concept of choosing a partner through a purposefully playful, colorfully lit televised format. Contestants
answered silly, but illuminating, questions in hopes of finding
their perfect match; think of them as the very first prompts
that app users are now so acquainted with. Casual social
spaces, such as TGI Friday's, also added to these increasingly
lowering stakes around romance. Yes, that restaurant where
the waiters wear "flair"—aka, as *Office Space* immortalized,
the different buttons and pins affixed to the uniforms of wait-
staff to display their personalities—was originally designed as
a singles bar. It was meant to create a new environment where
young adults could meet and socialize informally.

This shift from formal courtship to casual dating venues
reflected broader social changes, encouraging more spontaneous and relaxed interactions between potential partners.
Together, these developments—legal reforms, educational
advancements, and pop culture influences—have shaped the
modern dating landscape, making it more diverse, equitable,
and accessible. And it all started with a woman's access to a
bicycle!

As movies and TV shows were telling young people that dating with the intent to simply continue dating was all right, science also stepped in to agree. Oral contraception became available in the States in 1960. Within two years, 1.2 million women were using the Pill, according to the *American Medical Association Journal of Ethics*.[9] Suddenly, the threat of an "oopsie baby" while dating wasn't so dire. The possibility of a forced marriage went out the window right along with it. By 1973, *Roe v. Wade* ruled that every woman had a protected right to an abortion. Once again, singles were given the opportunity to get to know one another without a metaphorical shotgun pushing them to say "I do." Women and men no longer had to tie their lives to the person in front of them. They could date until finding the right one. Marriage became delayed, and the dating period lengthened.

In the late 1970s and 1980s, we had the introduction of video dating. Companies like Great Expectations[10] would allow their members to film a short bio of themselves and the kind of person they were looking for. To view these videos, other singles would also have to be members of the dating service, and they could watch the videos at member centers. For $200 a year, you could watch a few VHS tapes, find an acceptable match, and send in a postcard to the person you liked, hoping they'd like you back—after they headed to the service location to view your tape, of course.

Then, in the 1990s, technology allowed for the dawn of desktop dating. I call this the second wave of modern dating. Early in the decade, a Silicon Valley man named Gary Kremen was paying $2.99 a minute for telephone-based dating services. Although personal ads had been popping up since at least the 1600s,[11] they had never been a click away. Until now. Message boards and websites like Yahoo Personals also boasted endless personal ads. Kremen eventually became demoralized and exhausted by the process (and probably asked his loved ones "Where are they?" a lot). Sound familiar? Soon enough, it dawned on him: an internet database of available singles would make his, and everyone else's, search for a significant other so much easier. In 1994, Match.com was born.[12] So, you're swiping today because one guy wanted a girlfriend in the mid-nineties.

As Kremen was getting the first true dating site off the ground, AOL was revolutionizing our access to the internet. By 1997, AIM (AOL Instant Messenger) had arrived,[13] allowing everyone to send anyone a message. Unlike social networking sites today, like Instagram or TikTok, where we're all online all the time, you *had* to sign into AIM to receive a message. That was partially due to the fact that dial-up internet was king at the time, meaning you had to actively *go* online to be online. The feeling of always being connected to the internet didn't exist. When an AIM friend logged on, you heard the sound of a creaking opening door; most kids of this era can describe in visceral detail the feeling of hearing that noise, a door cracking open, and realizing your crush was back online. It was exhilarating!

As Kate Kennedy said in her book, *One in a Millennial*, "Like the personalized ringtones of days to come, you could adorn your crushes with custom sounds like 'moo' or 'cha-ching' when they signed on, putting out a Bat-Signal telling me to make myself available. I vividly remember the rush that went through my body seeing my crush sign on, the anticipation of hoping he would IM me first, while I waited with bated breath . . ."[14]

The adoption of AIM, paired with access to countless message boards and chat rooms, meant people were meeting and falling in love through faceless messaging for the very first time in history. While parents could have set up relative strangers to court by exchanging letters or starting a word-of-mouth campaign in previous generations, they weren't actual strangers. The prospective couple likely had culture in common and an entire shared community to hold them accountable to each other. But with AIM messaging, individuals truly had no idea who was on the other side of the screen. That didn't stop romance from blossoming.

Soon enough, everyone was booting up their computers to scroll through internet profiles. OkCupid even began as a desktop website that required an old-school mouse to peruse its contents. People no longer needed to rely on a real-life matchmaker, family friend, or shared social space like an office or a church picnic to find a potential partner. Now you could type in your zip code and religion, ethnicity, or even preferred kink (if you were on one of the more sexually straightforward sites) and get a list of hot singles in your area.[15] Sifting through the singles you found not so hot was part of the bargain.

While this dating strategy might seem efficient, it was abnormal to the ways people had located life partners for millennia prior. The original dating sites, which were created by men, taught singles to date by using filters. Height. Race. Exact location, down to the ten-block radius of a neighborhood. All these qualities became key factors in deciding who to date, even though they have little bearing on long-term compatibility. When everyone is a random face in a bottomless sea of possibilities, easily identifiable, unearned characteristics—

which are the ones genetics can bless someone with, like height and a strong hairline, no matter the person's character—slowly start to rule.

Those very characteristics took center stage in 2012, when the third wave of dating flourished. While dating websites had transitioned to smartphones as apps in 2009, Tinder launched that year; the OkCupid app and Hinge would debut in 2013; and Bumble would follow the next year. Religion-specific apps like JSwipe and JDate (which also began as a website in the 1990s) premiered in 2014. All these apps, along with a plethora of others that would come in subsequent years, have collectively been deemed The Apps. Suddenly, women and men were being socialized to not only date via filter, but to swipe on infinite stacks of singles. A thumb to the right means "hot" and to the left means "not." We're putting seconds—if not one singular *second*—into deciding what kind of person we want to spend our lives with.

In the height of the COVID-19 pandemic, I found something to laugh about: *The King of Staten Island*,[16] starring tattooed heartthrob Pete Davidson, alongside other sex symbols Bill Burr and Marissa Tomei. The semi-autobiographical movie follows Davidson's apathetic character, Scott, as he finally gets his life together. His mom has started dating a new man who, like his deceased father, is a firefighter. So it's time for Scott to open his heart up a little bit, too. Naturally, there's only one place for an emotionally stunted twenty-something to turn . . . The Apps. As Scott's friends attempt to rob a pharmacy, we get a scene that perfectly encapsulates online dating. Scott is supposed to serve as lookout as his friends commit a felony. But he gets distracted by the

Tinder-esque app lurking on his phone. He swipes on seven profiles in less than four seconds. "Yes. No. Yes. No. Yes, yes. No," he mumbles, slack-jawed, as he thumbs through women's first photos.

And there it is.

You don't know who's swiping; you don't know what they're doing while they're swiping; and just because they swipe doesn't actually mean anything. They might just be glancing at your introductory image when they *should* be helping their buddies pull off a burglary.

Obviously compatibility goes beyond a single image—which might be determined by an algorithm—on an app. You're going to need someone who shares your lifestyle and your communication patterns and expectations (which I'll help you figure out with this book). But with swipe culture, you decide who you're going to talk to, and ultimately date, before finding any of the important stuff out.

WHY DO I FEEL COMPLETELY OVERWHELMED BY MODERN DATING?

Everyone is burdened by the paradox of choice,[17] an economic theory that describes an inescapable psychological obstacle in which people tend to believe having multiple options will lead to *better* options, and a happier ultimate decision. But in reality, having too many options creates more work in choosing any single thing. And, in the long run, a chooser often feels unhappy with their decision, leading them to wonder if the next best thing remains out of grasp. App daters can swipe on people exactly one mile away, one hundred miles away, or in a city on the other side of the globe. The options are, literally, endless. To understand the magnitude of this dilemma, I'm going to tell you a story about my father, Taso.

Like all Greek men in the 1970s, my dad did his required two years in the Hellenic Army. He then went off and sailed the seven seas as a ship mechanic, enjoying a life of adventure as a young man. After twelve months of travel, he finally docked in Singapore. With a year's salary burning a hole in his pocket, he decided he was going to buy a Seiko watch. When my dad walked into the watch shop, he was confronted with hundreds of watches to choose from. Now he had to ask himself a lot of questions. What kind of metal finish did he want? How big should the band be? Which model was he looking for in the first place? After pondering all these possibilities, my dad finally made a decision. He left the store feeling defeated and without a watch.

The next day, he went into another store. This store had just thirty watches to choose from. He picked a pocket watch for his dad, and three matching watches for himself and his two older brothers. He left Singapore content.

It's a lot like when you want to watch Netflix but spend thirty minutes scrolling through all the shiny, unknown content instead of actually watching anything. Eventually, you just give up, press play on a familiar episode of your favorite sitcom (for me it's *Parks and Recreation*), and go to bed.

Choice paralysis will do that to you. When your breadth of choices is incomprehensible, it's nearly impossible to narrow anything down to just one. That's ultimately what dating with the intention of lifelong partnership is: picking just one. So a smaller pool of dating, let's say, within your community, can be easier.

I know you picked up a dating book, but I'm going to throw out one more economic theory to blow your mind: the secretary problem.[18]

Imagine a boss is hiring a secretary and knows she has ten people to interview. She also knows that once she turns someone down for the position, that individual is permanently out of the running. The boss can never go back to that person for the job again. While the first interviewee's chances of getting the position are abysmal, the fifth or sixth person has a great shot of landing it. Since The Apps are billed as "lifestyle" in the app store, they have little inclination to give you a slim set of profiles to make decision-making easier. They aim to keep your thumbs swiping on the app through hundreds of possible "secretaries" (or love interests)—not just ten.

I know this because, as a professional matchmaker, I encounter the secretary problem each day. How is it that a client will have swiped, swiped, swiped for years, across hundreds of profiles, but somehow gets into a relationship by their fourth or fifth match when they've suddenly hired me? I am a good matchmaker, sure. But I also believe that when I tell my clients in the beginning of their contract, "Look, you're only going to get six to twelve matches from me in the next six months," it sets a tone, one that I have had to learn the hard way is necessary to help set my clients up for success.

I once had a client, let's call him John, who was ready to get married. He was thirty-five, Catholic, and worked in midtown Manhattan at a big law firm. His long hours weren't giving him a moment to breathe and just meet someone. Upon his hiring me, I knew exactly who his first match should be. I set him up with Julia. They had a spectacular first date. I couldn't wait to hear when they would see each other again. But as we wrapped up our feedback discussion for the first date, I got a curveball. He wouldn't be scheduling a second. Instead, he had a gleeful expression as he said, "Julia was great. But I wonder if you have anyone greater? Who else ya got?"

He was a bull in the romantic china shop I had so carefully crafted. I was dumbfounded.

A few months later, after he had met six more women, John returned to me and asked the question I had been waiting for: "Can you set up a second date with Julia? She was the best."

Julia was dating someone else I had set her up with. They were in a serious relationship. John had missed his chance on what could have been a really happy experience. She, on the other hand, is married to the guy she committed to after John, and they now have three beautiful daughters.

This sort of dating FOMO (fear of missing out) has permeated matchmaking because of the Tinder-fication of the dating landscape as a whole. I attended a dating industry conference back in 2016 where one of the speakers, online dating consultant Steven Dean, demonstrated the results of a focus group he had conducted. In his observations as a dating coach, he revealed that if you matched with someone on Tinder, the chance of you meeting that match in person was less than 15 percent. But a match on Coffee Meets Bagel translated into a 90 percent likelihood of actually meeting up in real life. The key difference between the two apps? Coffee Meets Bagel, at the time, limited the number of profiles a user saw to a mere ten a day.

The conclusions that I took away from his presentation were twofold:

1. When presented with a limited number of matches, people weren't going to accidentally swipe away their soul mate or date like Pete Davidson in *The King of Staten Island*. They would actually read the whole profile, study the photos, and give some grace. After all, they only had a few options to choose from that day.

2. When presented with an unlimited number of matches, people would swipe away potentially great options based on surface-level details that have no real effect on compatibility. They would also take matches less seriously once made or over-swipe to the right for faux validation.

I like to call this faux-validation swiping. It's when someone swipes right on a potential match just to learn if that person likes them, too. It feels good to be liked. I get it. And so does science. Dopamine (the feel-good chemical) is immediately released into the brain when we see "It's a match" flash on our screen, no matter how we feel about the stranger.[19] But the next step is communication, and . . . does anyone really like their quick-swipe match enough to want to communicate? Probably not.

In her book *Dopamine Nation*, psychiatrist Dr. Anna Lembke explains that the "mechanisms in our brain that compel us to approach pleasure and avoid pain were evolved over millions of years for a world of scarcity."[20] We, as a species, are motivated to stay alive—to seek shelter, food, and safety. However, in our current environment, where we can get our food delivered with a few taps, we are living in an age of over-abundance. Our human instincts may compel us to overindulge. It feels good to be "a match," but are you *actually* a match?

Part of the problem is surface compatibility—or surface *in*compatibility. It can go either way, and often does. Someone might quickly swipe right for any reason, from immediate sexual attraction to liking the restaurant in the background of someone's photo. But that fickle nature can rear its ugly head once a thoughtless match occurs and you start to peruse the complete contents of someone's profile. Suddenly, you're searching for any reason not to go on a date. I recall one of my friends, Lucinda, complaining that men would comment on her Philadelphia Eagles jersey as a reason not to date her. How . . . absurd. Imagine choosing the mother of your children based on what football team she supports.

ASK MATCHMAKER MARIA

Do you feel the existence of online dating sites makes it easier or harder to find a companion?

This question doesn't feel productive to me, because regardless of how I feel, they exist and they are never leaving. They're like smartphones. They exist. They're never leaving. They have permeated every fiber of society and constantly evolve our behavior. And just like we assign "screen time" privileges to children, we are tasked to intentionally create boundaries with how we use any tool that provides us convenience. Online dating doesn't make the process of finding a partner easier or harder; it's up to you to decide how you want to integrate it into your life.

HOW ARE PEOPLE DATING TODAY?

All this brings us to today, where people do not trust The Apps even though they could be fantastic tools to meet someone, during a period when people are experiencing extreme dating fatigue.

It's important to remember that men and women swipe very differently. My team has observed that many men, regardless of their sexual preferences, swipe right based on the first photo. They'll only look at the rest of their match's profile if they match. They'll then promptly unmatch if the remainder of the photos don't match the initial one that caught their eye. They'll also unmatch if the prompt responses or personal data aren't to their liking.

Therefore, that dopamine hit of "Ooh, he likes me" you get with every match is a trick. You should actually be thinking, "Ooh, he *might* like me."

The reality of the situation is much closer to the feeling of walking into a bar (if everyone was looking around, and not at their phones). Each time someone walks in, the bell above the door dings and patrons look up. You might smile at someone or someone might smile at you. But that doesn't mean they're going to come up to you. It certainly doesn't mean they're going to buy you a drink or ask you out on a date. So now you have the power to limit the number of people getting your hopes up in the metaphorical bar.

ASK MATCHMAKER MARIA

Is it a bad idea to group-swipe with friends? I like to share my screen and talk about matches.

It's a 100 percent terrible idea if you're looking for a serious relationship. This isn't *The Bachelor* and your romantic future isn't a game show.

Women, on the other hand, regardless of sexual orientation, will put in Effort with a capital E. They'll not only read through your profile, but they'll take note of photos that have been tweaked with AI and share screenshots with all their friends. If you manage to get their swipe, they're hoping you'll message them back.

This complicated third wave of dating has crashed right into the fourth wave of dating, which we're still seeing the effects of today. That fourth wave is pandemic dating, which snuck up on all of society starting in March 2020 when people were driven into their homes, as social situations—like dating—could literally kill. Sharing air particles with the wrong person could have potentially led to a hospital stay. Most adults wouldn't get their first dose of the COVID-19 vaccine until the spring of 2021, meaning many singles spent about a full year alone in their homes.[21] Through conversations with clients, fellow dating experts, and social media connections, it's become clear a lot of women spent that time working on themselves. They got into therapy and read up on attachment theory (which we'll discuss in a later chapter).[22] Empty days led to hours scrolling TikTok, unraveling topics like weaponized incompetence (which occurs when one partner purposefully performs tasks poorly or appears incapable of them at all in order to avoid them. It is often played for laughs in sitcoms, when a bumbling husband off-loads basic house chores on his frazzled wife to a cheering audience; that behavior is then reflected in real life as if it's charming).

At that same time, men were either left deeply lonely or bombarded with dangerously anti-women sentiments.[23] In a vacuum of healthy male role models, social media personalities touting particularly misogynistic ideas and language took hold, influencing many vulnerable men and young boys, some just coming into understanding their own sexuality. They've recommended violence against women or "gatekeeping marriage"[24] and giving women less. In response, a large section of men started blaming their very reasonable trauma and loneliness on women, leaving them further from romantic connection than ever.[25]

Throughout all these waves, different deal-breakers have popped up. When I first started matchmaking over fifteen years ago, the biggest deal-breaker was smoking. A nonsmoker couldn't imagine kissing a walking ashtray for the rest of their lives—and a smoker didn't want to deal with the judgment. Then, in 2015, game show host Donald Trump announced he was running for president. The smoking debate was immediately overshadowed by the Trump deal-breaker. Clients told me their potential spouse either *had* to be a Trump supporter or absolutely couldn't be one. Party lines like Democrat or Republican didn't matter.

Since the COVID-19 pandemic began, however, deal-breakers have veered toward health-based values. I predicted in December 2020 that the dating apps would give users the option to apply different vaccine icons to their profiles. Sure enough, OkCupid rolled out the first one a few weeks later; the rest of The Apps followed suit soon after. The Biden administration even partnered with Hinge, Tinder, Match, Bumble, and OkCupid to incentivize getting the COVID-19 vaccine.[26]

Currently, women's reproductive health is a hugely important topic in dating. However, I personally believe the next big societal deal-breaker will be people's understanding and acknowledgment of climate change. In Europe, they've already moved on to this exact discussion.[27] After all, they don't need to parse people's profiles to figure out if they're on the same page about equal access to healthcare and bodily autonomy across genders. Abortion is legally protected there. Meanwhile, here in America, I've had countless conversations with my clients about their response to *Roe v. Wade* being overturned. Those talks are complicated, but fruitful. No matter what deal-breaker comes next, I'll be here to help you weather the storm.

Just like I helped weather the storm with Daniel. Daniel was a fan of my podcast and called in during a live hotline episode in March 2022. He shared his dating fatigue. He was five feet six and primarily dating online. So he knew many women's app settings were filtering him out before they even saw his charming photos and endearing prompt answers. To make matters more disheartening, he was a proud progressive in a really red state. I could hear it in Daniel's voice—he felt defeated.

My matchmaker brain instantly started to tingle. I knew that a lot of incredible women from Texas followed me online. It was time to play matchmaker in my Instagram Stories. I asked Daniel to send me a photo of himself with his pertinent details on it, like a baseball card. He told me his age (thirty-four), religion (Methodist), location (Austin), height (we know this one already), and his job (public sector consultant). I also instructed him to share his intention, which was a serious relationship that could lead to marriage. I posted Daniel's dating baseball card on my Stories and included his social media handle. Several women reached out to him, but one fellow Texas woman really sparked his interest. Her name was Melissa and she lived three hours away, in Uvalde. They set up a virtual date and it went well—no awkward pauses and no red flags. They planned an in-person date "in the middle"—aka San Antonio—soon after.

Love dripped from every word when Daniel would go on to tell the *Today* show (yes, that *Today* show) about the magical moment he first saw Melissa in real life. The pair went to Freetail Brewery in San Antonio, and she wore a white dress. "I was stunned. She truly was a wonderfully beautiful person inside and out," he said. This second date was a night that neither one of them ever wanted to end. From the brewery they went to an arcade bar. Then, the movies, and dinner at a Palestinian restaurant. By the end of the night, Daniel and Melissa both knew their connection was worth a long-distance relationship.

That May—only a few months after meeting—Daniel and Melissa's burgeoning love story was put to the test. An active shooter opened fire in Uvalde's Robb Elementary School, killing nineteen students and two teachers. Melissa worked nearby; the permanent voting site close to her office was used as a reunification site for victims and their families. Daniel left work and raced to be with his girlfriend.

"Daniel was there and held me while I cried. Ugly cried. The I-don't-know-if-I-can-breathe type," Melissa told the *Today* show. "And he was there for me as I woke up through the night in bawling jags, took me to work the next day since there was more to be done, and made sure I ate, drank water, and slept."

Afterward, Melissa knew Daniel was the man for her. She had proof that no matter what horrors life threw at them, they would stand together as a team. "And we would come out stronger and closer than ever," she said.

Daniel and Melissa got engaged that December, less than a year after a DM turned into a FaceTime date and a FaceTime date led to a brewery in San Antonio. Daniel had chosen the night of his company's holiday party to pop the question, since they would both be dressed up (there's a good tip, fellas). Melissa said yes before he could even finish asking. "Saying yes to Daniel when he asked me to marry him was easy," Melissa, who was previously married, told the *Today* show. "I know that sometimes, love is not enough. What we have is much tougher stuff. He will battle in my stead when I cannot, and I will do the same for him."

Their wedding was less than six months later in June 2023. This whole new life, all because one man called into my podcast and decided to take a leap with a modern-day matchmaker.

If Melissa and Daniel's story gives you hope, then you're in luck! I'm here to tell you that you should feel hopeful, because there are great people everywhere. And it's okay to feel overwhelmed. I'm going to provide you clarity and guidance on how to navigate this modern dating landscape. We need to look at how dating has evolved up until now, to see where it may go. We're going to discover strategies that will lead to meaningful connections. Holding on to hope and being open are the best ways to ensure you will find love.

2

HOW DOES A PROFESSIONAL MATCHMAKER MATCH, ANYWAY?

ASK MATCHMAKER MARIA

How much of your advice is based on knowledge passed down from previous generations?

Nearly none, as my grandmother didn't give dating advice. She was matchmaking. She set up people from a homogenous society with the same religion at a time when war was common and famine rampant . . . so the priorities were different. But she did think about people's temperaments a lot . . . and so do I when I'm matching!

My mom, Alexandra, worked for my company for two weeks. Incredibly short-lived. She couldn't fit into the world of modern matchmaking, which is balancing your own personal bias and thinking to yourself, "Okay, the search is crazy, but maybe I have this person who could be a good fit." Honestly,

I think she would have been happier doing what *her* mother once did.

I remember when I was single, she came home one time and announced, "I was talking to someone at church and they have a tall son."

"Okay?" I responded while simultaneously rolling my eyes. "What does he do for fun? What does he do for a living? How old is he? What do you know?"

"Well, it's so-and-so's son." Apparently that answer should have been enough to satisfy my curiosity.

She was playing by the rules of old-school matchmaking. The details of the match are secondary. The community and the family take precedence. Just go on a date, you'll figure out the rest later. Years later, I spoke at Matrimony.com headquarters in Chennai, India. In the lobby, they showcased the following quote: "Good citizens make a good country. Good citizens come from good parenting, and good parenting comes from happy marriages."

I felt like my mom's world and my world collided. I understood where she was coming from . . . but modern matchmaking has a different finesse to it as we'll soon discover.

As I tell people often, I'm a fourth-generation matchmaker. (I don't include my mom.) Not only has my family made matches, but we've turned to matchmakers in times of need. So we can trace my profession all the way back to my great-great-grandmother, who lived in Asia Minor at the turn of the twentieth century, in the small city of Αϊβαλί, now Ayvalık. Her daughter, matchmaker Despoina, would narrowly escape the atrocities of the time and flee to Greece in the wake of World War I. Despoina had been part of a traumatic population exchange triggered by the signing of the Lausanne

Treaty in 1923, which altered borders and lives forever. My great-grandmother went from living in a port town on the Aegean to completely starting over in the far-flung city of Kozani in northwestern Greece.

My father's side of the family had a similarly harrowing journey around the same time. The Pontic genocide rocked Asia Minor from the 1910s until 1923. My Pontic grandparents' families had escaped the carnage; my *yiayia* Maria was just four years old. My ancestors were relocated from the south coast of the Black Sea to Serres in northern Greece. They brought their rich heritage along with them and were determined to keep it alive. So when Pontic Greeks like my family were of marrying age, they sought out matchmakers to create marriages within the same subculture. During this era, matchmakers weren't women with businesses who gave advice on Instagram. They were whichever woman or man was keyed into the social conversation. They knew which families had young people of marrying age—and which families could be of mutual assistance to each other (or to the community). Wouldn't you rather dairy farmers and glassblowers got together over two cheese-making families that could create a monopoly on feta?

Still, other elders couldn't help but get in on the matchmaking game, too. It was commonplace throughout Greece until around 1980 for parents to play matchmaker for their kids. Rather than wait around for someone else to help, they would mediate a marriage for their children. You knew *of* the suitor. The young people courted. They got married a few weeks later. Cypriot Greeks, Karpathian Greeks, Cretan Greeks, and, of course, Pontic Greeks heavily relied on this practice to form alliances between families. Love and personal choice were secondary. And, like a modern prenup, matchmakers helped negotiate dowries and other financial arrangements. For instance, does this bride come with a house? Is the groom's farm under his name or his brother's?

My great-grandfather Lefteris was one of these active parents. He wanted his daughter to be with someone who had a strong work ethic and a good heart. After asking around, he was introduced to Miltiadis, a man seeking a wife. Lefteris decided his daughter Maria was a great match for my grandfather Miltiadis, who was thirty. And, like any respectful man at the time, Miltiadis asked Lefteris for Maria's hand in marriage.

As Miltiadis and Maria (who is my namesake, by the way!) were settling into Serres, my great-grandmother Despoina and my *yiayia* Chrisoula weathered World War II together. Famine, hunger, a civil war—it was one threat after another. But they survived. Like most Greek matchmakers (there was always at least one in every village), they were really good at building community—no matter the crisis or change. I imagine they were good at observing others. I've been told my grandparents were extroverted and fearless. So it's no surprise to me that I'm often told how similar I am to my *yiayia*, who came to marry her husband after he asked her brother-in-law if it was okay. My great-uncle, having taken the responsibility of matching his wife's sisters, was more than happy to oblige.

In 2011, I ran into an old friend of my grandmother's on the island of Alonissos. I think her name was Fotini. She stopped in her tracks as she was walking in the tiny village. "Chrisoula?"

I thought she was confusing me for my sister. We do look alike even though I'm quite taller. "No, it's Maria."

She nodded. "You look just like my friend Chrisoula." Recognizing she was speaking of my *yiayia*, I enthusiastically told her that I was her granddaughter.

My *yiayia* had matched her with her spouse. She had also matched her best friend with her spouse.

"What did you pay her?" I was curious!

"We gave her a fish!" Sure, that makes sense.

Even my in-laws came together through parental match-making. One fine day in the sleepy little town of Ierapetra, in southern Crete, my father-in-law, Yianni, was drinking coffee in the square. Suddenly, a beautiful woman walked by. Not one to miss a golden opportunity, Yianni immediately asked someone if they knew who the mystery woman was. Yianni learned she was Chrissy, the daughter of the town's most highly regarded teacher. Mind you, my father-in-law at the time was pursuing his PhD in education. So when Yianni returned home, he asked his mother to ask about Chrissy, the teacher's daughter, who, as it turns out, was also a teacher! Yianni had never talked to Chrissy. He hadn't even heard her voice. But he knew what he wanted his future to look like. And Chrissy was in it. So Yianni's mom and Chrissy's dad spoke, and together they arranged for Yianni and Chrissy to finally meet. Chrissy initially didn't want to do it. But her father told her Yianni had a car. She liked the idea of the car, and said, "Okay, fine, I'll meet him." A few months later, they were wed. A year later, George was born. Greek parental matchmaking at work.

Then, like the asteroid that hit the dinosaurs, something came for Greek matchmakers in the 1980s. The fearsome, the terrifying . . . women's magazine. Or, at least, that's my personal theory. The first issue of *Cosmopolitan* hit Greek shelves in 1979, bringing sex advice and sexy styling with it. Who needs a *theia* (auntie) for help when you've got cover models beckoning you inside glossy pages? Love marriages obtained through trendy tips became preferred.

Fun fact: I have a vintage 1979 Greek *Cosmopolitan*. On the cover,[28] the magazine promises readers it will explain the secrets of "true love" and shouts "Sex is not taboo!" Prepare to get seventeen clear answers to "hot questions." This would have been great advice, if it were culturally targeted. But it wasn't. Most of the writing was translated into Greek from a British or American issue of the magazine. They were repurposing content meant for a very specific section of the global population— thousands of miles, if not *oceans*, away—and sharing it with Greek women as fact. These women had no idea they were being given faulty advice that had very little to do with the lives they were living or their own dating ecosystem. It's a lot like telling a tiger that the only way to breathe is by sticking her head in a lake. Yeah, that works for fish. But it'll kill the tiger.

Greek women weren't living the breezy lives of their magazine-buying American or British counterparts, *yet*. Greece had been under a brutal dictatorship from 1967 until 1974.[29] People were only just starting to mentally adjust to newfound freedom and possibility. The smoldering *Cosmo* in their hands had no context for the conservative shadow hanging over its readers' heads. Just five years before *Cosmo* hit Greece's shores, women had strict curfews and modest dress codes. So those same women now reading the magazine wanted to believe the steamy, liberating truths it promised—who wouldn't?

Fast forward to 1983, when the Panhellenic Socialist Movement (PASOK) government in Greece led by Prime Minister

Andreas Papandreou implemented significant reforms that advanced the rights of women and established gender equality.[30] Changes included the abolishment of the dowry system, introduction of civil marriage, ensuring equal pay for equal work, and legalizing abortion with improved access to contraception. Women didn't even have to change their last names when they got married! (By the way, I think these reforms are excellent.)

The *proxenitra* (matchmaker), however, was no longer the nearby respected community builder. The task of matchmaking was moved from the matchmaker's hands into those of the meddling best friend.

The new matchmaker was your friend who was in a relationship, and co-ed outings and parties could be initiated by, let's say, her inviting all her girl friends and he inviting all his guy friends. Even with the rise of social media, Greek people have maintained this form of dating by clicking into the tags of your photos, and asking, "Who's this? Who's that? When are you inviting them out so I can meet them?" That's kind of how my parents met!

My parents met in 1982. My mom was twenty-four and my dad was twenty-eight, and they had both been invited to the birthday party of a mutual friend. My dad thought my mom was really cute and he loved how smart she was and how loud she laughed. He pleaded with the mutual friend to arrange coffee with all her friends so he could see her again. So, their friend invited six friends to coffee, and of course my mom and dad. At this café, my mom got to know my dad a little better. She thought my dad was super sexy. "The way he smoked was so cool." (It was the eighties . . .) So, naturally, she contacted their mutual friend and pleaded to do another coffee date and to invite him, too, not realizing my dad had done the exact same thing the day before. Anyway . . . I'm told it took four outings for these two to finally go on a solo date. And here I am now, telling you the story!

And look! No parents or matchmakers *or dowries* were involved in the process. In fact, my dad met my grandfather a couple of weeks before he proposed to my mom eighteen months later!

We've come a long way from my *yiayia*'s living room. While my ancestors simply wanted to maintain their culture in an increasingly fraught world, I have different goals as a matchmaker. My clients are dating across race, religion, and border. Rather than trying to keep a heritage alive, I'm looking to match two people whose lifestyles and temperaments are a long-term (and hopefully lifetime) match. For instance, my *yiayia* never had to think about all the different ways someone could be Christian, Muslim, or Jewish, let alone cross-match a client between religions, if the person was so inclined. She definitely never had to ask someone about their specific flavor of conservative, liberal, or moderate—and then find a fitting intellectual and moral match from her circle. Chrisoula, my *yiayia*, set up nice kids from nice families with other nice kids from nice families. At most she was worried about whether two people's energies matched or at least balanced each other out.

As a modern-day matchmaker, my job is to help people acknowledge and manage their loneliness and to help them find strong relationships in the process. Those connections could be romantic. But they could also be platonic friendships that end up leading someone to the exact right place to meet the love of their life. I believe that growing one's social circle is the key to finding the right match. Matchmaking is simply just one node in that system. By hiring a matchmaker, you're gaining access to a massive network that only they have access to. And that network must trust their matchmaker, too. I can't set people up with clients who don't *also* want to meet them.

And modern-day matchmaking is expensive. I'm not exactly being paid in fish and goats. None of my colleagues are. As a result, to be incredible at the art of matchmaking, you have to find creative ways to get our clients out of their own way, because the moment money is exchanged you have to balance a wish list with a reality check. And some clients are just not interested in reality. They'd rather you stick to the wish list even if it means they may not be successful in actually finding their match. It took me years to not take this personally, as I genuinely want my clients to be happy. I just can't make the best Starbucks drink if I don't have access to all the ingredients—and I definitely don't want to serve it if the client is actually allergic to what they ordered.

Unlike what my grandparents did, I'm not usually called upon by parents or other family members to help match their child of marrying age in their village (though it has happened in the past). Once, a very well-known and successful banker came into my office. I was prepared to meet a fifty-five-year-old man looking for his second chance at love. Instead, he came in to discuss his twenty-eight-year-old daughter's dating life. He wanted to hire me and told me that *he* had to approve any matches I found for her. Another stipulation . . . she could not know I was matching her. He planned to call me with her schedule each day, and in his rom-com fantasy, I would arrange a meet-cute with the guy to "accidentally bump into her," and he would be charming and ask her out. While this would make a fantastic movie starring Jenna Ortega and Tom Holland—with Matthew McConaughey playing the dad—this was real life. So I did what any reasonable young matchmaker would do and shooed him out of my office.

When a person who actually wants to hire a professional matchmaker for themselves comes in to meet me, I sit down with them and have a long conversation. I try to find an emotional connection with the person. I'll share a little bit about my life in hopes that they'll tell me everything about theirs. I recall a potential client once telling me that he did collegiate debating. I did, too, so we spent the first fifteen minutes of the call talking about different tournaments we had both attended and what our worst performances were. Then, he started talking about his debating partner, and how they worked well together. "Tell me more . . ." I asked. I wanted to know what it was about them that made him feel like he could trust the person each and every time they shared a podium at an international invitational.

"I just knew they saw the world how I saw the world. So I trusted that they'd be able to make a sound rebuttal when it was their turn to speak."

They saw the world how I saw the world.

From there, I asked him about his worldviews. "How do you see the world? What gets you excited? What keeps you up at night?"

I also ask my clients what their hobbies and interests are, not always expecting a well-rounded answer. Many will say travel, even though they only travel once a year. Some will talk about passions like playing the guitar or creative writing or mentoring. Others will give me a short list of how they stay active—think hiking or pickleball or CrossFit. I will also ask what media they consume. Where do they get their news? Do they listen to podcasts? Which ones? What kind of movies are they watching?

Then I will ask who they are doing these things with. Do they have a core group of friends? Is it an audience of one? Do they have a weekly guys' night or a girls' brunch they go to? I want to understand what community they have built for themselves, if any.

Sometimes I hit a brick wall during these conversations. Not everyone is great at talking about themselves, their passions, and their hobbies. In this case, I reframe the question. "What would you do this weekend if you had a significant other?" I ask.

Suddenly the floodgates open and information begins to flow. "I would for sure do a weekend trip by the Bay and hit up a food festival." "I would love to go to a wine tasting." "Maybe we would host friends for brunch and then binge-watch the latest new show." "I think we'd go to the dog park in the morning followed by a really long walk. Then we could grab a bite at this restaurant we have been meaning to check out."

I'm learning about the fantasy of what a happy relationship looks like, and for most, it's just the promise of doing enjoyable activities with your favorite person.

I ask my clients about their families, both biological and chosen. I want to learn if there is a sibling group chat and if they send funny memes to one another. I want to learn if they are expected to care for their parents when they get older. I want to learn what kind of jobs their parents had and what kind of relationship their parents demonstrated.

Some of my clients may reply with a really dry "I just don't talk to my family anymore." The door is shut, and I try not to pry it open. I'm a matchmaker . . . not a therapist! Instead, I will pivot the conversation and lean in to asking about their chosen family. How do they spend holidays? Who can they call if they're in a pickle? What do they envision their own family will look like one day?

A professional matchmaker has the ability to cut through the weeds and get these answers without feeling any shame. We are serious about getting personal.

To me, matchmaking is an art—the art of being a good listener by asking the right questions. But it's also about coordinating fun first dates, and calibrating the search based on the reams of date feedback we collect. We coach, we match, we cheerlead our people to the finish line of relationship success.

Good clients understand that a good matchmaking experience is one of cooperation. We will network and vet potential matches. We will coordinate your first and second dates. We will give you a ton of date feedback and cheerlead you all the way. We expect good date behavior, like showing up on time and being an active listener. We expect date feedback the following day that is helpful for us to get closer to finding your match. The more information we get, the better we can tune your romantic future like a radio dial in the nineties. We're all just looking for your favorite station. You can replicate this feeling by journaling about your dates and seeing what patterns pop up. What kind of people are you actually having the best conversations with? Who seems excited to get to know you? Those are the kinds of people you should be pursuing.

Good clients also understand that we matchmakers are

also human. We are limited to who is within our network and *their* enthusiasm to meet you, too. Maybe our client wants to date a doctor who has a house in the Hamptons, and maybe I know a few. If none of them are interested in meeting you, I can't exactly set you up, right? If you're noticing in your own network that a certain type you have in mind isn't responding how you like, it might be time to shake up your expectations. Don't worry—this book is going to give you a lot of strategies on revamping your outlook on what your type really is.

There's a lot going on behind the scenes. And I have not even mentioned the sheer amount of networking we do to recruit potential matches to meet!

I will go to networking events that I have no business being at, or tag along to a friend's Toastmasters meeting or creative writing class. I'll go to art shows or trivia nights and join a group looking for an expert on *Friends* episodes. I'll throw an election debate party or a Eurovision watch party for everyone who loves politics and European bops in Manhattan. I'll scour event listings for interesting things happening in surrounding communities that I'm not a part of and go there. I'm intentionally creating as many social circles as possible to cast a wide net of correspondence so when I need a match for a client, I know where to look. Not only should you be doing these things, but tell your friends to follow the same steps on your behalf. You need a legion of amateur matchmakers lifting up social rocks and finding out if there's romantic gold hiding under them for you. And don't feel shy about asking for this kind of help. Remind your friends and loved ones that they'll have to spend birthdays, holidays, and vacations with whichever person you end up with. Don't they want to like them? Well, now they can be masters of their own destiny.

But all that art sits upon the knowledge of understanding that each client has their own temperament and it is reflected in not only their personality, but in who they will connect with and how.

My *yiayia* had a unique way of matchmaking. Fascinated by Greek mythology, she used it as her tool for categorizing personalities and matching energies, creating her own system of personality typing. She'd label people as Zeus or Athena if they were ambitious and no-nonsense. Those who valued tradition and stability were either Hera or Hephaestus. Charismatic individuals were dubbed Apollo or Aphrodite, while the adventurous and independent were Poseidon or Artemis.

This feels very similar to the personality-typing system that I like to use when matching.

WHAT IS PERSONALITY TYPING?

Most people are familiar with personality typing. If you've opened up a *Cosmo* (oh, *Cosmo!*) and tried to find out "What Kind of Hot Lover Are You?" you've tried your hand at it. Or maybe you've asked Buzzfeed to tell you which *Friends* character you are, or what box of cereal you would be at the grocery store. Some people, however, will immediately associate personality typing with Myers-Briggs. Maybe you took the Myers-Briggs Type Indicator (MBTI) in college and now use a lot of letters to tell people you're friendly (aka "I'm an ESFJ"). The Myers-Briggs test assesses people across four categories: how they direct and receive energy (Extroversion or Introversion), take information (Sensing or Intuition), make conclusions (Thinking or Feeling), and approach the outside world (Judging or Perceiving). Depending on your answers, you'll get one of sixteen possible Myers-Briggs types, which is fun. A lot of people feel really well-defined by their type.

Yet here's the thing: Something like the MBTI is painfully unhelpful for matchmaking—or even dating. Because you don't have to only understand what *your* type is, but what it means in contrast to every other type there is. No one is remembering all that. This same adage applies to one of the most hallowed forms of personality typing there is: astrology. It's great that you know you're a Taurus and that means you probably enjoy luxury, greenery, and staying comfy-cozy inside. But what does that mean against a Scorpio? A Capricorn? A Gemini? This question gets even more complicated when you factor in the "big three" conversation going around that takes into consideration more elements of someone's chart (like the moon and one's rising sign) than *just* the popular sun sign.

My astrology and crystal girls and boys, I know you can answer all these questions. But what about everyone who doesn't follow three astrology accounts on Instagram? It's probably a lot harder to find a good match by categorizing people in this way. Especially if it's more focused on where the stars were when you were born over who you actually are today.

The potholes in a lot of personality typing have led me to biological anthropologist Dr. Helen Fisher's Temperament Inventory.[31] Maybe you know who Helen Fisher is— she's probably had a huge influence in your life. At least if you've dated since 2005. That was the year Dr. Fisher became the chief scientific advisor to Match.com. Since that time, Match.com has not only become an app itself, but evolved into Match Group, the dating app juggernaut. Match Group owns a dozen brands, including dating giants like Tinder,

Hinge, and OkCupid, and more targeted dating apps including Latin-marketed Chispa, Black-marketed BLK, and career-focused The League. Without Dr. Fisher's work, none of those brands would be where they are today—and neither would their users.[32]

Dr. Fisher's Temperament Inventory doesn't have the sixteen types of the MBTI, the twelve of astrology, or even the nine of the Enneagram, another popular personality-typing system. Dr. Fisher just has four. People can be broken up into Builders, Directors, Explorers, or Negotiators; one of these types is someone's primary type and another is their secondary. However, everyone has some percentage of each in their personality. I, for one, am a big-time Director. My secondary temperament is Builder. On the other hand, my husband, George, is a Negotiator first, and a Builder second. You should not take these titles literally. An Explorer shouldn't be the one in charge of reading the directions to brunch, and a Builder may not be the one you want erecting your new house. These are just the monikers Dr. Fisher chose. So . . . you probably have one question now.

WHAT DO THE TEMPERAMENTS MEAN?

This subject is one of my favorite topics to discuss in my monthly coaching classes. It's important to remember that no temperament or type is better than another—in dating or in life. They all have their benefits and setbacks, and help someone contribute in a relationship and act as a great partner. As proof, I'm first going to tell you a little marriage tale so you can see how differently George and I tackle a problem. Then we'll dig into the definitions of all four temperaments. However, after hearing this story, you'll understand two of them really well.

When I started my podcast, *Ask a Matchmaker*, I realized I needed to buy a proper podcast microphone. My AirPods were just not going to cut it. I asked George for help choosing one. What he didn't know was that I, a Director, already had a front-runner. To pick one, I went to Amazon and searched "podcast microphone." I looked at the ratings. I looked at my budget. And then I added the best one to my cart.

Then I waited for George, a Negotiator, to get back to me.

He had a completely different approach. He looked up the top ten relationship podcasts. See, he wanted to see what my future competition was using—and which mics had helped them get to such a successful place in the relationship podcast sphere. This information went in column A. In column B, he put a photo of the mic used in the corresponding podcasts that he sourced from their websites or their Instagram pages. He put a link to each microphone in column C. Then he put in the time and listened to a little of each podcast. He rated them for sound quality, and put the data in column D. In column E were the prices of the microphones. Ten days later, he came back to me with his selected microphone.

We picked the same microphone!

Directors, Negotiators, Builders, and Explorers might have different tactics. But it's totally possible they'll all end at the same place. So who are they?

Who's a Director?

I imagine my *yiayia* thought of Zeus and Athena when she met Director personality types. Zeus, the almighty god of all the gods, was known for his authoritative nature. Athena, the goddess of wisdom and warfare, was strategic, logical, and ambitious. Both were driven by their goals and were strong leaders.

According to Dr. Fisher, Directors are associated with the testosterone system of the brain. We're independent thinkers and deeply analytical. From my experience, Directors are quick and precise thinkers because they live life with contingency plans for their contingency plans. We have a mental Rolodex of everything that could ever possibly go wrong, and then create fixes for all those scenarios. We are really great at identifying patterns! We are the people who need whiteboards in our showers for the moment inspiration (or, more likely, solution) strikes. I'm saying this from experience.

If you're a woman Director reading this—welcome to the very small club. Only about 12 percent of women are Directors. That makes a lot of sense, because it's difficult to be a woman Director. Most women, especially of my generation and older, were taught to care for people from the moment they could sit up and talk. We were given dolls. We were given kitchen sets complete with Easy-Bake Ovens to practice for our future roles. But Director women are problem solvers first. They *can* care deeply and thoughtfully, but it doesn't look like traditional feminine caregiving. We would rather help you solve a problem or learn a new skill than cradle you in our arms while you cry. Our binders full of solutions are our caring.

Director men, on the other hand? Congrats. You're often seen as the master of your own universe. Socialization benefits Director men with their take-charge attitudes and pragmatic approaches. Still, they have one big catch to look out for: narcissism. Between their natural behavior and our social values, narcissism can be easily cultivated in Director men. They should maintain solid, honest relationships and routinely seek out viewpoints beyond their own to keep this threat at bay.

Who's a Negotiator?

I imagine my *yiayia* thought of Apollo and Aphrodite when she met Negotiator personality types. Apollo (the god of the sun, music, and prophecy) and Aphrodite (the goddess of love and beauty) were diplomatic, empathetic, and charming.

In some ways, a Negotiator is the equal and opposite temperament to a Director. While Directors have traits linked with testosterone according to Dr. Fisher, Negotiators display traits linked with estrogen. In the same way there are women Directors, men can be Negotiators. And it doesn't make them any less masculine. Remember: my husband is a very sexy Negotiator guy.

Negotiators are intuitive, instinctual, diplomatic, and authentic. They think big-picture and try to consider every variable—including everyone's feelings—before making a decision. My favorite example of a Negotiator is President Bill Clinton. He is legitimately one of the most charismatic people I've ever seen. When you're in a room with Bill Clinton, no matter how big it is, you'll feel like he's only speaking to you. All my clients who have observed him say the same thing. Negotiators care about making people feel heard and attended to. That habit, when wielded properly, makes them incredibly magnetic.

But their empathy can also be their biggest problem. In my experience, a Negotiator can appear indecisive or like they're playing both sides of an issue. To avoid this problem they should keep their boundaries clear and let their own ideals influence their decision-making.

Who's a Builder?

I imagine my *yiayia* thought of Hera (the goddess of marriage and family) and Hephaestus (the god of blacksmiths and craftsmen) when she met Builders. Builders are often traditional, practical, and reliable. It's just a coincidence that craftsman god Hephaestus also happens to be a Builder.

My sister, Chrisoula, is a classic Builder in many ways. She's the kind of person who can't go to bed until all the dishes are clean and put away. When she got a new waffle maker, I gave her my waffle recipe. It calls for two cups of flour. It makes a great, thick batter, which in turn becomes great, thick waffles. But when Chrisoula called me, she asked if the batter was supposed to be all soupy. "*Soupy?*" I responded, confused. Yes, soupy, she confirmed. So I asked how she had added the flour into the batter. "I picked up the cup, I took a knife, and I cut it," she said. Chrisoula likes things precise and orderly. Cutting-flour-with-a-knife precise. This is not how I make my waffle batter. When I take the cup of flour out, and it has a little extra mound of flour on top, I leave it as is. That extra is what makes the batter good, whatever mystery amount it is. I don't care—as long as it gives me results.

Builders care. They care about tradition, process, and rules—how things *should* be done. Their traits are linked to the serotonin system. So they love nothing more than order, and that order makes them feel safe. They're more inclined toward the military or organized religion because of these tendencies. But that doesn't mean every Builder is hitting the pulpit or strapping on a uniform. My sister certainly isn't. But most Builders find their order somewhere or another. I've found that Builders tend to be well-liked because they're reliable, trustworthy, and dependable. When they say they're going to do something, they always do it. And they bring logic and a detail-oriented approach to their actions.

Netflix's *The Crown* gives us an inside look into the life of my second-favorite Builder (after my sister), Queen Elizabeth II. For Elizabeth to become queen, her father, King George VI, had to die. The tragic moment comes early in season 1, when Elizabeth is in Kenya and must fly back home. When she lands, Elizabeth changes into mourning blacks and reads a letter from her grandmother Queen Mary. Elizabeth is told not to let "personal indulgences" eclipse her duty. "The Crown must win—must always win," Queen Mary writes. These become the words Queen Elizabeth lives her life by. She may have stepped onto the plane Elizabeth Mountbatten, princess and young wife. But she stepped off of it Queen Elizabeth, one with the Crown. And she never wavered.

Who's an Explorer?

My *yiayia* was definitely thinking of Explorers when she'd call people Poseidon (the god of the sea, earthquakes, and horses) or Artemis (the goddess of the hunt and wilderness). Both gods are unpredictable, adventurous, and seek novelty.

There is one temperament that would never understand the unshakable conventions of a Builder: the Explorers of the world. Linked with the traits of the dopamine system, they're brimming with energy and vitality and are very curious and creative people. They're people who value joy in their lives, and are not afraid to remove whatever is keeping them from those feelings. It also means they're very direct and sure of what they value in relationships, people, and experiences. My Explorer clients are the ones who tell me about their passions, the exciting places they've lived and the ones they travel to for work or pleasure. Still, they're not all thrill seekers or literal adventurers. Some are ER doctors and nurses chasing the rush not available in the rest of the hospital, or work as day traders, doggedly pursuing the next great stock. Although they're almost definitely investing, either emotionally or financially, in a creative outlet like guitar playing, painting, or an interesting new workout.

A lot of your favorite TV characters are Explorers. Think: Samantha Jones in *Sex and the City* or Ilana in *Broad City*. Samantha would never be caught dead doing something (or someone) who doesn't bring her joy; many of her *Sex and the City* plotlines feature her actively communicating her needs or leaving situations that do not meet those expectations. In one of my favorite episodes of *Broad City*, allergic Ilana has planned to stab herself with an EpiPen just to attempt to eat a shellfish dinner with her best friend, Abbi. A bowl of Alaskan king crab stew could kill Ilana. But it's also way too seductive for her to pass up before trying everything in her power to try to consume it.

While Explorers might sound too focused on ephemeral pleasure to commit, that's not true. They simply will only commit to a relationship that fully serves their outlook. They are resilient and consciously making relationship decisions. I once had a Builder client who had recently left a twenty-three-year marriage. I asked her, "At what point in your marriage did you know that it wasn't working?" Her answer? About twenty-two years earlier, when her son was born. So why did she stay? "Because that is what was expected of me from my community," she explained. She was terrified of what her community would think of her. She couldn't take the idea of being judged. So she decided she would get a divorce once her son graduated from college. And that's exactly what she did.

An Explorer would never do that. They wouldn't be able to remain where they were unhappy. They would either leave or find a way to *make* themselves happy. Yes, they might be more likely to get divorced. But they're also far less likely to keep another person in an unhappy situation any longer than necessary. Their goal isn't to hurt someone, but to ensure everyone is in a better situation quickly.

WHAT ARE THE BEST TEMPERAMENT MATCHES?

Like I said earlier, personality matching is so important to me because it's something I use daily in my work as a matchmaker. I'm very good at assessing what someone's temperament is after hearing them talk for a little bit. Give me your ninety-second elevator pitch, and I'll be able to tell you (with a 90 percent success rate) whether you're a Director, Negotiator, Builder, or Explorer. I bet my *yiayia* could determine if you're an Athena, an Apollo, a Hera, or a Poseidon using the same method. So when I start to recommend matches for my clients, I'm looking to balance out their personalities and find someone they can comfortably build a life with.

I see a lot of people chasing the wrong choices for them. For example, a Builder might see an Explorer and get excited.

"Oooh, shiny!" they'll think. And I'll have to remind them that person isn't for them from an anthropological and biological standpoint. That person will leave dirty dishes in the sink and want to jet to Peru after seeing a particularly fascinating documentary. The Builder will feel so out of their mind.

So, which temperaments should you scientifically be looking for?

Director/Negotiator

This is the marriage I ended up in. And I'm so thankful for it. My husband slows my Director brain down so I don't do something in haste. In return, I speed him up so we stop counting variables and start making decisions. Negotiators help point out all the competing details and Directors make executive decisions. At its best, this is the relationship equivalent of a perfectly working machine.

Builder/Builder

Unlike the Director/Negotiator dynamic, Builders do not do well with their opposite, Explorers. If you're a person who likes rules—as Builders do—it's beneficial to be with someone who also likes rules. And no one loves rules like a fellow Builder. Explorers, on the other hand, will grow to resent or refuse a Builder's routines.

I saw this exact problem rear its head in real life. I once had a client, let's call her Jackie, who appeared to be an Explorer. She was an artist-turned-academic with a chic accent and well-used passport. Jackie was the kind of person who would be happy to fly off to Italy for the weekend and return to work on Monday. She tended to date jet-setting men who were *definitely* Explorers. But every relationship crumbled. All those men were temperamentally not a match.

Finally, I asked Jackie to figure out her temperament. Turns out, she was a Builder through and through. Explorer was way at the bottom of her results. The reason why she traveled spontaneously was because she was a single woman with disposable income. At her core, she sought stability, routine, and reliability—traits that she said were missing in all her past relationships. I told Jackie, jokingly, "I see you with an accountant, instead of an international man of mystery." For a long-term relationship, she needed an anchor who shared her need for order. Her flings could explore as much as they wanted, but her husband needed to build.

Months later, during a barbeque, Jackie overheard a man say he worked at a big accounting firm. She immediately pulled him to the side for a chat. See, Jackie needed to be the one pursuing this accountant. She presented as a flashy Explorer, the kind of person who might leave on a red-eye to a city the accountant had never even heard of. But that wasn't who Jackie was or what she wanted. So after they began to chat, sensing positive vibes, she asked him out. Soon they started dating. They eventually got engaged, and then married. Last year, they welcomed their first child. I'll never know if Jackie's husband is *technically* a Builder, but based on all that she shared of him he certainly sounds like one.

Explorer/Explorer

Similar to the Builder, Explorers do well with their own. But, more than anything, Explorers need to look for the person who wants to, metaphorically speaking, sail the seven seas beside them. I instruct my Explorers to find the balance. For instance, one of you is going to be the ship captain, and the other the cruise director.

To me, the captain is manning the ship. They have a goal in mind for you as a couple, and they're sticking to that goal. Shiny objects don't distract them and they will get you to your destination come hell or high water. Even with this determined attitude, this half of the Explorer couple still values the freedom of being on the metaphorical ship—a vessel that can take you anywhere on your journey to the people and places you need to get to.

The cruise director of the couple is the one finding the fun stuff along the way to the destination, whether it's literal or figurative. If you're going from Barcelona to Seville, they're figuring out what you can learn about each other on your journey and picking the entertainment on the way. If there's a can't-miss restaurant in the middle, they're the one putting it on the itinerary. And they're making the entire experience all the more lighthearted for both of you.

WHAT IF I FIND MYSELF ATTRACTED TO A PERSON THAT'S NOT MY "BEST" TEMPERAMENT MATCH?

If you just read the previous "best" matches as, say, a Builder, looked up, and realized the person sitting across from you is an exuberant, whimsical Explorer—don't worry! Or if you're a Director planning date number two with another resolute Director—everything is okay. No relationship is doomed, whatever temperaments the two people in a couple might have. Personality typing isn't here to tell you exactly which person to marry and which one to dump. You just might need to communicate more with some people over others. But humans are complex, like a delicious multilayered lasagna. Your temperament is just one single layer of pasta. And it'll be tasty with marinara, pesto, or Bolognese.

While I usually feel like my life as a modern matchmaker is so different from my *yiayia*'s experience so many decades ago in Greece, discussing personality typing reminds me we probably have a lot in common. I talk to clients until I can figure out their temperament. My *yiayia*, and other matchmakers of the time like her, also started their process by talking to people. That good coffee that brought in all the gossip? Those stories probably told her oh so much about so-and-so's kid's temperament. The parents' meddling built matchmaking on shared values and long-term goals and stories. Stories of who was deeply analytical or deeply empathetic. Stories of who was outwardly particular and traditional or who lived with an entrepreneurial spirit that their tiny village was just too small to hold. With these findings they might recommend one match over another, but they didn't want to get in the way of true love, either.

Following in the steps of the Greek gods, the *yiayias* once had their role in orchestrating love and destiny. Now, with the help of this book, the power is in your hands.

The more you understand yourself, the better you can navigate the complexities of relationships. Personality typing takes your story and acts as a compass for assessing problems and opportunities. It's a superpower to have that level of knowledge of yourself: Who are you? What lifestyle do you want to lead? What things do you find absolutely annoying about yourself? What kind of partner will you need to pick up the slack? What strengths do you bring? By learning these things about yourself, you will understand that others have their own compass, too. It's easier to connect when you can understand. It's easier to take the initial spark from Zeus's lightning bolt and turn it into an eternal flame.

3

ARE WE TOO DIFFERENT TO MAKE IT WORK?

IN 2023, I BECAME ENAMORED with a new internet trend. Suddenly, women began asking their male partners how often they think about the Roman Empire. To their shock, they learned that many men really do think about the Roman Empire a lot. Like, *a lot* a lot.

Soon enough, the conversation evolved. And those same women asking the "Roman Empire question" turned the camera toward themselves. They started sharing the topics that consistently captured their hearts and minds. Unforgettable celebrity moments from the early 2000s were brought to the forefront (think the teenage feud between Lindsay Lohan and Hilary Duff). Others eulogized their favorite TV shows that were canceled too soon (Oh, *Santa Clarita Diet*, we hardly knew you!). It's not that women don't care about ancient culture. Ancient mythology is many women's metaphorical Roman Empire.

But what this conversation really showcased for me is how differently men and women tend to see the past. For men, the Roman Empire is a dazzling feat of success in architecture, engineering, military strategy, and politics. Women, however, will look at the Roman Empire and see that something was missing: themselves.

Conversations around the Roman Empire often lack the mention of a single woman's name. Generally, it's all "Caesar" this, and "Nero almost burnt down Rome" that. In fact, there are almost fifty total speaking roles in Shakespeare's Roman epic *Julius Caesar*. A whopping two of those parts are for women—and they're both the wives of the actual main protagonists. This is how so much of history has viewed women: as the appendages of much more important men.

But our culture is moving past that narrow view. A media mogul like Oprah can be a billionaire—and so can a sparkle-sporting popstar like Taylor Swift. Many women no longer need a man in the way they used to. Instead of expecting a man to provide supreme financial and physical protection, many women want someone who can offer emotional and mental stability—a safe harbor in the unpredictable squall of modern life. Millennia-old priorities are quickly getting put to bed in favor of quickly adjusting, progressive dynamics. This development has led to some very big questions, like, "Do I need to share the same political party as my partner?" This is one I answer daily, it having grown increasingly popular since 2016 and exploding with the 2024 election. It's because most everyone, even those not particularly interested in politics, wants to date someone whose values align with their own. This comes up in my coaching classes, in my weekly #AskAMatchmaker direct messages, and even in casual conversations with single friends. My advice always boils down to one simple truth: you don't need to agree on all the details with your partner, but you must live in the same reality as the person you're building your life with.

The same idea of sharing one reality applies to this book. You may not agree with every recommendation I give, or even want to wait twelve dates to hit the sheets with your latest match (more on this later). But we have to be in agreement on the state of the (dating) world, and how we're looking at it. This way, no matter whether you're a man or a woman, a single dater or long-married spouse, we're all on the same page when it comes to love.

In the US, our echo chambers have led to polarized opinions on issues like women's access to comprehensive healthcare, LGBTQIA+ rights, gun control, and vaccinations, creating a massive divide among singles. Sharing the same reality doesn't just apply to politics; it's a crucial element in understanding how we view every facet of the world—especially in the realm of dating.

And the state of dating is this: Straight men and women are dating on different planets. But guys aren't bumbling their way through Mars, and women aren't nagging from Venus, as John Gray suggested in his famed 1992 psychology book *Men Are from Mars, Women Are from Venus*. Instead, men and women are spread across a billion different planets, moving through reactive galaxies that are more often pulling them apart than bringing them together.

HAS POLITICS ALWAYS INFLUENCED RELATIONSHIPS?

It's easy to believe that politics influencing dating is a new phenomenon, but it's not. It's the way we talk about it that has changed. Think back to how financial and social class colored every nineteenth-century romance you've ever read (or watched the swoony adaptation of on Netflix). One of Western literature's most famed romantic heroes, *Pride and Prejudice*'s Mr. Darcy, finds his love interest Elizabeth Bennet embarrassing because she's from a slightly lower social class. They're both attending lavish balls in the English countryside—but he's undeniably wealthier than her.

Or consider the fact that interracial marriage wasn't legal throughout the United States until 1967, long after many readers' parents and grandparents were alive and, probably, dating themselves. All of these rules around partnering are, at their heart, political issues.

ASK MATCHMAKER MARIA

Can you get past political differences in a relationship?

It really depends. How much of your politics is tied to your own morality? Are we debating putting up some streetlights and increase funding to public schools? Or are we talking about women (and families) having the freedom to make their own medical decisions? You can probably build a life with someone who disagrees with you on the first question. But when it comes to the latter, I hope you see eye to eye.

Before modern dating became modern dating, people tended to stay within their very niche microcommunities.[33] Families had much greater control over who their young people married. So hyperspecific political opinions didn't matter as much; a couple probably shared a race, religion, or class—and often all three—meaning they probably shared a lot of the same values. And they were probably going to marry whomever their parents wanted anyway. The goal here wasn't always happy marriages, but a variety of outcomes, from the consolidation of wealth to simply removing one more mouth to feed from an over-filled home.[34]

Today, we no longer play by those rules. We are dating beyond the microcommunities and cultures we were raised in, possibly across entire continental borders. Someone in Los Angeles could be swiping on blokes in London, as long as both parties have functioning Wi-Fi. With so much unknown about a potential match, politics has become the quickest way to understand a stranger's values. With a single tick of a box (Democrat or Republican, Liberal or Conservative, or even the much-debated Moderate), anyone can get an efficient picture of whether their moral compass aligns with someone else's. Over the decade and a half I've spent matchmaking, I've witnessed this become one of the greatest sea changes in dating.

Part of the reason shared politics feels so important in this era of American dating specifically is due to a political divide that's getting more contentious every day. According to research by professor of political science Lilliana Mason, Americans have become deeply socially divided along partisan lines since 2016. Rather than a national "we" outlook, many people have gravitated toward an "us versus them" attitude. "As the parties have grown racially, religiously, and socially distant from one another, a new kind of social discord has been growing," Mason writes. "Partisan battles have helped organize Americans' distrust for 'the other' in politically powerful ways."

In other words, our collective political polarization isn't merely about policy disagreements. Our political affiliation has become a building block in our very identity, leading to a complete mistrust of anyone who feels differently. And since the United States only has two main parties, we're stuck in a binary. Friend. Enemy. With very little wiggle room in between. It's a miracle when you can find it. And, honestly, I don't always recommend bringing across-the-aisle tactics into your bedroom. But sometimes it's worth it.

ASK MATCHMAKER MARIA
How do you match based on politics?
One of my intake questions asks how a client aligns politically. Instead of using American political party labels, I ask if they "lean liberal," "lean conservative," or if they're "in the middle." Following that question, I ask how important politics are to them. Some people want a partner that shares their political leanings; others are open to someone with a potentially differing opinion. Some are apathetic to the discussion, encouraging me to move past this part of the conversation. I try not to—no matter the results, these questions are a great stepping-stone to identifying someone's core temperament. I care less about the political affiliation and more about how a client identifies the problems in the world and their reactions to those problems.

Once I was matching a celebrity. When we started to talk about politics, she told me that she cares less about the political affiliation of her match. What mattered was if a person could identify the issues in their community and feel motivated enough to improve the lives of their neighbors.

She told me about how she had recently learned the homeless shelter in her neighborhood was out of resources. Quickly and quietly, she wrote a check. Her boyfriend at the time, a man of generational wealth, couldn't fathom why she cared so much. He had always been at the highest perch of society and was used to keeping his eyes forward—or even further above, as his parents had taught him. He believed looking down at the income inequality below was how you fell. But my client had hustled her whole life. Although she had picked herself up by her Manolo Blahniks, she never forgot where she came from. So she was determined to answer any call for help.

In her story, I understood that she was deeply empathetic and motivated to respond to the needs in her community. Based on this one example, I realized she was driven by empathy and a desire for harmony. She needed someone who shared those same motivations. Her partner, on the other hand, was more detached from the struggles of those in his community, focusing instead on maintaining his position in society. It immediately made sense why these two had broken up, and that this woman was looking for a new relationship. There would always be another homeless shelter, another soup kitchen, another family in crisis. My client would always want to roll up her sleeves and help. Her ex would have never even noticed anyone asking for help. My client and her boyfriend had been existing in two different realities and expecting the other to have the same conclusion. It was never going to work.

HOW DO ALGORITHMS AND ECHO CHAMBERS SHAPE OUR POLITICAL DIVIDES?

There is a difference between a value divide and a *perceived* outlook divide. My client and her ex-boyfriend did not prioritize the same things. But this fact had nothing to do with their voter registration. In fact, they shared the same political party. That's why I want you to look beyond a single label on a dating app profile to figure out if someone is worth dating. You could share the same political affiliation. It doesn't mean you're a long-term match. Or maybe they have ticked "Moderate" or "Other." I encourage you not to assume it's nefarious. It's possible that they may have a nuanced perspective that doesn't fit in a tiny box on a screen. Maybe they would love to tell you about it, and they'd be open to hearing yours, too. Not only could you find a great match in an unexpected place, but you'll be encouraged to dig deeper into the actual beliefs of someone who technically shares the same label as you.

After all, we live in a digital world, and many of us have content fed to us through algorithms designed to keep us online as long as possible. Meta, TikTok, Google, Netflix—they all utilize formulas to deliver content that aligns with our existing beliefs, which creates an ever-intensifying echo chamber. A lot of that echo chamber shapes our politics and assumptions about others.

In 2022, I attended a community theater performance. As I waited for the show to begin, an acquaintance of mine asked if he could sit next to me, and I replied, "Of course."

"Are you sure? I don't want to make you uncomfortable because I'm a Republican," he said. My jaw nearly dropped, but

I kept my composure. I didn't understand why he said that, so I called out the elephant in the room—pun not intended.

"Could you help me understand why you said that? I don't think we've ever talked about politics."

He never explained how he knew I was a Democrat. To this day, I assume he had caught some social media post of mine and tucked it away for a moment like this one. And, boy, did he capitalize on it. He explained, at length, with few breathing breaks, that my political party cared about nothing as much as they cared about "making children trans." I don't know how I kept it together, but I used my poker face just to see where this diatribe was going.

I asked him if he really believed that topic—little kids' gender!—was all Democrats talked about whenever we met. He confidently said yes—"You must!"

I asked him where he got this news from because no one had bothered to tell me, a card-carrying Donkey. I couldn't believe this conversation was happening. But I knew he would repeat whatever I said to his conservative enclave. So I tried to be as diplomatic as possible. I took a breath and put together my best response. "I can't speak for all Democrats, but the ones that I know think about having bodily autonomy and equal rights. Surely you agree with these two things?" I asked.

And of course he did.

Because he agreed, I tried to pivot to what he and I had in common. I wanted to step away from our echo chambers, which emphasized and distorted our differences, turning our very real similarities into blurry, funhouse mirrors of themselves. "Look, we're both here because we want to support our community, right? Look at all the incredible things you do for your own children to make them feel empowered here." I started to list the things I admired in him as a parent. He was attentive, confident, cared for others, and vocal when he perceived an injustice. These are qualities I think I share. I leaned into them, to prove our connection, and that maybe—just maybe—we shared more of a reality than he assumed. "You're scared your kids are being influenced to be something they are not because they are being taught to be more inclusive of others," I told him. "I don't believe that what you described is something any family takes lightly. It's a monumental change. The way I see it, anyone who is trans should have access to the healthcare they need. And privacy to make their own medical decisions. I would say the same on a host of other subjects."

And somehow, we came to a place of understanding that every family should be able to make their own private decisions.

Everything about this conversation was political. Some people would never have it with someone they're dating. I don't expect *you* to have it with every person you date. In fact, people break up over politics. Not everyone deserves your energy—especially if they hold beliefs you find to be dangerous, racist, or generally hateful. But if you take a step back and look at the off-line reality, you may realize you're more compatible with some people than you would expect.

HOW DO CHILDHOOD GENDER NORMS SHAPE OUR ADULT RELATIONSHIPS?

Like most parents, I was really excited to watch with my children some of the classic movies I had grown up with. First, we started with *The Little Rascals*.

I should preface this by saying that my husband and I are

raising a son and daughter in the twenty-first century. We are both self-described feminists, just as our respective parents were, and exhibit an equitable household. There are no "boy toys" or "girl toys" in our house. It's "the kids' toys." The pink crayon is used in my son's Crayola box as much as the blue crayon is used in my daughter's. We've done this intentionally, not only to have our daughter believe that she can achieve anything, but for our son to understand that he, too, can embrace any interest, emotion, or aspiration without the confinements of traditional gender roles. This approach not only nurtures their creativity and confidence but also fosters a sense of respect and understanding for the diverse world they are growing up in.

So, we watched *The Little Rascals* with our little rascals. Immediately, the nostalgia drifted away and I became hyperaware of how young boys and young girls have been socialized into understanding the rigid set of norms of what it means to be a man. My son picked up on it, too. He was in kindergarten at the time and was surprised and sad that the boys in the movie had created a "He-Man Woman-Haters Club." No girls allowed! My son has so many friends at school that are girls. He loves spending time with his sister; he often calls her his best friend. It never dawned on him, at the ripe age of six, to hate girls simply for being, well, girls.

In the movie, the boys build go-karts, pull pranks, and grin their way through mischievous adventures. The girls have perfectly decorated slumber parties, dainty ballet recitals, and pretty little dresses. Alfalfa and Spanky are the two main characters. Alfalfa has a crush on Darla. He is torn between his loyalty to the club and Darla. Meanwhile, Spanky is disturbed by Alfalfa's public displays of affection for a girl.

A lot of what this movie exhibits, in my eyes, is Man Box Culture,[35] an idea initially conceived in the 1980s by Paul Kivel of the Oakland Men's Project. His work on issues related to racism, violence prevention, and gender equality, and then further developed in the 1990s by A Call to Men founder Tony Porter. Man Box Culture refers to society's narrow set of rules for being a man. In Man Box Culture, men are expected to be less emotional, more surface-level, and only show feelings when those feelings are aggression or apathy. This stoic indoctrination begins in boyhood and increases over time. Men are often punished by both other men and women for attempting to get out of this emotionally constrictive box. They are also led to believe they'll be rewarded for following these rules. But that's a trap. The expectations of Man Box Culture leave straight men not only isolated from deeply relating with other men, but from the ability to connect to women as loving romantic partners.[36] Yes, the patriarchy is dangerous for women, but it's also leaving men out in the cold.

But *The Little Rascals* also helps to show how to deconstruct Man Box Culture. Darla challenges the boys' gender norms by pointing out their sexist attitudes. She's assertive, confident, and kind. She stands up for herself when she feels she's being disrespected. She even kicks Waldo to the literal curb after it's revealed to her that he is cheating to win the go-kart race. By the end of the movie, the boys begin to see the value in forming friendships with girls, moving toward a more inclusive and less stereotypical view of gender relationships. I was hopeful that by the end of *The Little Rascals*, my kids understood that membership in a woman-haters club isn't something to aspire to. Which brings us to . . .

WHAT IS THE MALE GAZE?

American pop culture has mostly viewed love through the "male gaze."[37] Film theorist Laura Mulvey first defined the term in 1973, despite the fact that it started coloring our perspective long before then. Through the male gaze, women are posed as sexual objects and rewards for men's good behavior, whether that be working out, financial success, having a charming personality, or pulling off an epic adventure.

If you're not quite sure what the male gaze is (or if it's real), watch 1988's *Twins*, starring Arnold Schwarzenegger and Danny DeVito as Julius and Vincent Benedict, the titular, inexplicably fraternal twin brothers. The most famous scene in that movie involves a dance sequence nicknamed "the butt grab waltz." The butts being grabbed belong to the twins' sibling girlfriends, Marnie (Kelly Preston) and Linda Mason (Chloe Webb).

The Mason sisters do nothing but squeal in delight when their rear ends are squeezed by a pair of mismatched brothers in the middle of the dance floor. Marnie and Linda become even more excited when Julius and Vincent pick them up by their hips, revealing the women's underwear to an entire crowded bar.

No woman I've ever met would smile so widely throughout such a disrespectful encounter. But there are Marnie and Linda's blank grins as they're manhandled in neon lighting. The male gaze tells us this kind of behavior toward women is normal, and this is what women like—that it's proper flirting. Now go find the nearest woman you can, and ask her if the butt grab waltz is actually her dream encounter. Likely it's not.

The downfall of Victoria's Secret can be attributed to the prioritization of the male gaze.[38] The company's marketing strategy historically focused on playing into and appealing to men's fantasies, using hypersexualized imagery of women. The brand promoted unrealistic beauty standards using supermodels, the Victoria's Secret Angels, whose looks are generally unattainable without extreme dieting, possible plastic surgery, and some very specific genetics. This approach created a disconnect with its consumer: people with boobs who want to carry those boobs through a variety of stages in life.

Following the birth of my son in 2017, I was absolutely shocked that Victoria's Secret didn't have maternity bras. Looking around the store—already feeling so much discomfort from my changing new-mom body—I was defeated. Who was this store for anyway? This brand did not represent my needs. Did it ever represent my values?

With the body positivity movement dominating conversations by 2021, Victoria's Secret did begin to make some changes by creating the VS Collective, a group of models chosen for their achievements over their looks with diverse body types.[39] But their reliance on the male gaze for decades made their inclusive reinvention an uphill climb.[40]

However, in 2021, they did finally launch maternity bras.

The male gaze for too long has been used to distort and limit men's understanding of the opposite sex, reducing them to mere objects and reinforcing harmful stereotypes.[41] A lot of sitcoms tend to rely on the weaponized incompetency[42] of their male characters for laughs. Think: *The King of Queens* or *Family Guy*. Those shows, and many like them, suggest it's okay for real-life women to be in charge of the emotional labor of their household, as well as the physical upkeep of housework. Those women are left exhausted—but that's okay because it's hilarious in these shows. This skewed perspective not only freezes men's perceptions of women but also limits how they interact with the world around them.

CAN THE FEMALE GAZE HELP US BREAK FREE?

The female gaze can thaw that freeze, giving men the chance to enjoy real emotional intimacy and even nonsexual touch. By moving away from Man Box Culture, you can move into the kind of wholesome masculinity represented by men like Travis Kelce, who spent a lot of 2023 and 2024 lovingly staring at girlfriend Taylor Swift as she performed in packed stadiums across the globe, or Alexis Ohanian, cofounder of Reddit and husband to Serena Williams, who cheers for her every chance he gets as publicly as possible. I mean, she really did marry her biggest fan!

Wholesome masculinity, in my eyes, is the idea that an emotionally expressive and emotionally resilient man's energy is conducive to promoting well-being. His collaborative nature and attitude toward finding solutions resulting in net positives is contagious to those around him. He doesn't feel emasculated by allowing others to share the stage with him. In fact, he welcomes a compromise or an ally, even if they are of the opposite sex. People feel safe around him because he is safe and secure at his core.

I don't think it's an accident that Stanley Tucci, Pedro Pascal, and Ted Lasso, the fictional American football coach played by Jason Sudeikis who goes to the United Kingdom to help a struggling soccer team win the title with his positive and charismatic leadership, became the internet's lovable zaddies—or sexy grown-man crushes—once President Biden was elected in 2020. We had all spent four years watching a president proudly make rude and offensive remarks about women. We were told to think of it as "locker room talk" despite our discomfort. We were more than thirsty for wholesome masculinity. We were parched. A trio like Stanley, Pedro, and Ted quenched us.

The female gaze erases the idea of a woman as an object and instead puts her in the driver's seat of desire.[43] Minute, purposeful details and the feeling of empathy are king—or should I say, queen. The female gaze powers this book, along with many cultural touchstones I'm willing to bet you already love.

While "female" might be in the name, this perspective on romance has as much to offer anyone as it does women. In reality, it's welcoming to all and can improve anyone's dating life. Don't believe me? Well, in no particular order, here are some of my favorite examples of the female gaze.

Any TV show made by Shonda Rhimes: Anyone who knows me knows that *Grey's Anatomy*, created by megaproducer Shonda Rhimes, is one of my favorite shows. In fact, beyond the soft comfort of *The Office* or *Parks and Recreation*, the soapy drama of *Grey's* is my comfort show. But the long-running medical drama is more than just a good time. Powerful women run the halls of Grey Sloan Memorial Hospital. The show's female stars get their power from their own confidence—not by making their male colleagues look or feel small.

Rather, men are just as smart, talented, and sexy as Grey's

superheroine doctors. Grey Sloan is populated by the kind of men who know how to take care of themselves. These genius surgeons can cook, clean a home, and even have a dream house built from scratch in the middle of nowhere as well as stitch up a body. You can find similarly empowered men in other Rhimes series like *Scandal* and *Queen Charlotte*. In Rhimes's world, it's never a man's job to save a woman—or a woman's job to fix a man.

Stanley Tucci: This man right here is the star of one of my favorite theories, appropriately named the Stanley Tucci Theory. I created it in 2020, just after I rewatched *Easy A*. When I look at Tucci, I think to myself, "This is a man written by a woman." He appears to be far more interested in crafting the perfect negroni cocktail or pasta dish than dominating any conversation. He can play a convincing villain precisely because he is acutely aware of what makes someone feel villainous.

While I don't personally know Tucci (yet!), he appears comfortable with women and their spaces. He never seems imposing or like he intends to demonstrate his strength in an overpowering manner. When he makes a cooking video, he speaks softly and is more encouraging than condescending. It looks like he listens, learns, and contributes afterward. I bet he's great at pillow talk. So I'm inclined to believe that men who like Tucci and connect with his behavior are probably more giving in the bedroom. If they can find such a wholesome and caring man entertaining, they probably understand that women have needs, too.

Other celebrity men who fall under the Stanley Tucci Theory umbrella include John Legend, Dev Patel, Andrew Garfield, Giannis Antetokounmpo, Jack Black, and Keanu

Reeves. Throw in all the men from BTS, the South Korean boy band, too!

Fleabag: The male gaze tends to prioritize winning—after all, it's the only way to get the girl in the end. But in *Fleabag*, there is no way for its unnamed character to win (or lose). *Fleabag*, starring and created by Phoebe Waller-Bridge, isn't a zero-sum series. Instead, it's a relatable show about a woman experiencing the complications of life. She misses her late mom and her best friend, whose death she holds immense guilt over. She loves her family and especially her sister, but feels like they'll never understand her. Her love life is a never-ending mess. None of us may want to be Fleabag, but we can all empathize with her. And that feeling of empathy is an asset in any relationship.

HOW CAN YOU LIVE THE FEMALE-GAZE LIFESTYLE?

Letting the female gaze into your life isn't hard. You're probably already doing it. When you send your friend a *Grey's Anatomy* meme, you're doing it. If you've ever stood in line for a Greta Gerwig film, you've done it. If you watch the first half of *Titanic* with the same enthusiasm as the second half, you did it!

But if you're not sure why it's worth your while, I can explain. Incorporating the female gaze into your dating and relationship strategy—no matter your gender—will generally improve your life. You'll notice your relationships become more egalitarian. You'll start to correct power imbalances while increasing respect. You'll start to feel closer to your loved ones, and like you're finally getting on the same page—whether that is about emotions or decision-making. This attitude won't just be a win for you, but for everyone else in your social (and romantic) orbit.

Recently, I got a new "Roman Empire." I became so moved during the 2024 presidential election watching men like Doug Emhoff, Vice President Kamala Harris's husband, and her running mate, Governor Tim Walz, model a modern version of masculinity for the country—one that welcomes emotional vulnerability, partnership, and very emphatic love for the women and children in their lives. These are the kind of family values I want to see in the world. And I hope after reading this chapter, that kind of behavior becomes your Roman Empire, too.

As you work on welcoming the female gaze into your life, it's very likely that you'll find yourself either starting to evolve your behavior or what you're looking for in a partner. If you are a man who wants to date women but doesn't feel like you're giving off Stanley Tucci vibes just yet, you can start changing that today. You can enroll in the next breast cancer walk in your community to involve yourself in something meaningful and connect with other good people, for example. What opportunities are there in your community or workplace? For example, my husband helped create a women's empowerment group at his office. If there's one at your workplace, can you ask them how you can volunteer or be a better ally? And, if there is no group, can you follow in George's footsteps and make one of your own?

As you focus on this expansion and settle into those spaces, try to work on listening first and speaking second. A warm and curious attitude will only win you new friends, both male and female. And remember, friendship is all you can ask for in these situations. This isn't the time to expect sex or a relationship in return for good behavior (that's the male gaze!). And if you're a woman seeing men in these spaces, try welcoming them with an open mind—and being as honest and open as you feel comfortable. Inviting men who are there "for the right reasons," to quote dating-show parlance I hear about so often, into more feminine-friendly spaces will create a greater positive social ripple effect than you can imagine.

This empathy allows us to share a life together more cohesively. If you can see the same reality as someone else, you can build a life with them—even if you don't agree on every single detail in that world.

4

I THINK MY PICKER IS BROKEN. HOW DO I FIX IT?

WHEN I TELL PEOPLE I am a matchmaker, many start telling me that they have this one friend I *have* to meet.

"Tell me about them!"

"Well, they're picky." *Ha*! I'll be the judge of that. We've just laid the groundwork of why we're here and what our goals are, and now we can dig into the real reason you picked up this book: figuring out how to track down your perfect match. So, we're going to need to figure out if you're picky or if your picker is simply off.

I've determined a threshold to tell if someone is really picky—it's much higher than you're probably thinking. Most people I have met are not picky (and I've met a lot of people). Instead, they're just terrible at articulating what they're looking for. For instance, some will resort to the old mental list they made when they were twenty-two, probably after a particularly bad breakup. Others will say, "You know . . . tall, dark, and handsome." And I'll quickly level with them: "Okay, but for real now."

"Okay, they're family-oriented, confident, intellectually curious . . . ," I'll hear. Now we are getting somewhere.

The response I dislike most is "I'll know it when I see it." Because, sure, that makes sense! But how quickly will you realize it when it's in front of you?

To be picky, in my professional matchmaking eyes, is to limit your dating pool so much that it's more of a dating fish tank. And to be really picky is to lack the self-awareness to even realize you're doing this to yourself. Pickiness is to believe you're going to catch the perfect fish out of that tank, and that same, singular fish will have been looking for you all along, too. I bet you'll never think of that "plenty of fish in the sea" platitude the same way again.

To avoid true pickiness, consider how your picker is working in the first place. What do you value in a life partner? How have your past dating experiences (if any) influenced which people you're naturally drawn to? How do you pick the right people? Also, who is driving your picker? Is it you? Your parents? *Your psychic?*

I had a client once, let's call him Liam, who insisted that he be set up with a woman from Europe who was a Gemini who would be interested in getting married and having children. Now I don't match people based on horoscopes, so I made some assumptions. I figured he wanted someone who was a worldly expat with a chatty and adventurous side. Luckily Manhattan is full of them. This part of his search was not picky. I can find female expats in their thirties who want to get married and have kids in a New York minute. However, how many will I find who also want to meet him, a highly religious, twice-divorced father of three?

Oh yes! Liam, forty-four, was the founder of a hedge fund and had three children by two ex-wives. He wanted to get married and have at least two more children. And while he didn't care if his match had a religion, he really cared that his children shared his religion and actively practiced that religion.

And yet, even with his complicated background, I still found Liam matches! So, as any matchmaker would do, I prepared to share the good news. One day, we hopped on a Zoom so we could discuss my initial choices. "When are their birthdays?" he asked, as he looked over my suggestions. This is when things turned picky.

"Why does that matter?"

"I need to determine their horoscopes."

"I don't do astrology-based matchmaking. I'm not going to share their birth dates with you."

I was ready to set up some dates. Why was he stalling?

This is when he revealed that he had a psychic.

Listen, it's okay if you have a psychic. Or an astrologer. Or an energetic coach. Or a Reiki practitioner. I think all these professionals can have a profound effect on teaching you how to use the metaphysical to discover new opportunities. But my job as a matchmaker is to find people who are enthusiastic to meet you. There's no crystal ball here. It's just first dates.

He made me meet with his psychic so that she could check each individual match's birth chart in confidence. According to her, only one of them was a match.

I set them up. Their date took place in one of the glass

igloos that had sprung up on the streets of New York in response to COVID-19 protocols. I don't believe they ever went on a second date. She didn't feel a romantic connection. I guess it wasn't written in the stars.

When I think of picky, Liam is my threshold.

As you've learned from the previous chapters, there are just so many factors at play when it comes to long-term compatibility. Leaving long-term love up to your sun sign is too simple and leaves your future up to too much chance.

It can feel discouraging when the pool of potential partners you envisioned turns out to be a fish tank. But I'm here to help you fix your picker and hopefully make the process easier.

I never want one of your friends to call you picky ever again, because I think it's very possible that you aren't! This chapter will go a long way in boosting your confidence when it comes to describing what you want—without thinking you're acting unreasonably. You're about to learn exactly what you value in the person you hope to call your life partner one day.

Grab a pen and a piece of paper. Yes, a real pen! Figuring out the contours of your future deserves your full attention—not some Notes app tapping that will instantly be forgotten for an Instagram notification.

Now that we all know *how* we're looking at the dating world at large, it's time to start looking for our specific partner.

Open your phone—yes, you can use it *now*—pop over to your Clock app, and set that timer for sixty seconds. It's time to get honest with yourself and answer the following question with a bullet-point list, one characteristic per line. *And go!*

"What qualities or values am I looking for in a partner?"

It's been sixty seconds! *Bing, bing, bing,* goes your alarm. Good job! You're already on your way to cracking your personal compatibility puzzle.

This exercise is simple and straight to the point, but incredibly revealing. As you were writing, you may have noticed you started to list the same criteria you're used to applying while swiping on The Apps. "He has to be over six feet tall." "She should share my religion." "He needs to be ambitious." This is all normal. We're simply trying to figure out how you currently recognize what kind of person is right for you.

Sometimes, my clients think that kind of unicorn person comes with a certain size bank account. They'll require at least a $200,000 salary—or even $1 million! Technically, this makes sense. Major cities, like New York City, Los Angeles, San Francisco, and Miami, where many of my clients happen to be, are pricey, and only getting more expensive by the day. But if you're also looking for an equal partner, you may want to reconsider your salary minimum. Because the person bringing in seven figures every year might already be treating their job like their spouse. It's possible they won't also have time to supply the emotional and practical support you're looking for in a partner.

Now it's time to ask yourself another question:

"What qualities or values do I bring to a relationship?"

Set that timer for another sixty seconds, and get to work. While we're used to constantly evaluating potential partners in our phones and across the bar, this is your chance to get introspective. Don't be afraid to brag. There's a reason you're looking for someone amazing—because you are, too.

Bing, bing, bing! Again, your alarm is going off. If you notice your first list is much longer than your second list, don't despair. That's how 90 percent of people have approached this exercise during my years of leading hundreds to fix their picker. As we're dating, we rarely consider all the attractive qualities we bring to the table. But keeping that list in mind is exactly what will tame the tendrils of anxiety when you find the person who truly checks all your compatibility boxes, which will evolve by leaps and bounds by the time you finish this chapter.

Although I'm happily married to my perfect penguin and soul mate, I know what would go at the very top of my list here if I were dating today. Every morning, I read through two newspapers. Not only does that mean I'm well-informed (and can therefore keep a partner equally well-informed), I'm a delightful plus-one for dinner parties. My college-debate-champion past also helps in that arena. I'm a whiz in the kitchen who can whip up layers of traditional Greek pastitsio and a tray of brownies for dessert, so my household will never go hungry. I'm an active listener, an honest friend, and great with kids. I'm pragmatic to a fault. I'm caring and compassionate. I'm no-nonsense. No one will ever have to wonder "What is Maria thinking?" You'll know in the most direct way possible.

This second list will remind you that the potential partner making you swoon over dinner is equally lucky to enjoy your company and that the person who disappears after a first date is the one missing out on you. You're an incredible human. Once you know that, no one can take it from you. If you don't feel like an incredible human just yet, go out there and cultivate the kinds of hobbies, interests, and experiences that would make you feel incredible. The period before you find the love of your life is the best time to focus on becoming the optimal version of yourself. Not only is this when you'll have the most time to prioritize yourself, but you'll be able to enter a relationship as a confident and whole person, rather than someone looking to be completed by another individual. This is a great way to make sure you're only partnering with someone who improves the beautiful life you already possess—and leaves little room for someone who may want to capitalize on your vulnerabilities.

I like to think of your Good Qualities list as your backpocket list. Never again should you feel the pang of anxiety after a first date. I think so many singles focus on "Oh jeez, did they like me?!" when really . . . did you like *them*? Having this list in your back pocket (or saved as a note in your phone) will serve its purpose: reminding you how lucky someone is to be dating you. And if they're acting like they are not lucky, they're missing out.

Now that you've reminded yourself who you are and what you think you're looking for, we can work on perfecting that perspective. That's where the all-important five pillars of compatibility come into play. I have the pillars listed in the order that you will learn about them in a person. I will tell you right now that these also happen to be in the order of least important to most vital:

- physical compatibility
- spiritual compatibility

- intellectual compatibility
- financial compatibility
- emotional compatibility

You might be surprised to see physical compatibility coming last in terms of significance. After all, it's what is whispering in your ear as you swipe through your app of choice before bed and the one coloring your scan of the singles table at every wedding. But the promise of physical compatibility can't be king. I would know, I've set up over five thousand first dates.

Think of these pillars like the columns that make up the Parthenon in Athens (it always comes back to Greece). If you were to remove a middle column in the Parthenon, the entire structure wouldn't collapse before your eyes. There might be some strain. It might need some extra support. But the temple would continue to stand. Physical compatibility is like that: it helps the relationship survive, but the whole thing won't buckle if those feelings sometimes wane while everything around them is strong.

On the other hand, the Parthenon could fall into the dust if you removed a corner column. There is just so much weight on both ends holding up the structure. Financial compatibility and emotional compatibility are your corner pillars for love. Without those, a strong gust of wind could easily topple your relationship. If you don't believe me, take the story of one of my clients, who was in a billionaire marriage. When you think billionaire—with a *B*—you probably assume there's no need to fight about money anymore. It's effectively endless.

But this real estate couple could never agree on how to spend their money. Private jet or business-class commercial with all the normies? The Paris Ritz or a lowkey Airbnb to live like a local? International boarding school for the kids or a local private school? The questions never ended—or aligned. Inevitably, one half of this couple ended up back on the dating scene and under my tutelage. Their former partner's looks certainly didn't put them there.

So how do you figure out what metaphorical materials make up your pillars? I'm going to tell you, of course.

WHAT IS PHYSICAL COMPATIBILITY?

Imagine you're in the time before The Apps. You can enjoy the feeling of relief spreading through your body for a few seconds before we continue. One, two, three, *ah*. Okay, it's the pre-Tinder era and you're standing at an open bar at a work friend's wedding. If you're a straight woman, a man who is a *bit* taller than you approaches. If you're five feet four, he's five feet six; if you're five feet seven, he's five feet eight, and so on. He's present. He makes you laugh. You wouldn't run away screaming. You may just be genuinely attracted to this man. Other people may just be genuinely attracted to him, too. I need you to start applying this thought experiment to how you're swiping and judging people in real life. Even if someone doesn't meet the height requirement you've set—or whatever other physical line in the dating sand you may have started to employ—they could still be the right person for you.

If you don't believe me, let's dig deeper into how real-life experiences tend to offer much more grace than a three-second swipe. I don't love to use scales, but for this purpose, we will. Let's say we're back at that wedding and a woman finds a man at face value to be a 6 in terms of attractiveness. But then he proves to be a great dancer. He goes up to a 7. And he's an attentive listener. Now he's an 8. And then there's that all-important, feel-it-in-your-bones quality: the C factor (or creep factor), which he thankfully lacks. He's a good guy and doesn't make your skin crawl. After a short conversation, that 6 has become a 9, or a 10 if he remembers to open a door or mention his love of Stanley Tucci. On the flip side, if you talk to a man who appears to be a 10 for, well, ten minutes, you might learn he possesses that dreaded Creep factor, or maybe he is arrogant. Maybe he never asks questions, or body-shames nearby women. Then, that 10 starts to look a lot like an undatable 5.

ASK MATCHMAKER MARIA

If a guy sexualizes your profession (i.e., fantasizing you as a "hot teacher") is it a red flag?

I don't know if men know this but anytime a woman meets a man, she judges him on his C factor, or creep factor. If a woman was on the subway or walking to work and someone started sexualizing her based on her profession—or her race or body type—she would be able to immediately detect the imminent danger. She would say to herself, "That's a creep. I'm going to ignore him. I'm not going to talk to him." Unfortunately, I think one of the consequences of online dating is a woman's ability to detect the C factor has diminished. We might excuse creep behavior because of all the other information we are provided on their profile, like photos of them with their friends, their correct grammar, and even their height. However, it is disrespectful. It is a red flag.

As we've already learned, dating apps were created by men, who tend to determine their attraction at lightning speed. The attributes they may be attracted to can be a wide gulf, but their dedication to a pass/fail rubric is singular. So they naturally created all the search filters that have been powering the dating site game since the dinosaurs like Yahoo Personal ads and Match.com roamed the earth, to find that ideal woman. This new approach flattened the ephemeral parts of physical attraction that used to rule analog dating with a dangerously simple (and fast) "yes" or "no." You've probably swiped left on your potential soul mate three times because of a wonky photo angle, thinning hairline, or embarrassing outfit (don't worry, we will still find them!).

As a five-foot-eleven woman, I searched for men five feet nine and up during my dating search. That means I was open to men who were shorter than me. Really. If you are a five-foot-five woman exclusively interested in dating men six feet and above—as many clients have initially told me—consider one thought experiment. If I had applied that same logic to my single life, I would have been claiming I could only muster up a scrap of attraction for a six-foot-six man and above. You can laugh, it's a ridiculous picture.

Having a man who is seven inches taller than you will not actually lead to a safer life in the twenty-first century. In fact, you'll be much better protected by washing your hands and keeping your passwords secure than needing a step stool or a running start to kiss your husband. Germs and hackers are the enemy—not a five-foot-six man.

Instead of focusing on unearned attributes like height or hair patterns, ask yourself what physical needs will truly make you feel fulfilled in a relationship. Physical compatibility is not just about looks. As someone whose love language[44] is physical touch (tied with words of affirmation), I feel most loved when my partner holds my hand or rubs my arm while we watch a movie together. (My sister, Chrisoula, always laughs when she recalls how she once witnessed me ask my husband, "Why don't you love me?" when he neglected to rub my arm while we were watching an episode of *Hacks*.) If your love language is quality time, you might be physically compatible with someone whose perfect Sunday is spent lying in bed doing a crossword puzzle together.

As you consider what you require for true physical compatibility, also ponder what makes you feel sensual, inside the bedroom and out. Is it someone who appreciates the effort you put into an outfit or a thoughtfully prepared homemade meal? What gestures make you feel safe enough to experience intimacy and vulnerability? When are you at your most playful? Once you start to answer these questions, you'll realize physical compatibility is so much more expansive, and exciting, than liking a pretty picture on a screen.

Sometimes, physical compatibility can be as simple as being with someone who makes you feel confident in exactly who you are. I got proof of this fact when someone sent me an Ask a Matchmaker Wednesday question I had never heard before. A thirty-seven-year-old woman revealed she was insecure about her thinning hair. "What's a bigger turnoff to men: thin hair or wearing a wig?" she asked. I said that I didn't know—but people are attracted to confidence. I told her to do whatever made her feel her best. Soon enough, I was flooded with messages from women who shared in the original follower's dating experience.

"I wear a hair topper (like a half wig that clips onto the top of your head) because I have the same insecurity. Guys never question it when I tell them about it and the ones that do aren't the one. What makes you feel confident is something they should support. They should embrace all of you," said one person.

Another said, "I wear a halo extension, which isn't the best when I'm horizontal. ;-) No men have ever batted an eye when I tell them I'm taking it off or when they put their fingers in my hair when making out. I agree. Being confident is most important!"

I even had a few men chime in saying they don't care. One of them shared, "Most men would likely not notice. My wife's hair was thinning before she started taking her hair meds. She wore a wig at our wedding! Never noticed. Never cared."

Physical compatibility is rarely the same as being a peak physical specimen, whatever that may be. It's about finding the person you feel your safest and sexiest around without any shame.

Dating app culture gives people permission to ask for age ranges, height ranges, and body types. They mistake these desires for their physical compatibility needs. My colleagues and I cannot seem to shake this. It often feels like people concoct an imaginary perfect person in their minds and think, "Oh, a matchmaker can find this magical unicorn person and bring them to me." Like I'm a headhunter for the empty space in their Instagram photos. But that's not what I do. Instead, my job is to understand who a client is, find them a person who aligns with their lifestyle, values, and attractions, and hope both parties see a future in each other. These details are what actually help maintain physical compatibility.

One of my clients, let's call him Rohit, insisted he could only be physically compatible with Jewish white women, though he was South Asian. His reasoning was to maintain a status quo in his co-parenting relationship with his ex-wife, who was also a Jewish white woman. However, after each date, Rohit's feedback always revolved around them not connecting on a "soul level." I had to keep asking questions, and I found that the root of the problem was that he wasn't feeling a cultural understanding. There were things he wanted to express in how he was raised that just didn't translate into words.

I told him, "Look, we've tried it your way. Let's try it my way now."

I set him up with an accomplished lawyer with beautiful eyes and long, thick hair. She was South Asian, too. The feedback was positive right away. During their date, they talked about their favorite music and recipes. They talked about "back home." Her familiarity was comforting, and he was absolutely buzzing with excitement the next day. "The conversation just didn't stop. We already have plans for a second date!" His assumptions about physical compatibility were keeping him from finding a partner he was compatible with *at all*.

Sometimes the qualities you assume are a physical dealbreaker are actually keeping you from your perfect match.

WHAT IS SPIRITUAL COMPATIBILITY?

When I started my business, I used to simply ask, "What about religion?" Many would say "not religious" or "spiritual." I knew this was the wrong approach about a year in when I had a new client who had been raised Jewish and wanted to meet someone who was also Jewish. When I searched my database, I couldn't find anyone who was Jewish in Manhattan. Something wasn't right.

I changed my questionnaire and conversations to "What religion were you raised with, if any?" The follow-up question to that was, "What's your relationship with your faith now?" The possible responses to that second question were:

- "I'm serious about my religion."
- "I'm somewhat serious about my religion."
- "It's just part of my culture."
- "I'm not serious at all."

Suddenly, many of the Jewish women I would attract into my pool of singles would check off "Jewish" and in the following question, "It's just part of my culture."

It also opened up a conversation about faith. For instance, someone could say, "It's just part of my culture," and then say they wanted a match who shared that exact culture by also sharing the same faith. Others would say they weren't very serious about their religion, but they *did* go to church every Sunday—and they expected their partner to share their faith or have the same commitment to religion as they did. I would also ask what faith they hoped their partner might have, and while most were really open, many were not. Whatever the case was, I was receiving critical information early on.

I have seen so many clients burned by having the religion talk far too late into a relationship. No one wants to ruffle the feathers early on, so they tiptoe around religion. Meanwhile you might be dating someone who expects you to convert to their religion for marriage and kids to be on the table.

You might think spiritual compatibility comes down to a simple question: Do we share the same religion? That's how many modern daters simplify the swiping process. But there are shades to that question. Some people grew up with a certain religion, but hold little connection to it now. Others may identify as Jewish, for instance, but consider it more of a cultural signifier than a defining religious factor. Someone else may identify as Jewish and practice very actively, keeping kosher and observing Shabbat every week.

When deciding whether to set my clients up with someone outside of their religion, I ask what their relationship with that religion is now, and what faith (if any) they plan to teach their children. The point is for you to pay attention to how open (or closed off) you actually feel to the idea of raising an interfaith family—or if you're prizing a same-religion relationship just to please parental figures. Your mother's approval of your spouse shouldn't take precedence over your daily happiness with a partner who may not be compatible in any other way. If you're feeling unbearable pressure to live up to your family's dating expectations, it might be time to talk to a therapist or even go to family counseling to get through this very legitimate issue. Though having a different belief system from a prospective partner may understandably pose some challenges, a shared faith doesn't equate to shared values.

As someone in my Ask a Matchmaker Wednesdays DMs recently told me, she's a white woman who was raised Hindu and continues to practice today. When she was trying to exclusively date other Hindus, she felt like her option pool was constricted. So she started dating men who shared her *values* as a Hindu versus focusing on finding someone who already shares her spiritual beliefs or wants to convert. She's never been happier or felt like her pool was wider.

However, through the process of matchmaking, my client Zain, a non-practicing Muslim, realized how important his faith ultimately was to him. He thought he was open to dating women of all faiths. Then we actually started talking about religion. I asked him, "Do you expect your children to share in your faith?"

"Of course," he replied. Looking at my notes, his last girlfriend was Mormon. "So, why didn't it work with your last girlfriend?" I asked. "Because, when we talked about our future, she didn't want to convert," he said matter-of-factly.

"And you're still open to dating non-Muslim women?" I said. "If you're hiring me, let's make this easy on all of us. Let me focus on just meeting women who share in your faith." It never dawned on him to zoom in on one (clearly more compatible) type of woman until I held up a mirror that said, "We're not merely looking for your next girlfriend, but potentially the person you may have kids with."

Clearly, you can't determine spiritual compatibility by checking a box. So you should attempt to apply an understanding of the Greek word *agape* to this category. Not to get all Philosophy 101 on you, but Aristotle defined *agape* as the soul's recognition of another soul. A soul mate in this instance will make you feel like you're on the right path. You'll exist on the same vibe frequency, whether you share a religion or not.

To decipher whether you can share a vibe with someone, start to interrogate what makes you feel spiritually connected and respected. Do you see eye to eye on subjects like evolution (like . . . literally. Do they believe in evolution? Do they believe dinosaurs were real, or did the devil put their bones in the ground to confuse us?) and acceptance of other people's lifestyles? What matters most to you about family quality time and holidays? Do you value the specific celebration of religious observance or the basic comfort of regular time with loved ones around nostalgic foods? Does your purpose align with a prospective partner's purpose?

Even a lifestyle practice like veganism can fall into spiritual compatibility. If your connection to animals and the environment is so powerful you're willing to forego the earthly pleasures of butter and cheese, something divine is surely afoot.

I know a lot of dating books say not to talk about religion on a first date. But if your faith is a cornerstone of your worldview, you should talk about it early in a manner that welcomes questions and showcases your values. That means saying something like "The more I connect with my faith as a Christian, the more I realize how important giving back to my community is" versus "I can only date another Christian because that's what my family expects." One is a conversation starter, and the other is a conversation ender.

When I was dating, I was open to dating non-Greek men. In fact, I dated a lot of men outside of my culture. At some point in my early dating, I also shared my precise values for how I wanted to raise my future children. It didn't matter if I was talking to a German atheist, a Catholic guy, or an alien. This individual needed to know what I wanted, and they could be in or out. On one date, I proudly said that I fully intended to raise my children in the Greek Orthodox Christian community I was raised in and to take them to Greece every summer. I would expect them to go to Greek school once a week, go to Sunday school (every Sunday, duh), and to be involved in the youth group that would teach them Greek folk dances and Greek theater. The man I was dating had a different religion and said he expected his kids to share it as well. But as I asked more questions, I realized he didn't belong to a particular community or hadn't practiced his religion in years. I knew we wouldn't work out long term.

Some people might tell you I should have been more open-minded. But that wasn't honest. I wanted my kids to follow one religion and for that religion to be Greek Orthodox Christian. I envisioned them participating in the same community that I had as a child. I could date someone of a different religion who was open to raising our kids in the Greek Orthodox community—but could never build a life with someone who wanted those children to be an entirely different religion, especially if they didn't want to participate in the community I love. If I had forced myself to partner with someone who saw that future, I would have ended up resenting them.

From that fateful date forward, I knew what I wanted. I would either marry a fellow Greek Orthodox man or look for a person who would come along for the ride. Think: Ian in the movie *My Big Fat Greek Wedding*. He leaned all the way into Toula's culture once they fell in love. My desire never had to do with winning, or even, exactly, Jesus. I simply knew how I wanted to build my family around my personal spirituality, which is based in my lifetime Greek American community.

Obviously, I ended up with a Greek guy following my plan. But that doesn't mean your values will lead you to someone just like you. George and I actually have different approaches to our culture. We just needed to be aligned on how we saw our future—not on every detail of our personalities.

The role that spirituality plays in your life can and will be different for everyone. Once you realize what *your* true perspective is, you'll be setting yourself, and any future partners and kids, up for a much happier life.

WHAT IS INTELLECTUAL COMPATIBILITY?

Once upon a time, a friend of mine started dating a man who seemed generally promising. They had fun. He expressed straightforward interest in exploring long-term dating on their third date. But he didn't read. His apartment was disconcertingly free of books (at least that she could see). And she was a successful writer. Still, she told herself she was being a snob and different people are smart in different ways. It was fine. It was all very fine. Yet, even when friends met him, they praised the couple's connection . . . while wondering if he could keep up with her.

After nine months, they broke up. At around eight and a half months, he asked her if she thought he was a bum because he did not read books. It became clear in that moment that no matter how much these two cared for each other, they were fundamentally intellectually incompatible. Not because he didn't read, but because they just weren't smart in ways that enriched the other.

Intellectual compatibility is more than merely being, well, intellectual. It's about ascertaining what makes you feel mentally fulfilled and at ease. One of my favorite questions on OkCupid used to be "Do you think morality is relative or universal?" While you don't need to share the exact same answer with your partner, your individual approaches to that question can reveal a lot about your critical-thinking skills and attitude toward the world. Pay attention to those findings.

But this pillar of compatibility doesn't have to feel like studying for the SATs all over again. It's also fun. Sharing the same sense of humor is an example of intellectual compatibility, as is enjoying the same genres of films.

In an effort to continue romancing each other years into our marriage, my husband and I have a weekly Marvel Mondays date to maintain our intellectual intimacy. We watch a superhero movie and then talk about it in depth. It's a meeting of the minds and our mouths to popcorn.

If you're not interested in watching Hollywood's finest battle it out in spandex, you could attend lectures with a partner, a creative writing class, read the same book or article and then discuss it, or take a wine seminar. What matters is that you learn together—and enjoy expending your mental energy in complementary ways.

FINANCIAL COMPATIBILITY

In the beginning of 2012, I attended a dating industry conference in Miami. I met a guy and, well, long story short, we began to date. He told me he had a few master's degrees—I guess one wasn't enough for him—and he was thinking of starting a dating social network app soon. I asked him what he did for work. He said "yacht broker," and was apparently based in London. I didn't really think to look up on Glassdoor what exactly that is. I figured the man was a yacht salesman. I don't know?!

Anyway, I told him I'd be heading to South by Southwest soon, the conference-slash-festival that celebrates the convergence of tech, film, music, education, and culture. I would be specifically going for interactive events. I proudly said I was able to score a room at Motel 6 a couple of miles down the road for $250 a night! I would be there for four nights. He was welcome to join me if he could get his hand on a South by Southwest pass on such short notice. I didn't think there would be availability. Two days before I left, he said, "Okay, I'm coming. But I don't want to stay at a Motel 6. I got us a room at the Hilton Convention Center." The very convention center where all the panels we would be attending were located. I couldn't believe it. That place had been sold out forever. Then, I started sweating, thinking about the cost of splitting a room at the Hilton Convention Center during peak conference time! "Don't worry about it," he said nonchalantly. Like the money was nothing.

When I rolled my suitcase into the glittering lobby of the Hilton, I was expecting something nice. It was clearly a nice hotel. Then, my bags weren't taken to some basic king suite with a solid view. It was there I learned *we were staying in a suite with a skyline view of Austin*! My new beau was paying per night what I paid in rent for a whole month, and, at that time, I counted every single penny. Hell, just a few months before, I'd swiped my card at my local pizza spot praying to God it would not put me in the red! He insisted on paying for it all. And thank god, because even if I had wanted to contribute half, I couldn't.

That first night, I got thirsty. I remember going to the minibar to get a bottle of water. He woke up and said, "No. Don't do that. They overcharge! I'll go and get you water."

So he got up and walked two blocks in the middle of the night to buy us a dozen waters at the nearest pharmacy. This (apparently secret) billionaire would rather do all that literal legwork than let us pay four dollars for a bottle of water.

You might think this story proves that I value convenience more than I valued my ex. It doesn't. Instead, it shows that convenience meant different things to us. He didn't want to wake up an extra hour early every day to pack into the Motel 6 shuttle to the convention center with a bunch of strangers. He preferred to just take an elevator down. I didn't want to walk half a mile for water when there was perfectly good (if pricey) H2O right in front of me in the room; paying the extra two bucks was worth saving the physical effort. I left that trip with crystal-clear proof my "yacht broker" and I weren't actually a match. For weeks I had been ignoring obvious signs that we probably weren't financially compatible. We approached monetary obstacles in really different ways.

In hindsight, I think about the stories I would tell him of my childhood or the origin story of my business. He would react like an anthropologist uncovering the quirks and mysteries of middle-class culture. Eventually I asked him more about the yacht broker business. I had to. Money had been flowing on every date, but the South by Southwest experience was unlike anything I had ever done before—even with him. Turns out, he wasn't a yacht broker! He was a shipping heir.

Look, I, too, can rise up the rungs of the social hierarchy. The guy would have been so lucky to have had me as a long-term partner or wife. Yet our connection never felt fully real. Our time together felt more like a vacation from my real life than the process of finding a life partner. Which makes sense. We were raised so strikingly differently from each other. I was getting a peek into the mindset of a different type of person and class than I had ever fathomed. Still, there were downsides. My productivity had completely cratered. I hated it. And he just didn't get it. He thought I wanted to "hustle." He had no idea that no one *wants* to hustle. But I had to. It was the only way the company I had put so much of myself into would thrive. I didn't have generations of family wealth backing me. Instead, my success was actually one of the best chances my family had for long-term prosperity. They were relying on me—not the other way around. Sadly, my handsome, wealthy shipping heir and I were ultimately . . . not compatible.

The equation for financial compatibility is a surprisingly simple one, as it encompasses two parts: how you value the way you spend your time and how you value the way you spend your money. Remember that billionaire couple from earlier? They fundamentally could not agree on the answers to these questions. They simply did not have the same lifestyle.

To avoid finding yourself in a similar pitfall, begin determining your own five- to twenty-year goals. Is buying a home a necessary milestone for you? What is a perfect vacation for you? How often does that happen? Do you want to become a parent? If so, do you plan on public or private schooling, and do you want to pay for that? Or, do you want to skip parenthood and allocate your funds somewhere else? What do you consider a splurge, and what exactly is worth that kind of money for you? What do you hope retirement looks like for you? Would you sign a prenup?

A key word in all those questions is "you." These boundaries and expectations are for you to share with a prospective partner. Rather than quizzing them on a first date about their net worth and fifteen-year plan, share your own vision of the future when the timing feels natural and appropriate. This openness will hopefully inspire a discussion about your shared and contrasting goals, rather than feel like a surprise job interview in an ax-throwing bar. Knowing the answers to the above questions will make it much easier to have a conversation rather than reacting to the information you are uncovering.

Still, I know conversations around money make even the most confident people nervous. So I have a foolproof question to painlessly kick off any financial compatibility chat: What would you do if you won $1 million from a scratch-off gifted to you by your boss? Instantly, you'll learn about a prospective partner's relationship with work and how they think about financial planning.

Fellow matchmaker Paul Brunson told me he would put all his imaginary winnings in a certain electric car company—and his wife would agree. I, on the other hand, experience stress around the concept of student loans. Therefore I would pay off my student loans, along with my sister's. Then I would create six education trusts, one for each of my kids and niece and nephews. (These winnings are after taxes, obviously.) Without asking my husband, I know he would say the same, because we're aligned on our financial concerns and goals.

Of course, our financial advisor and accountant would advise us to do something completely different. (Hello, compound interest!) And these kinds of people can also be really helpful when you start to have serious conversations about potentially combining your finances.

Before any of that happens, you have to be comfortable talking about your lifestyle. How do you spend your time? How do you invest in yourself? How do you see your future?

You also have to assess your financial triggers. What are the things you learned about money? What are the things you need to *unlearn* about money? How do societal norms or peer pressure influence your spending habits?

Developing financial self-awareness and envisioning the life you want to share with a partner will help you find someone whose goals align with yours.

WHAT IS EMOTIONAL COMPATIBILITY?

Welcome to the final, and most important, pillar of compatibility. Pull that pen back out, and take a minute to write down the three things you need to feel acknowledged in a relationship. Everyone's answers are different. Think about the level of communication you are looking for. Some people may need to hear from their partner every day. But I also once had a client who put little value on quality time and constant communication. She dated a man she would only see on Saturdays; they did not text or call each other between dates. They're married now.

ASK MATCHMAKER MARIA

My boyfriend doesn't have any friends. Should I be worried?

I would be. I think men having friends is paramount to their emotional resilience. The more internal fortitude someone has, the stronger their ability to be a good partner who can adapt to stressful situations and cope with life's ups and downs.

While toxic masculinity may suggest that resiliency is born

out of a refusal to cry or show feelings in public (or private), the real answer is much more, well, emotional.

You can recognize an emotionally resilient partner based on how they predict and react to challenges, their ability to think positively, their commitment to goals, and their range of social support. That social support acts as a compass. While a romantic partner is a wonderful person to have in your life, men can only be good boyfriends and spouses if they are good friends. It also lessens the pressure of their romantic partner to be all things, thereby improving emotional compatibility in a relationship.

While outside work can certainly bolster emotional compatibility, the pillar also comes down to the people intimately inside the relationship. To further understand what you need, think about the moments in your life that made you feel emotionally safe, or what circumstances would create that feeling for you in the future. What kinds of behaviors embody reliability to you or make you feel listened to? What are you sensitive to and how can a partner respect those possible triggers?

Emotional compatibility, like financial compatibility, takes more than a few dates to discover. In fact, it can take anywhere from three to six months to learn how you align as you go through the initial milestones of a relationship together—being intimate, meeting friends, your first fight. As you keep dating, you'll discover their emotional triggers and their coping mechanisms as they will discover yours. Throughout this period, if you're emotionally compatible, you'll feel supported and comfortable sharing personal thoughts and feelings.

If at any point you feel anxious or confused, and they're not providing crystal-clear clarity, that's not a good sign.

Think of emotional compatibility as your load-bearing pillar; you need it to stand up in a relationship. But it's only with all four other pillars (physical, spiritual, intellectual, and financial) that the Parthenon can withstand the centuries.

Below, I have created a word bank for you for each pillar. As you glance across the words, circle the ones that speak to you the most. What do those words mean for you? Expand on why you found them important.

Do you notice that the word "respect" is in each of the pillars? Respect—both mutual and for self—are paramount to long-term compatibility as they lead to creating a sense of trust, balance, and boundaries, making it easier to manage conflicts.[45] In any relationship, you should expect differing thoughts, opinions, and solutions to everyday problems. Mutual respect will make you more likely to listen to your partner's perspective, helping you decide the best path forward for yourselves. Self-respect involves communicating your own needs through self-awareness and recognizing your own

Five Pillars of Compatibility Spark Words

Physical	Spiritual	Intellectual	Financial	Emotional
Desire	Comfort	Humor	Goals	Empathy
Touch	Purpose	Ambition	Lifestyle	Balance
Sex	Peace	Values	Respect	Attentive
Connection	Acceptance	Equality	Retirement	Thoughtfulness
Activities	Pride	Respect	Vacations	Intimacy
Attraction	Values	Goals	Habits	Sensitivity
Intimacy	Family	Equity	Upbringing	Reliability
Playfulness	Commitment	Thirst	Comfort	Comfort
Attuned	Understanding	Support	Safety	Receptiveness
Giving	Participation	Conversation	Freedom	Temperament
Respect	Open	Education	Opportunity	Appreciation
Open-mindedness	In tune	Career	Family	Respect
Communication	Respect	Communication	Communication	Communication

worth. You're less likely to tolerate mistreatment and you may be better equipped to show respect to your partner as well.

In the next chapter, you will be ready to fill out your very own Compatibility Matrix to manifest your true perfect match. You don't need to use the exact words from the word bank. Instead, just use them as a stepping-stone to figure out which characteristics from each pillar you hope to see in your future partner. Let these words inspire you and help you dig deep into your desires. Because we're about to start fixing your picker and help you manifest your dream relationship.

5

HOW DID YOU MEET YOUR HUSBAND? AND HOW DO I DO THE SAME THING?

A WEEK BEFORE I TURNED twenty-eight years old, I went to a bar on Stone Street for a beer with my friend Bianca. It was one of those mild November days where you could sit outside in downtown New York and let the heat lamps warm your cheeks. Bianca is a little *woo*. She believes in astrology, and, like so many of my friends who share that interest, talks about it passionately. I love listening to them talk about it passionately. It's my ASMR.

Since Bianca knew my birthday was coming up, she started to explain that I was about to enter my Saturn Return.

As the astrologer Aliza Kelly once told *The Cut*, Saturn Return happens when Saturn in the sky aligns with Saturn in your birth chart. After twenty-eight long years away, Saturn once again occupies the same place in the sky as it did at the moment you were born. As Kelly explains, "Because Saturn is the planet of responsibilities, time, and wisdom, a Saturn Return is, basically, your astrological coming of age. Think of it as the push you need to enter true adulthood. Saturn demands that you take full and complete accountability for your choices, propelling major—albeit challenging—transformation."[46]

At twenty-eight, I already had a pretty robust date-coaching program with Agape Match. I helped singles understand the five pillars of compatibility, like I just helped you. I asked myself, "What if . . . I utilized this new information to manifest my own partner? Why not just lean into the 'woo' for the sake of Saturn?"

So, on my twenty-eighth birthday, I wrote out my pillars into a matrix. From there, I converted my matrix to a manifest. I didn't add nearly as much as I have encouraged clients to do in the years since, but it was clear: I was looking for someone who admired me as much as I admired them.

Now, I had to put it out in the world. I . . . published it on my personal Tumblr (it was the early 2010s!). I posted it to Facebook. I emailed every person I knew. This is the man I am marrying. If I build him in my mind, he will come.

And then I thought to myself: My Saturn Return is asking me to take full and complete accountability for my choices. How can I supercharge this transition? I went through my mental Rolodex. I considered which of my friends were dating the kind of guy who would be friends with *my* guy. Birds of a feather flock together, right? I thought of two men who fit the bill: my friend Maria's husband, Taso, and another friend named Maria's boyfriend, Panagioti.

The reason I chose these specific couples in my quest was

because I admired them. In our interactions, I saw equitable relationships. I saw outspoken women who were dynamic as hell, and their partners were so damn proud of them. Taso, who was Greek American, was also my lawyer. His advice was always pragmatic, and I appreciated his honesty. Panagioti, who was born and raised in Greece, was finishing his PhD in a foreign country (our United States). He was resilient and inquisitive. Both men had a really strong work ethic and appreciated the same in their partners. Surely they had good friends with similar qualities.

Panagioti and Maria called me a week later—they said they'd be going to a bar in Boston with friends on Friday. Did you think I was going to scoff at the distance? I had given them a homework assignment—*Invite me next time you're out with your friends!* They did it. Give me an Amtrak ticket! I'm going to Boston!

A few days later, I was walking into Lolita Tequila Bar on Dartmouth Street with Maria and Panagioti. I probably met nine of their pals, along with some people in their extended social circle. Four of the men in attendance were single. And one of them . . . was really smart, funny, and clearly liked me. I could feel his interest from the way he actively listened to every word I said. His name, obviously, was George. I wanted to get to know him more, so I got his number by saying something super lame like "Oh, you're originally from Crete? Show me on the map." He put a pin on the address on my Google maps and then I said, "Okay. I'm gonna save this pin so that if I ever go to Crete, I will contact you to go for a coffee. [Mind you, this man lived in Boston.] What's your number so I can call you?" He gave me his number. And as I was typing, he said, "Send me a text, so I can save your number. Otherwise, I'll think you're spam and won't pick up."

Cue the "Mastermind" lyrics from Taylor Swift. Looking back, I see we were both trying to get each other's numbers. Duh. Anyway . . . I texted him and instead of texting him my name, like a normal person, I texted him a cute photo of myself. It was of me looking into the camera, drinking a Greek coffee from a small mug (that's what they are served in) with my pinky up. With a single tap of "send" I had scored two big wins: my new crush had my number *and* a reminder of what a cutie I am.

He texted me back one minute later: "You're cute." I felt my face go red. We were literally with all his friends in a crowded bar, and this is what was happening, while everyone was about eight inches away from us.

Anyway . . . it worked. Feel free to steal this move whenever you need it. It's much more clever than sharing your Instagram handles and agonizing over when to DM five days later.

If I hadn't had my manifest absolutely memorized, I never would have realized what a good man I had standing right in front of me—honest to God. George resembled none of my ex-boyfriends. That was a good thing. But if you're only familiar with a certain kind of person—whether that's a race, height, hair color, or body type—you're destined to repeat the same dating mistakes without the guiding light of a concrete list of what qualities you are looking for. That list helps point you toward a *person* instead of the familiar outline of a type.

As I got to know George, I realized he was actually exactly

what I was looking for. And really cute to boot. He was just a different cute from what my eyes were used to chasing. So, hell yes, we went on our first date the very next day. We took a four-hour walk in the frigid cold of a Boston winter with the friends who introduced us. We walked the Freedom Trail while our chemistry, also, knew no bounds. Then we had our second date that very evening for cocktails at The Hawthorne. I'm so sad to report that this incredible venue closed during the pandemic.

By the way, George loves to tell people that it was on this date I told him that one day, when I got engaged, I wanted a sapphire ring, because my mom had one. He loves telling people that I was talking about rings on our first date. But really, we were just walking past a jewelry store, and I was just . . . talking. Still, he did hold on to this detail for two more years. When he proposed, I got the sapphire ring I had always wanted. I'm proud that I shared my dreams that early. Never forget: the right person won't be scared off by honesty.

Now, back to our second date—I recall thinking I was having the best time with this man. We weren't asking each other questions like a job interview. As we stood by the bar, side by side, we conversed about our favorite *Friends* episodes, and he shared his passion for mixology and cooking. I shared my passion for Eurovision. I felt comfortable to just be myself. Were we both nervous? Probably! Were we both excited? Absolutely! When he went to the bathroom, I snuck a coaster from the bar into my purse. If he was The One, I wanted a memento from the day. I have that coaster framed in my office. It was the best second date ever.

ASK MATCHMAKER MARIA

Is it true that when you know, you know?

The only people who say that are married people who want to throw their ring in the dating advice pool. I think it's dumb and useless advice. Like, yeah . . . after five years, it's easy for them to say, "When you know, you know." But when they first started dating, they didn't know. They just loved how they felt around the other person and they kept dating them.

With only a weekend to get to know each other, because George would be heading back to his hometown on the isle of Crete for Christmas break, we didn't waste our time. When a person is in the right place to date you, they'll display the same eagerness as you, without reservations about maintaining a cool (read: detached) appearance or the fear of going "too fast." Your anxiety will fall away when it comes to concerns like "asking for too much" or rushing some imaginary timeline.

Despite our distance, we continued to date, and I studied my manifest after every encounter. The more I got to know George, a lot of it through video chatting, the more it became clear he checked all my boxes, and then some. Three weeks later, after he returned to the States, we were boyfriend and girlfriend. We became Facebook official two months later (*remember*, it was the 2010s). I still read my manifest each month to confirm that George continued to match what I was looking for, and I stayed grateful to the woo-woo and my ability to follow it into saying "yes" when the right one came along.

ASK MATCHMAKER MARIA

My brother's friend says he's interested but thinks I'm "off limits." What now?

The only people who say stuff like that are people with bad intentions. If he was actually interested in something serious, he'd ask you out . . . date you . . . and be well prepared for the most epic wedding roast of the year by his best man (your brother). But he doesn't want to date you. He just wants to sleep with his best friend's sister. After such a manipulative opening, he doesn't deserve the honor.

In the previous chapter, you were given some instructions on how to identify what direction your picker should be set at. Now that (I hope) you're feeling inspired, it's time to write your manifest. When I say manifest, I mean that I want you to think of a detailed declaration of what you hope becomes reality. You will detail the exact kind of partner and relationship you hope to attract into your life. You might be thinking this exercise sounds way too woo-woo for a person as practical as you—or, even me, a CEO and mom of two with a master's in global affairs (and not a single crystal in her home). But, like you've just learned, writing mine is what brought me to my husband, George. Or, at least, it helped me realize he wasn't just some random guy when I met him. He was The Guy.

So here's how you'll write your own manifest:

I want you to start by writing down the values and characteristics you are looking for in your ideal partner. I'm obviously not going to look at your matrix, so if you put a certain word under the wrong column, don't worry—you can't get in trouble. For some columns, you might realize you only have two or three words. For other columns, you'll have seven or even ten words. That's okay. As I explained in the last chapter, that just means one pillar is more important to you.

I remember when I did this, I had just two characteristics under spiritual—"is cool with me raising our kids Greek Orthodox Christian" and "if they don't believe in God, they won't make me feel stupid because I do"—and eleven under intellectual. "Is a feminist and understands the definition of the word," "knows current events," and "is a logic-based thinker" were some of my favorite qualities under the intellectual pillar. George has all of these good characteristics and more.

Let's get started!

Physical	Spiritual	Intellectual	Emotional	Financial

Now I want you to look over all the characteristics you just listed in your matrix and circle your top ten. Then, I want you to rank them from most important to least important and contextualize them. For instance, maybe you tell me you want someone ambitious. Okay. What makes them ambitious? I once had a woman tell me my client wasn't ambitious enough. I was surprised to hear that feedback since he was the CTO of a major tech company. I asked her why she felt he wasn't ambitious. She responded that she didn't like that he had no plans to leave in the next five years. She measured ambition as hustle and not someone settling into a high position they had presumably worked really hard to achieve. The stock options didn't matter to her—nor did the salary—only what was next. Maybe you tell me you want your future partner to be a strong communicator? Excellent . . . What is a strong communicator to you? Do you expect to be spoken to each day? (Reasonable ask by the way.) What level of contact do you need to feel secure?

What qualities does the partner you want to be with have? Contextualize it!

1. _____

_____

2. _____

_____

3. _____

_____

4. _____

_____

5. _____

_____

6. _____

_____

7. _____

_____

8. _____

   _____

9. _____

   _____

10. _____

   _____

Okay! Now on to the next part: your manifest. I really believe that you should kick this off with a wonderfully affirmative statement like "Let me tell you about the person I am meant to be with!" I have done this exercise over one thousand times with my clients, and I've seen it all. I have seen people write everything from letters to their friends in the present tense, "Dear Jessica, I have to tell you about my boyfriend!" to proper wedding vows. I want you to feel excited!

Once you're finished, you'll have a tangible reminder of what you're actually looking for in a long-term partner or even the future co-parent of your kids, if that's something you're interested in. And you'll have concrete proof of what doesn't really matter during the hunt for a spouse. Qualities like a specific height, body type, or belonging to a single profession will start to seem so much less important than how a potential partner makes you feel or shows up in a relationship.

Before we get into the work of writing your manifest, I thought you could use an example of what one can look like. Every time this subject comes up in my monthly dating crash course called the Agape Intensive, students light up the moment they see a manifest that works. So I went into my Notes app archives and found you one very special example. Of course, I'm talking about my own.

December 5, 2012

Let's talk about this awesome man I am meant to be with. He's going to rock! You know why? Because he'll think my sass is sexy. He will admire my brain and my can-do attitude. He'll come from a family where the female figures in his life were treated with respect, honor, and loyalty. He'll have a passion for life. He will be social, friendly, and generally an all-around nice guy. He'll want to impress me, just as much as I'll want to impress him without a hint of competitiveness to glory. Maybe he'll be taller than me and hopefully he will speak Greek (so he can talk to my dad), but meh . . . these characteristics are not that important. What's important is that he is a man of his word, that he is dedicated to his dreams with ambition and drive, and that he has positive energy to want to inspire "us" to be better each and every day.

So, yes, I admit, 99.9 percent of men are probably intimidated by my personality, my career, my lifestyle, even this post! Who cares about the 99.9 percent though? If I am meant to be with someone exceptional, he's probably not going to be in the general populace segment. I am willing to wait and play those odds because . . . the rest of our lives is just so flipping worth it.

I met George nine days later.

You've probably noticed my manifest isn't flowery—I'm not a flowery woman. Like I mentioned before, I'm pragmatic to a fault. But over the years, my Agape students have gotten quite imaginative with theirs. One woman wrote hers as if she were on a road trip with her new fiancé. She detailed the way his hand felt on her leg, along with the scenery rushing by her window. The story transported you to her very own love story. If that's the kind of manifest that sounds more natural to you, here's an example from another one of my students.

Hey, let me tell you about the amazing man I'm spending my life with. I enjoy every morning in his arms and it's the safest and happiest I've ever felt. He loves and supports me as much as I love and support him—it shows. He communicates his love and commitment to me not only verbally, but also physically with his actions every day. Therapy and lots of friends of all genders help him support me. In a minute we're going downstairs to have our morning cold brew together.

Ever since the beginning, my fella made his intentions clear, and our connection has only grown from there. He is smart, sexy, secure, funny, and successful in his own right. He loves when I win and is my biggest cheerleader. My own playfulness and silly-goose behavior only makes him love me more. As my friends say, he can keep up with me.

We align in our passion for our friends, loved ones, and progressive politics. We're looking forward to a beautiful (child-free) life together, and I still have my IUD to make sure that happens. He teaches me about his interests and is always excited to learn about mine. Although we're always out and about in LA, we also spend time watching our favorite shows and weird new movies. He also always watches the dog when I want to take a nap.

Just like the woman in the car with her imagined fiancé, this manifest gets specific. Not only does this woman outline precisely how her partner makes her feel, but she reveals where they align on future values . . . down to the IUD in her uterus. No detail is too small if it matters to you and could affect your relationship. And something as serious as family planning will affect a marriage. As proof that women aren't the only ones who can write a manifest, here's one from a man who absolutely knocked writing his out of the park.

Dear Past Bob,

I met the most incredible woman during my travels. She's brilliant and passionate about everything she does. We're constantly challenging and supporting each other as we learn about the world around us, and it's so much fun teaching each other new things.

She brings so much balance to my life, with just the perfect amount of adventure. She shares my desire to explore the world, and we're on the same page about being the cool aunt and uncle instead of raising children of our own. She's also incredibly playful and shares my silly sense of humor, so we're constantly joking around. She makes my sides hurt with laughter. We keep each other up, talking through the night about life, the universe, and everything, having to remind ourselves just how important proper sleep is.

We communicate openly and honestly with each other. I always know what she wants, needs, and feels, and we have very clear intentions toward and expectations of each other. Her words and actions show me exactly how much she cares for me. She knows I love to be close to her and initiates physical contact just as much as I do. Honestly, we can't keep our hands off each other.

We are each other's biggest cheerleaders, and we spend each day building a psychologically and emotionally safe environment for our relationship to flourish as we move through life, together.

Keep going. She's right around the corner.

Future Bob

One feature you might notice in all three of these is that none of them include negative speak. My student looking for a man writes that her partner is her "biggest cheerleader," instead of saying he "isn't afraid of her success." My student searching for his wife describes her as someone who is "incredibly playful" rather than someone who "doesn't take themselves too seriously." The most obvious signs of negative speak in a manifest are words like "no," "not," or "but," although verbs like "lose" can also fall into this category.

You might be saying, "Maria, why *wouldn't* I say that I want no cheaters in my dating pool?" And I would tell you that not only will this approach set you up for an unnecessarily pessimistic dating journey rife with self-criticism, it's also very hard for the human brain to actually conceive the idea of nothing.

In human history, we have proof of Mesopotamian numerical systems from about six thousand years ago. And while the Babylonians created a symbol to express a blank space in the abacus in 300 BC, it wasn't until the fifth century AD that Indian mathematicians transformed zero from a symbol to a number.[47] Imagine . . . humans built the pyramids in Egypt and the Parthenon in Athens before we could understand the concept of zero!

When I attempted to explain the concept of zero to my five-year-old son, he had a difficult time grasping it. And that's because we all do. For proof, try to imagine literally nothing. You're still seeing *something*, even if it's a vast black void. So if you tell yourself "no cheaters," all your mind will do is fixate—and therefore actively search—for cheaters. And that's how you'll end up sitting across the table from one. If you train yourself to instead focus on someone who is, say, emotionally available and ready to commit to one person for lifelong partnership, *that* is who you'll find.

Before you start writing, decide if you want to do a straightforward manifest like I did or a scenescape manifest like some of the women from the Agape Intensive. We will talk through how to do the former first. You can also write one with just bullet points, if that sounds easier to you, and luckily you already did a lot of that work in the previous chapter.

You already know what values a partner needs to bring in terms of physical, spiritual, intellectual, financial, and emotional compatibility. Write all those down.

Now, close your eyes and think about how you really want your partner to make you feel. Does safety feel like making dinner together every Sunday? Or a forehead kiss whenever you ask for it? Do you need someone who asks if you want to vent or problem-solve when you come to them with complaints? Are you the big spoon or the little spoon? Get all these thoughts on the page.

If you notice that an unexpected piece of negative speak has crept into your manifest, that's okay. That's normal. Let it hold up a mirror to what might be holding you back, and adjust to something more positive.

Some examples of my past clients' negative speak and how I shifted it:

1. "They don't shy away when things get tough" changed to "They jump in feetfirst when we experience a challenge."
2. "He doesn't overreact to my anxiety" changed to "He provides me balance."
3. "She is never disrespectful and does not dismiss my feelings" changed to "She treats me and others with respect and is open to hearing how I feel."

If you're feeling the urge to write a scenescape manifest, you're going to need to dig into your imagination a little bit more—and tap into your last creative writing class. To start, close your eyes and take a deep breath. Now, close your eyes again (I assume you opened them back up to continue reading this book) and imagine the kinds of moments you want to share with your significant other. For some, this event can be big, like an annual family event. One woman's manifest included matching Old Navy shirts for every Fourth of July family barbeque. For her, that's what love looks like. Another mentioned taking down his tree on December 26, which is anathema for me, but hey . . . it's his manifest! He and his future partner don't have to celebrate the Epiphany. I don't care. What I do care about is that these students put in what I call *identifiers*. I want you to look back at your manifest one day and identify your person through this specific moment you're sharing. For others, the scene is more intimate. It could be the nightly conversation someone has with their spouse about anything. What shape does a life together take for you? Jot it down with as much detail as feels natural and needed.

As you start to conjure your future relationship in your mind's eye, ask yourself more questions. What kinds of traditions and routines do you hope to build with your partner? How do you interact at parties with your friends? Is there a shared wink across a crowded room? How do you tackle big family events together? Do you want to be the couple that hosts Thanksgiving dinner every year or are you catching flights to faraway lands for the holidays? Are they the kind of person who's down to join brunch with the girls every few months or playfully trash-talk in your annual fantasy football league? Do you go running together every weekend or are you more of a Sunday-morning farmers market kind of couple? Or both? You'll notice as you plan the mental map of your future relationship, you never actually think about a specific hair color or height—just the way you *feel* sharing the life you've always wanted. Remember, as you prepare to write your very own manifest, the goal is not to manifest the perfect relationship, but the relationship that is perfect for *you*. You're not trying to write the next hit Netflix rom-com, or describe the kind of romance that would make your parents (or your group chat) happy. This is about taking what you've learned so far in this book, and using those lessons to picture the kind of relationship that would actually make you feel safe, acknowledged, happy, and loved. That image is different for everyone—but everyone's is valid and worth bringing to life.

6

HOW DO I MAKE MY MANIFEST MY REALITY?

I REMEMBER BEING FILLED WITH an overwhelming wave of excitement when I finished my manifest and read it over. I couldn't *wait* to meet this person. It was the same feeling I got when hearing that one famous line from *When Harry Met Sally*: "When you realize you want to spend the rest of your life with somebody, you want the rest of your life to start as soon as possible." Only I hadn't actually met the guy yet. I just knew how much happier and easier my life would become once he was a part of it. Gone would be the shame other boyfriends had made me feel about my body size, or take-charge attitude. In their place would be a true sense of unconditional love and belonging.

And I wanted that connection faster than a *Grey's Anatomy* patient needs Epi.

Okay, before we dive into what comes next, I'm going to need you to go back and double-check what you've written for negative speak. Like I said, that's totally normal—even I technically let one piece of negative speak slip into my own manifest: "He'll want to impress me, just as much as I'll want to impress him without a hint of competitiveness to glory." So don't feel bad if you need to turn some metaphorical frowns upside down. But, once you're done, it's time to release your manifest into the world. This is how you step off the sidelines and squarely into the game of finding your person.

Remember, I posted mine to social media. Then, at my birthday party, which was the exact same day, I asked each person in attendance if they had read it. If they hadn't, I showed it to them so they could read it. No one was allowed to sit down for dinner until then. Suddenly, I turned twenty people into headhunters for my eventual spouse. They understood that I was meeting my husband that year, and they were helping me do it. Even if they thought I was being over the top—and I was—I didn't care. Finding the love of your life is worth a couple of eye rolls from your nearest and dearest.

Within days, I had met George. My manifest kept me honest about what I was looking for in a man—and what didn't actually matter. In hindsight, by our second date, I knew he was the guy. We still kept dating for another two years before we got engaged. But I knew, quickly, that he was different from (and better for me than) anyone I had ever dated before.

ASK MATCHMAKER MARIA

Two dates with a guy. I like him, but I'm still curious. Can't help but think about all the other options. What do I do?

Welcome to dating FOMO! All it will do is confuse you. Look over your manifest. If you see who you're dating in there . . . keep dating them.

About a decade after my twenty-eighth birthday, I watched a new group of women create the same magic I had used to find George. It was during my Agape Intensive retreat to Tulum and on one of the most beautiful beaches in the world. The trip was almost over and everyone had just finished writing, editing, and rewriting their manifests. As we were chitchatting, one of the women told us she had woken up one morning at 6 A.M. to watch the sunrise. You could hear how moving the experience was from her voice. As we looked around at one another, the next step was obvious: we all needed to do the same thing the next day as a way to release everyone's manifests.

I expected everyone had talked a big game, but ultimately wouldn't wake up literally before the crack of dawn the next morning. Yet, there were each of my students at 5:45 A.M. the next morning, ready to go. As they released their manifests to the sunrise by reading them out loud in the direction of the new day, you could feel the energy radiating off of the women. They were crying. They were hugging. Immense pride and gratitude were practically bursting out of my pores. I looked over at my sister, Chrisoula, who is my co-leader in our intensives. Even we started to cry. "Look at them! Look at what we've done!" we said with our eyes. It was a wonderful reminder that everyone in the group believed in love. They knew it was inside of them and would be found outside in the world any day now. And that kind of hopeful romanticism wasn't merely okay—it was beautiful.

A year later, I asked one of the women on that trip, a New York City–based product manager named Alexis, how the experience had changed her approach to dating. She called her manifest her "blueprint," which is how I want you to think of yours. Because you can't build a great house without one—

and you need to bring in a lot of people to help with construction. Some people are builders and other people might decorate the place. But you're never going to get your dream home on your own.

Now that Alexis has *her* blueprint, she has noticed she's carrying an unshakable picture of her partner in her mind. That had never happened before for her. But she's not imagining physical qualities. Instead, when Alexis moves through the world, she now notices when someone makes her feel the way she describes in her manifest. That could mean a man shows emotional maturity or financial competency and confidence, which are important for her. As Alexis continues to date, she tells the people around her what kind of man she wants to marry. She's sharing the blueprint to get her metaphorical house built faster.

Because writing your manifest isn't enough. Memorizing it isn't enough. Letting it be a personal secret doesn't push you to the next step in finding your partner, which is holding yourself accountable for who you're dating. Part of the magic that makes a manifest so special is putting it out there, so it doesn't just stay in the void. And there's no wrong way to release yours. You could

- go to the public library or nearest independent bookstore and slip it in a book;
- read it aloud with your loved ones during a full moon;
- post it to the social media platform of your choosing; or
- force your friends to read it before you treat them to a birthday meal (like I did).

Now, whenever you pick up a book, see the moon, or scroll through Instagram—depending on your release method of choice—you'll think of your manifest. You'll consider whether you're putting yourself in the places you need to be to find your person, or, if you're dating someone, whether that person fits the very reasonable expectations you've set for romance. As long as you've shared your manifest with another person or created a habit of consistently thinking about your manifest, you've released it properly.

For nearly seven years, I instructed my New York–based students to take their manifest to the main New York Public Library location and put it into a book. I'd venture to guess that there are approximately two hundred books in the New York Public Library with manifests in them!

Even if you just text your best friend your manifest right now, that's enough for me. Because you've suddenly created a stakeholder for your romantic future. The more people who are invested in your happiness—and understand intimately what it would look like—the better. Not only will your friend (or, hopefully, *friends*) be on the lookout for your prospective partner, but you'll know to leave a relationship that is stealing your time faster. When everyone cares about your future, it's much harder to hold on to someone who doesn't fit the vision.

If you're not quite sure which friends to tap into the mission, look at the relationships around you. Which ones do you admire? They don't need to be the people closest to you. This couple could be acquaintances or members of your wider community. In fact, I had only met Maria and Panagioti—the couple that would introduce me to my husband—just three months before! Should you still not see anyone worthy of your appreciation, ask your friends which couples they admire. If there's still no one to pick from then, it's time to widen your social circle. *Make new friends,* as I say! Hit up an event that intrigues you. Join a professional organization. I'm sure that by then you'll have some great candidates in the pool. So you need to get talking. Reach out to the couple in question and tell them how much you admire their relationship. Then ask them to be stakeholders in your romantic success. Ask them to be on the hunt for your person—and be willing to hold up a mirror while you're dating. It will be a massive ego boost for the couple. Absolutely no one would say no to such an earnest and open question. George and I agree to help complete strangers when they ask. We're always honored to be a part of their love story.

One of the many reasons I love my coaching classes is because they come with built-in stakeholders. Each student discovers a wide new friendship group of ten to fifteen people. And, on top of that, when they come on my annual retreats to Greece, they get dozens of more new friends. With each new friend, they gain exponentially more new connections that could lead them to their person. Strangers become platonic soul mates. Everyone has invested in the same dating philosophy. They're passionate about boundaries, communication, and reasonable expectations. They might approach dating differently—with some sprinting toward their person and others taking a slower walk down the winding path of dating—but they're all cheering one another on to find their dream relationship.

Each coaching group also releases their manifest differently. I have had students do the following:

- Send each of their classmates a postcard with their manifest written in, so each person has ten-plus postcards of manifests plus theirs. Their postcard book becomes a physical reminder that there's people around the country rooting for them.
- Burn their manifest on the day of the winter solstice with the smoke releasing it into the atmosphere. They chose that day because it symbolizes new beginnings. I do love the woo-woo for finding love!
- Put the manifest in a bottle and swing it out to sea.

One of my coaching clients, a New Jersey woman named Erin, has always wanted to go to the Lost Kitchen in Maine. It's infamously impossible to get a seat at the Michelin-starred eatery, which is only open from May to September. So she writes her manifest on a postcard every year, and sends it to the Lost Kitchen as a bid to get a reservation. Simply having her manifest out in the world in a very physical way makes Erin feel hopeful about what will come next. She says the Lost Kitchen is going to keep getting her manifest until she's in love, has a reservation, or (hopefully) both.

Some of my students prefer to really lean into spirituality to get their manifests out into the ether. That's one of the reasons the retreats have become such a hit with my clients. During one of the trips, I take my students to Delos, an island in the Cyclades chain in the Aegean Sea. Delos is the birthplace of Apollo and Artemis, and has been an epicenter for global spirituality since antiquity. Not only will you find sanctuaries on the island for the twin gods who call Delos home, but also ones for global deities. The Egyptian gods Isis and Anubis, the Syrian gods Haadad and Atargatis, and the Greco-Egyptian god Sarapis all have sanctuaries. And you'll even find ancient Eastern Orthodox Christian churches and a synagogue on the island.

While I am a bit of a history nerd, I'm not telling you about Delos for my own benefit. It's important to understand the many millennia of spiritual history found on this island. It grounds you to the four elements, as you sit directly on the Cyclades, feeling the wind and seeing the water. You walk the sand, connecting with the earth. From above, the bright Greek sun beats down on you, connecting you to fire. Each year, I try to lead my students in releasing their manifests on Delos. Because I don't want to get in trouble for littering, I ask them to take their manifests written on paper and first rub them against the dirt and then, after a few moments, bring the manifests up above their heads so that the wind may take the dust with all their powerful wishes from them. That way, a piece of their manifest lives on what UNESCO calls "the most sacred of all islands."

Once your manifest is out in the world, the truth becomes undeniable to you and everyone else. You will be able to acknowledge that what you're looking for is reasonable.

You will also break up faster. This might sound like a downside, but it's the greatest win imaginable. You should break up with people who do not fit your expectations or life goals. You can give yourself permission to go on a first date with someone without thinking, "This is my future boyfriend," or "This is my future girlfriend." Just ask yourself if you could drink a single cup of coffee or glass of wine with this person. And if you like them and you're curious about them and you want to see them again, now you're going to start getting into the mode of "Could this be my partner? And if they are, am I marrying them?" Do they fit the manifest or not?

This approach will keep you from falling into a lot of relationship traps. One of the most dangerous ones I've noticed is the problem of the sunk-cost fallacy.[48] The sunk-cost fallacy is a cognitive bias that occurs when individuals continue an endeavor or make decisions based on previously invested resources (time, money, effort) rather than the current and future benefits and costs. When you're not dating with a manifest in mind, you might end up giving a lot of time to someone who isn't aligned with you (or you with them). And as you start to see the red flags, you might ignore them because you've already invested (or, you might assume, "lost") so much time on this person. And every passing minute could feel like further proof you have to stay.

A follower, let's call her Natasa, reached out to me right after Valentine's Day via email. Matt, her boyfriend of four years, had not proposed like she thought he would. They had already been living together for two full years. So she communicated her disappointment to Matt. She was sad they weren't getting to the next step. She was thirty-seven. He was forty-two. She wanted to get married and have kids. Matt had started a business six months ago, and asked her for patience. "I just want to get the business off the ground first. Give me a year," he told her.

I should also mention that Matt didn't get Natasa a gift for Christmas or for Valentine's Day. Yeah . . . sit with that for a moment.

I'll never know what kind of answer she was hoping for,

but Natasa crumbled at the truth that I perceived. This man was wasting Natasa's time.

Let's do some math: If Matt had proposed on Valentine's Day, *maybe* she'd be married within six months. Now she's thirty-eight. If they tried for a baby *right away*, and got pregnant *right away*, with no issues, *maybe* she'd have a child by thirty-nine.

But instead, he wants to put a pin in it. I sounded the alarm! *He's a time thief, Natasa!* I'll never forget her reply. "I'm thirty-seven. I don't want to start from zero. Dating sucks. I'll just wait for him."

I sincerely hope she gets what she's waiting for. But as a fellow entrepreneur, I'm here to tell you that when you own a business, there will always be *something*. I cannot imagine what a year would change in their relationship. And I definitely cannot imagine what would be going on with his business that would make engagement seem more appealing. *They already live together!*

Natasa, I believe, is a victim of the sunk-cost fallacy in dating. She didn't want to start from zero so she chose to settle for toxic characteristics or misaligned values rather than a fresh shot at happiness.

When you live by your manifest, you'll start to have important conversations faster. By about six months, you'll share your very reasonable expectation that, at this point, you're dating for serious commitment, including marriage (we'll dig deeper into dating timelines in chapter 12). You'll talk about whether you want kids, and how you hope to raise them. These discussions won't scare the right person. In fact, they'll be excited to have them. Because, if your manifest says anything about marriage or children, you'll need to be able to speak about these subjects after many months of dating. If you can't, how will you weather the truly difficult things over the course of a life? The right person says yes. The wrong person says, "I'm not ready." And if they do, believe them.

As you get to know people and learn who fits your manifest, you'll start to see which qualities aren't actually deal-breakers—and therefore what's worth sticking around for. Just like the excitement I felt when I finished my own manifest, you'll find that each new connection brings its own wave of anticipation and discovery. You're off the sidelines. You're running. And your friends—your stakeholders—are rooting for you along the way. So hold on to that initial excitement, and let it fuel your path forward. I believe your person is out there, and with each new encounter, you're one step closer to starting the rest of your lives together.

7

WHAT'S THE 12-DATE-RULE METHOD?

DATING IS NOT A PUNISHMENT or a burden—it's a privilege. It's a privilege to meet new people, figure out what works for you, and ultimately (if you follow my advice) find the wonderful person lucky enough to be your life mate. I want you to sit with that for a moment. Think about all the men and women who came before you . . . how many had this unique privilege. It's an easy fact to forget amid all the swiping, first-date nerves, and possible disappointment that comes with dating. But if you continue to remember how lucky you are to be on this journey, it will all be a lot less painful.

To put your best foot forward, start with a goal for dating. For some of my clients, their ultimate objective is to marry the person they want to grow a family with. For others, it may just be having more positive dating experiences, not necessarily attached to any particular outcome. But maybe you've been frustrated with online dating, and just haven't transitioned an internet match to an IRL meetup in a while. Or, you might just be "picky"—and hopefully the past few chapters have shaken up your priorities for a partner. So your aim might simply be to go on a date right now. No matter the challenges, you have to be honest about your dating intent and open to the process.

One way I've figured out to help people determine what they want—and if the person sitting across from them can offer that—is a little something I call the 12-Date Rule (12DR). First, I'm going to explain to you what that is, and then I'm going to tell you how to actually accomplish this strategy.

WHAT IS THE 12-DATE RULE?

I'm best known for creating the 12DR.[49] I promise it will be your fast track to determining real, long-lasting compatibility. The key to the 12DR is pretty simple: as you're dating someone, you should wait to have sex until your twelfth date, whatever you define sex to be. The goal here isn't to limit sex. I love sex. I recommend hoe phases in multiple situations (more on that later in this chapter). But if you're looking to pursue a long-term relationship with someone, it's very helpful to wait twelve dates to introduce the distracting chemicals associated with sex into your romance. By abstaining for twelve dates, you have the opportunity to really get to know who someone is and how they behave as a partner without the seductive appeal of a great orgasm covering up all the red flags.

When dating intentionally, it takes only three weeks to actually complete the 12DR. You rarely need more than a month to figure out how you feel about a person and whether you want to be their boyfriend or girlfriend. Many people who use the 12DR tell me they're saying "I love you" by the twelfth date or defining the relationship. I can't even count how many people have told me the 12DR led to engagements, marriages, and babies in the long run. At the time that I am writing this, over two thousand people have written to say the 12DR has brought them the happiest relationship of their life. They're even spending their cold hard cash on my 12DR Bride merch. Cute tank tops for everyone!

You—like everyone else who first hears about the 12DR— probably have a lot of questions. I understand that this may be a shift from your previous approaches to dating, so I'll answer the most frequently asked questions here. No, you don't need to do the 12DR with longtime friends or cowork- ers, as you probably already know their temperament. Yes, nonsexual sleepovers are okay, as long as you have commu- nicated your boundaries, and they respect those reasonable boundaries. Sure, if you want to have oral sex, it's fine. If it will leave you feeling emotionally vulnerable and connected to someone you barely know, don't have oral sex in the first twelve dates. If you're not in danger of those very common emotions, eat up. No, you don't have to tell your partner about the 12DR. It's completely normal to tell someone that you'd like to get to know them before you become intimate with them without having to be defensive. If they act weird or like you owe them access to your body, it's on them. They never deserved to be your partner anyway. If you want to, you can blame me. Say a matchmaker told you waiting a bit is a great way to test long-term compatibility—but you're excited to discover that part of them, too, and will share the exact moment you're ready to hop into bed together.

SO HOW DO YOU DO THE 12-DATE RULE?

Over the years, I've come up with what I call Matchmaker Maria date math to help you navigate the process of getting to know another person. You see, I noticed that in the dating process people would get stuck in the vocabulary. "I'm seeing this person." "We're in the talking stage." Squishy, purposefully obscure phrases like this lead to confusion. Confusion is the great enemy of healthy, committed relationships. The point of my work—and this book—is to exorcize romantic confusion from your life.

In Matchmaker Maria date math—or "MMM date math," as my followers like to say—certain experiences count as dating and others don't. You can use these guidelines if you intend to follow the 12DR with someone:

- A date can be an in-person experience or over the phone or via video chat.
- A date must be at least twenty minutes, and can go as long as three hours.
- You can have a maximum of two dates in a day, even if you have a marathon eight-hour date that includes brunch and a live show—that's still two dates!
- You should try to go on twelve dates before getting intimate (more on that in a bit).
- Three of those twelve dates have to be in person.

Texting isn't dating. Same for audio messages or voice texts.

ASK MATCHMAKER MARIA
Does sexting count?

No.

Dates should be enjoyable. There are no prescribed regulations on the specific location where a date needs to take place. So if dinner isn't fun for you before you feel comfortable with someone, stop having dinner dates. I had a client that insisted on wine bars. The problem is that after every single date, his dates would say, "He really felt the need to fill up every single pause in the conversation. The date was exhausting!" After hearing this feedback, I banished him from going on a wine date again. "Tapas and mezze dinners for you or bowling dates. These are your options," I said. This way, he could nibble on some food or go hit a strike and allow some natural pauses of silence to happen.

One of my favorite challenges is to tell singles to think like a tourist when they plan dates. Write down the ten things you've always wanted to do in the city you live in. These are your new date ideas.

"Oh, I've always wanted to go to the botanical garden. Would you have time Saturday to check it out?"

"I heard they're doing a beer tasting at the brewery by the pier this weekend. Do you want to go? Get some drinks and look at some boats?"

"There's a Chinatown food tour?! Let's go!"

I encourage singles (and couples) to even scroll through the Eventbrite app and look for date ideas, too! Nineties trivia night, a cocktail-making class, painting with a wine pairing, whale watching, and oyster shucking—the possibilities are endless and so much more fun than sitting across from each other and sharing a caprese salad.

Now that you've started to imagine your twelve wonderful dates with your perfect match, you probably missed something that is at the core of your current dating strategy. And that's on purpose. *Texting isn't dating.* Texting is a useful way of conveying information to someone, but it's not a real avenue to building a relationship. It doesn't tell you anything about a prospective partner (other than their texting habits). Many of my clients end up having entire "relationships" with strangers from The Apps and then want to sleep with them based on text-based banter. But you don't really know anything about them. You certainly don't know how they would behave as a partner during the best—or worst—times in your life.

That's why spending time with your possible partner is the only way to accomplish that. A phone call checks this box. You're able to have a real conversation, and gauge the other person's mood, temperament, and reaction to your words. Half of texting, on the other hand, is just your perception of reading someone else's words on a cold screen. Phone calls—or even video calls—also help you work on communication early and see if someone is willing to put in the effort of actively spending time with you for twenty minutes or more. You can fit in texting from a toilet. The same doesn't apply to a FaceTime call. Heck, you can even make this experience extra romantic by investing in a throwback physical telephone—curly wire and all—to increase all those nostalgic middle-school-crush feels.

ASK MATCHMAKER MARIA

How and when do I tell someone about the 12-Date Rule?

You have three options: 1) You don't tell them. You just say, "I'm enjoying getting to know you. I just want a couple of weeks to learn more about you before we get physical. I will tell you the moment I am ready"; or 2) You have them go to my Instagram page and read the highlight labeled 12DR; or 3) You give them this book to read this specific chapter. I promise. Someone respectful of your boundaries will not get scared off. The ones who had no intention of dating you will. And that is okay!

WHY TWELVE DATES?

Now, I'll be honest with you, the number twelve is my favorite because, as humans, we *love* the number twelve: twelve months, twelve horoscopes, twelve hours on a clock; even the Babylonians loved counting to twelve using the segments in their fingers.[50] I like twelve because it's memorable and easy to digest. Yes, you can wait more than twelve dates, or fewer than twelve dates. This rule is really about figuring out what you need to assess someone's capability as a partner. And no, you're not going to make it twelve dates with everyone.

In fact, you *shouldn't* get to twelve dates with everyone. That's the point—not every person deserves to have you for a committed partner. I realized this truth when I started dating

George. I was on an airplane and started pondering the trajectory of my previous relationships. All the ones that went a longer distance had a delay in sexual gratification by accident. I got to know one college boyfriend through class, and then we properly got to know each other on dates. Without thinking about it, we did the 12-Date Rule.

While relationships like that weren't my forever loves, they were very different from the ones that damaged my psyche for months (if not years) after they ended. Those were men I had slept with somewhere between the first and the third date. Suddenly, I had oxytocin—the bonding chemical, which is involuntarily released in women during sex—running through my body.[51]

I was figuratively wearing rose-colored glasses. The red flags were so hard to see, and the pink flags were invisible.

If I had waited a few more dates, I would have realized these were men who couldn't be vulnerable with me or completely lacked emotional maturity. Without the lure of sex, I probably wouldn't have even given some guys the chance for a fifth date. But, instead, I fell for them and gave them attention they never deserved for far too long.

ASK MATCHMAKER MARIA

What am I supposed to learn during the 12DR?

There are four things I want you to learn in doing this process:

1. How do they treat you when they're having a good day?
2. How do they treat you when they're having a bad day?
3. How do they behave when you're having a bad day?
4. How do they behave when you're having a good day?

That last one is the most important. I cannot tell you how many people have told me how often their partners emotionally shat on them when they simply went out to brunch with family or got a promotion at work. Instead of "Congrats, darling! I'll go get the bubbly!" it was "Great! Now I'll never see you." If they're consistently picking a fight with you on your birthday . . . it's time to go.

While writing this chapter, I saw a video of *Outer Banks* actor Chase Stokes surprising his girlfriend Kelsea Ballerini (I have no idea what their current relationship status is—they could be engaged by now!) with a birthday cake *at his own movie premiere*. It was his night to shine, and he turned the spotlight on her. Then he invited everyone to celebrate along with him. I want you to be with someone like that—someone who uplifts you when you're already on a high. They don't find your glory as a slight to them—they respect you and celebrate you. You'll only find out if someone is this person by giving them time to prove it. And there will be opportunities even in your first few weeks of dating.

WHAT HAPPENS IF YOU'RE SEXUALLY INCOMPATIBLE?

Countless people end up worried about this exact question. So I'm here to assuage your fears. No matter what happens, you will likely survive. And you will survive happily. On one hand, if you make it to twelve dates with someone, you really like them, and if you end up not immediately being a perfect match in the bedroom . . . you'll figure it out together. If you've managed to get to this place, you've actually been working on your communication skills and connection this entire time. You're perfectly prepared to tackle an issue like this one, even if you don't realize it. If you're committed to each other and want to make this work, you can weather most first-time jitters or conflicting sexy styles. All you have to do is talk through the problem and share what has gotten you *there* previously.

Also, as a reminder, you're encouraged to explore as much physical intimacy as you're comfortable with during 12DR. This strategy is about protecting your heart and allowing you to determine compatibility without sex clouding your judgment—not strapping on a chastity belt for a month. By twelve dates, it's likely you know *something* about your sexual compatibility with a partner before hopping into bed together.

While many couples can talk through their sexual incompatibility, not all decide to stay together. And guess what? That's okay. Any client I've had who has decided to end a relationship after 12DR has looked back on the experience positively. Not only was the breakup easy, but they enjoyed the relationship. They were happy. They found a real connection. It simply just wasn't the one they ultimately could commit to forever. They're more equipped to find their person and be an even better partner to them. No matter what, it was never a waste of their time.

Now that you know date math, it's time to prepare to actually date. Here are some of my other biggest rules and theories to help you be the best dater you can be.

WHAT IS GREEN (AND LILAC) THEORY?

Trust me—you should wear green on your first dates. I've been teaching this tried-and-true theory since 2012. At first it was just a yearlong personal experiment when I was still a single woman. Around this time, I started to notice that anytime I wore green, I would get compliments from anyone. Men. Women. Little Pomeranians on the street. *Anyone.* I knew this because I tallied my positive encounters throughout the day by outfit color. As a tall woman who is often called "intimidating," I wanted to know what actually encouraged strangers to go out of their way to speak to me. Green was the overwhelming answer, particularly from men.

So I started telling other people about my findings, and encouraging them to wear green as well. This strategy makes sense in terms of color theory.[52] Green is vibrant. It's welcoming. It literally means "go" across cultures. And it's associated with life, growth, luck, and health. Who wouldn't want to spend time with someone wordlessly exuding these characteristics? It doesn't hurt that green is also a universally flattering color. Play around with the shades, find the green hue that really makes you feel your best.

While green works great for women looking to date, I've started recommending a different color for men looking to date: lilac. Light purple generally gives off a friendly vibe. Women like when men seem approachable and safe—like they could be friends. Personally, I can't help but speak to a man when he's wearing lilac or salmon (pink). And I instantly see the confidence he exudes when I compliment him.

Ultimately, dating color theory is meant to help you; it isn't just about catching the eye of someone special. It's also intended to help you walk through the world with your own internal confidence. Your posture improves. Your smile is brighter. You flirt with abandon. You become the very best version of yourself.

Since we're looking for this kind of favorable outcome, there are many colors I don't recommend for a first date. At the top of the list is black. I know black is often perceived as sophisticated, and I'm not denying its simplicity certainly can have that effect. However, in the color wheel of emotions, wearing black is a missed opportunity to spark a positive feeling from someone new you're meeting, in the way that blue, green, and yellow do. I also advise against wearing white, gray, and red when going to first dates or networking events. White is "clean," and I do wonder if people will subconsciously avoid you if they're holding a dark beverage for fear of getting you dirty. Gray . . . is just light black. Come on. And red. Well, red is capital-P Powerful. Red is five-chili-pepper-emojis sexy! Red is not the right color for a first date when you're just trying to get to know someone and possibly start a relationship down the road. But it is the perfect color if you're in need of confidence as the keynote speaker at a conference. Maybe wear it on your next date. I know many of you will scoff, but I'm just asking you to leave the little black dresses and the black shirts for your second dates. You can do it.

THE APPS ARE A TOOL AND NOTHING MORE

Of course The Apps are branded as dating apps. They technically are. But you can (and should) take pressure off of swiping by seeing them as *meeting* apps. Now you can perceive them as a helpful way of getting to know a person in your community, rather than stressing about whether this two-dimensional image will be The One. Yes, once you make plans you're going on a date. Yet the outcome doesn't really matter. You're just taking a nice stroll with a new person or sitting for a drink with a cute stranger.

By treating The Apps as a meeting tool, you'll also start to unravel one of the biggest misconceptions about them: A slow response means someone isn't interested. That's not true. Time is flat on dating apps. If you've messaged someone and they've taken a while to respond, it's not a personal slight. You're both online dating, which means that person may have just gone on a great first date yesterday. Maybe they don't want to give that person the wrong idea by letting them see they're "online" on the app so soon. Maybe they're so infatuated they spent the day retelling their friends the details. Or maybe in a week they'll realize their latest crush was actually a dud. Or, maybe, they really, genuinely, *were* just "busy," as so many people say. Suddenly they're back in your DMs, exactly where they should be. Everyone is single until they're not, so don't stress about what they might be doing when they're not typing to you.

THE SPARK IS BULLSHIT
(AKA, GO ON THE SECOND DATE)

The point of a first date is to go on a second date. The point of a first date is to go on a second date. *The point of a first date is to go on a second date!* I will say this mantra until I'm blue in the face and you believe me. I often hear that someone doesn't want to go on a second date with someone because they "don't feel the spark." And I tell them that's great. The spark is a lie at best and a twenty-story-tall billowing red flag at worst.

Because the spark is exciting. When we hear the word

"exciting," we think it's positive. But it's merely a basic adjective to describe an experience. To fully understand what I mean, let's consider the roller coaster a lot of people find themselves on while dating. First, you go on a great first date. You stare at each other over candlelight and you feel the tingles. After some sexy shared plates, your date whispers in your ear, "Let's do this again." But then they take five days to text you. Eventually, after spotty communication, a second date is set up. It's good. They greet you with a tight hug. The conversation flows well. Still, the next day, it's crickets. Actually, it ends up being crickets for days. Rinse and repeat until you break things off, or they finally fully disappear. This is a romantic nightmare. It's also exciting. Your dopamine is sky-high throughout this entire process, and then you're flooded with anxiety. It's all so very exciting. That's why you'll keep wanting more, until the toll is undeniable.

After all, Britney said it first—hit me, baby, one more time. This is what she meant. The loneliness was killing her. It's toxic.

So we tend to feel "the spark" with people who trigger that aforementioned excitement or remind us of old relationships and old wounds.[53] As you know, those old romances didn't work out for one important reason or another. You shouldn't become excited that a potential partner is triggering dormant feelings inside of you. Rather, you should question if this person is actually long-term compatible with you, or just familiar because you're repeating a pattern.

On the other hand, the person you lack "the spark" with might be exactly what you need. They could offer you stable emotions, straightforward communication, and consistent support. For our adrenaline- and dopamine-addicted brains, this kind of steady experience lacks a spark. It might even feel boring. But it's not boring, it's safe. And you should feel safe with the person you partner with for life.

However, you won't know if your spark-y date is just a carbon copy of your ex or if your stable match is the love of your life without a second date. You need to spend time together to understand that. The only reasons not to go on a second date is if someone gives you that dreaded creep factor or commits another unforgivable dating sin, like they're rude to the waiter or disrespectful to you. So if you had a nice time and feel curious about someone—say it with me—go on the second date!

If you're still not feeling attraction to someone by the third date, though, let it go. It's okay, you tried. That's all I can ask.

ASK MATCHMAKER MARIA

What is the difference between anxiety and butterflies?

The easiest way to differentiate anxiety from butterflies is that anxiety stems from confusion and, typically, lack of acknowledgment. But with butterflies, you're excited to see them. You can't wait for them to look at you, and you feel like the prettiest or handsomest person in the room.

WHEN YOU'RE ON A DATE, STAND/SIT NEXT TO THEM

This one is simple. The way I see it, sitting across from a complete stranger gives off job interview vibes, forcing you to look straight into their eyes and ask a lot of questions, some you may not have the established history to inquire about just yet. First dates are to have fun, not to ask what their strengths and weaknesses are. It's just so . . . unsexy. Instead, sit next to each other, either side by side or perpendicularly. This way, your neck, head, and eyes have the freedom to move and look around as you're talking. It fosters connection effortlessly.

YOU CAN HAVE A HOE PHASE

As you date, you might discover that not everyone is worth long-term investment. This is when I would tell you to *hoe-phase* this person, if you still want to sleep with them. You cannot hoe-phase someone you would want to date or have emotional or romantic feelings for. You can only hoe-phase someone that you recognize you differ with on at least one core value. (Remember, we still have feel-good hormones coming through. I need you to be able to snap out of it.)

Hoe-phasing can mean anything, depending on your personal sexual comfort. It can mean going on a date just to go have fun, or a few great make-outs on a couch. Or it can mean penetrative sex. But either way, you must know it's casual entertainment that will never, ever lead to a relationship. Deviating from these expectations will lead to heartbreak, a life-altering situationship, or both. This person is never, and will never be, your partner. And, if they are a hoe-phase candidate, you should never want them to be. The key to making this work is finding a fatal flaw in this person—like she hates dogs and I have two French bulldogs—that will keep you from romanticizing a life with them.

EVERYTHING SHOWER THEORY

If you're going out to meet new people or you're in your season of dating, I encourage you to make all your showers Everything Showers. Everything Showers are the kinds of showers that consist of a few more steps than our typical showers, leaving us feeling extra fresh afterward. Ritualistic in nature, they may include exfoliating from head to toe, shaving, applying a hair mask or body oil. By doing this, you *will* have an extra pep in your step and that *will* help boost your dating confidence.

Following this advice will get you on the best dates of your life. But if you need one last cheat sheet, I've got you covered. Here are your lightning-fast dos and don'ts of dating that I haven't covered yet. We're starting with the don'ts so we can end this chapter on a positive note.

Your must-remember dating don'ts:

- Don't go to their house for a first, second, or third date.
- Don't say your city sucks for dating.
- Don't agree to a long-distance relationship that you cannot afford.
- Don't turn down a friend who wants to set you up. (And if you are open to a long-distance relationship, head to their city ASAP—it's how I met my husband.)
- Don't make big future plans with someone you've been dating less than a month.

Your must-remember dating dos:

- Do have a sense of humor about dating. Dating is supposed to be fun!

- Do get an online dating photography shoot done.
- Do build your social calendar with dating *and* non-dating events that seem appealing.
- Do expand your digital environment in ways that diversify your perspective by following new and interesting people or topics.
- Do say yes to meeting your date's friends. Whether it's a group date or someone's birthday party, always say yes. Even if it's early on . . . like a third date.

This chapter's goal is to help you adjust your attitude and make you as confident as possible. The more confident you are, the more open you'll be to meeting new people, setting your boundaries, and letting the right person into your life. So, if all else fails, take the advice I tend to give women clients: Pretend everybody in a room wants to sleep with you. That doesn't mean they do, or that you want to sleep with *them*. But moving through the world believing you are an all-attracting goddess will give you that extra spring in your step. Your shoulders will be pushed back and your smile will be brighter than ever. And if you're a man reading this, I have a hack for you, too. Tell yourself that everyone in the room wants to be your friend—they want to get to know you and spend time with you. You'll end up becoming your most affable and charming self. Everyone will remember you as the guy who made them feel welcome and happy. That's the kind of man people want to continue getting to know.

Now you're truly ready to get out there and date.

8

HOW DO I MAKE THE APPS WORK FOR ME?

WHEN I STARTED MY PROFESSIONAL career as a matchmaker, smartphones were rather new on the market. In fact, I remember attending a dating app launch party in 2009 with my friend Patrice, and they gifted each of us an iPod Touch just so we could download their app. They didn't trust that our mobile devices were all App Store–compatible. They were right. I had a Blackberry. For those too young to have experienced the iPod Touch, it was the exact same size as an iPhone but it didn't have call-making capabilities. While the dating app never got off the ground, my interest in the booming app market at the time did. I could see with my eyes that there were scores of people in my zip code currently logged into the same beta app, and yet, I was on my couch watching a rerun of *Law & Order: SVU*.

I purchased an iPhone a week later and gifted the iPod Touch to my sister. Then, I downloaded another app that had just come out called Foursquare.

Foursquare, like the other geo-location-based apps at the time, was centered around social discovery.[54] You could use the app to find cool things to do and meet new people in the process. What made this app stand out from the others was that it gamified the whole thing by awarding users with the title of "mayor" (a clear badge of honor) if you were the most frequent person to check in at a venue.

This did something to my brain, along with everyone else's. I felt encouraged to go out, so I went out! Foursquare gave out badges if you did certain activities or checked into a variety of experiences. If a lot of people were at a venue at the same time, you created a "Swarm." It was so much fun.

It also cured going-out anxiety and replaced it with extreme FOMO. *Everything was low stakes with high accessibility.* You could open the app, search for nearby places to be, and see how many people were currently "checked in." If you went to the bar around the corner (or the neighborhood library or even someone's apartment during a house party), you could also check in. By checking in, you were suddenly part of a virtual networking soiree—you could view who had checked into the venue in the last ninety minutes—and get a look at their username and photo. (Of course, you could make your profile private, but why would you want to?)

The act of checking in, in my extroverted eyes, meant you were game to be approached by a stranger. I met so many of my friends, and I even laid the foundation of my matchmaking business using Foursquare as my social capital playground. We all have some level of social capital. It is, essentially, the value in positive connections with other people who live and work in a particular society, enabling that society to function effectively.[55] Right now, growing yours will give you more opportunities to meet people to date. At that time in my life, however, increasing my social capital was integral to improving my business. You see, my profile said "Matchmaker Maria." People would come up to me asking, "Are you the matchmaker?" Yes, yes, I am!

Courage flowed through this app. I used it every single day, multiple times a day.

Foursquare's ability to provide a geo-locating tag was so monumental that it created the foundation for companies like Uber, Nextdoor, and Redfin to help you find what you need where you're at.[56]

But then a little digital behemoth called Facebook implemented those same geo-locating tags in 2010. Since Facebook was more mainstream, *everyone* was suddenly getting into the location-based game. Whenever someone would post an album of photos from the night before—which ranged from blurry to envy-inducing—they would "tag" the post with the location of their latest debauchery. My beloved Foursquare was quickly being boxed out.

And then Instagram launched months later, creating a brand-new social media stressor. Rather than dumping dozens of photos into a Facebook album called, let's say, "LaSt NiTe My bLuePrinT iTs SympHoniC xX," people were tasked with picking one single perfect photo to share with the world (and to define their evening, friendship, or aesthetic). At the time, all the way back in the early 2010s, that picture almost always included a plate of food and a Ludwig filter. An entire society was being conditioned to judge others on what one image said about their entire personality and social capital.

And our focus on judging a book by its cover has only gotten worse since the advent of The Apps. Dating outlets were no longer just available as desktop sites—the kind you scrolled with your wireless mouse from your house, or the coffee shop where you cribbed their Wi-Fi. They became app-friendly, which meant your next date was sitting in your pocket, just waiting to be found. And the key to making it all work was, really, that little geotag that made me Foursquare Queen. Only now, you weren't sharing your location to meet fun strangers at a bar for happy hour. You were telling the app exactly where you lived—or worked, or were hanging out with friends—to figure out which hotties were closest to you. Depending on your location filters, your options were, literally, endless. By the time Tinder launched in 2012, most people knew how to rate others on a single photo (thanks, Instagram). A perfect storm of nearness bias and encouraged snap decisions was upon all of us.

FOMO was no longer an in-person social discovery experience, but a swipe, swipe, swipe away. Not only were you worried that the most entertaining evening of your life was just around the corner—but that your soul mate (or perfect-for-the-night mate) was, too. Just one more match, just one more date to find them. The question "What if the next person is better?" began to stare you in the face all day, every day. Especially if you had notifications turned on. Date, date, date. Fatigue, fatigue, fatigue. But it didn't have to be like this. You didn't have to feel bogged down by a little app—or apps—on your phone. You could actually make them work *for* you, in the same way that I made Foursquare work for me, and that I've helped make The Apps work for my clients since the very first swipes well over a decade ago. I've seen and heard everything, and figured out a way to solve every obstacle you might encounter along the way. And I'm going to tell you it all right here in this book.

DO I REALLY NEED TO USE THE APPS?

Every day, I hear from people who don't want to date on The Apps. Some of those people are self-proclaimed "private" people. They're in positions of power—think: CEOS, politicians, etc.—or in careers where it's a little tricky to date, like teachers who are scared of swiping on one of their students' parents. But most people speaking to me are "time people." As in, they have better things to do with their time than swipe.

Hopefully, this chapter will cut down on the number of times I have to try to coax those people into giving swiping an honest try. After all, as I often tell my clients, to not participate on The Apps is like not having an email address. Everyone else is using these very mundane technologies, so you're probably missing out on important conversations without them.

Assuming the most basic numbers, I estimate that the people swiping from their couch are probably going through at least twenty-five profiles a day. Again, as we learned from Pete Davidson in *The King of Staten Island*, that doesn't mean these are mindful swipes. But let's say the average person is glimpsing at least twenty-five singles a day, minimum. That means they're possibly seeing about 125 fellow daters per week. They might have up to ten matches. Now imagine if they have multiple apps on their phone, like many people you and I know. That's *a lot* of romantic options. If you're not on The Apps, you're removing yourself from the opportunity to consider a variety of eligible individuals—and keeping yourself from being seen by them. I know that people looking for relationships would love to meet someone in the wild, but the computer in your pocket is also an undeniable tool. Knowing you're leaving no stone unturned can be a good feeling when you're intentionally dating. Why would you get in your own way?

Notice I just said the word "tool." The key to using The Apps is understanding that they're just that: a tool. Once you know how a tool works (and doesn't work) you can use it to your best advantage. Many of The Apps use the Gale-Shapley algorithm,[57] or something similar. The Gale-Shapley algorithm is designed to solve the stable marriage problem, which attempts to match an equal number of men and women looking to date. The aim is to make sure each man and each woman is most pleased with their match. If someone could be happier with another possible single over their current match, those two become a pair. The person who just lost their match now must find another match. All these decisions are based on how each single rates a possible partner. That attraction is usually boiled down to photos, prompts, and biological data (like age or height), which most swipers make snap judgments over (after already filtering down their pool).

While it doesn't sound particularly kind, the algorithm therefore orders users by perceived attractiveness, preferences, and likelihood of matches. So the most attractive person in a given zip code will see the first and second most attractive people in their area and so on. It's a brutal truth, but understanding brutal truths—like people *really, really* judge your first photo and have preconceived biases based on their possible trauma, their past, and societal stereotypes—is the only way to make The Apps work for you. And that's what we're here to do. So here are your biggest tips to making this process of swiping as painless as possible—and maybe even fun if you're open to it.

Winning Strategy #1: Get the Photos!

Most dating apps require you to post at least five photos on your profile. We are going to aim for eight great photos that you'll have on a rotation, in which you'll update your profile each week, replacing one photo from the reserves to let the algorithm do its thing. The algorithm loves a consistently updated profile.

STEP 1: Go through your phone and begin favoriting some of the photos that you love of yourself from the last year. I know most of your photos will include friends. Can you crop them out? Any photos of you at a concert? How about your last trip—did you take any solo shots there? Do you have a photo of you with *your* pet? Don't be scared to crop your own photos and fix the brightness, too.

STEP 2: I'm going to need you to call up whichever one of your friends is most talented at mobile phone photography. (They're the most active on Instagram.) You're going to treat them to a fun day date with you while you visit a variety of places. Go for brunch, a walk around the park, and visit a landmark or a museum. Tell your friend that their job is to take as many photos of you as possible.

Follow these two tips for really good photos:

1. As your friend is snapping photos of you, have them ask you questions about people you love or things you enjoy. "Tell me about your cute niece!" will snap you out of any resting bitch face (RBF) in a split second, leading to better, more candid photos.

2. When you're looking at the camera, pretend it's a door that has just opened and the person coming through is someone you wish you could give a hug to, dead or alive. This isn't as dark as it sounds— you'll feel at ease and, in my opinion, your smile will shine in its most natural state. For me, I always imagine my late aunt Georgia. She was the best! I would visit her most weekends when I was in college in Athens, and she was so excited to hear every drop of campus dating gossip I had to share. We also had the same celebrity crush—Sakis Rouvas—so we'd swoon over his music videos together. Anyway, I always think that she would have loved my husband if she had met him, and that always makes me smile. It's my best smile, really. So, who's your Aunt Georgia?

As you're going from place to place, you may see a well-lit historical building, or a colorful mural, or a pier with a bunch of boats. Take a snap there, too. We're looking for variety! End the day with a drink at a rooftop bar or a barcade. Again, snap a photo, bestie!

At each new location, change your clothes. That's right! I need you to raid your closet for three shirts, blouses, and/or dresses you can change into before moving to the next place. The dress code is essentially: what I'd wear on a first date and also what I'd wear to a backyard barbeque.

Do not pack a scarf or a turtleneck; there's no need to cover up your neck. I have always felt that people tend not to approach people who appear shrouded. Think about tech CEOs wearing turtlenecks or flight attendants with their neck scarves. To me, it screams, "I'm above you on the hierarchy here. Speak to me only if I speak to you or if there is an emergency."

Leave your sunglasses and hats at home, too. If you have them on, people will wonder what you're hiding.

These interesting photos will also serve as *message bait*. Now you can prompt people to "meet you here" at a Skee-Ball bar, or ask someone who's liked a photo of you at the museum if they've ever been to the same museum. "I am so glad you liked this photo of me. Did you know they host first Thursdays with free wine and a gallery tour?" Suddenly you've shaken up your profile and made it one of the most exciting options on the app.

And if you don't have any friends you trust to take your picture, you're not getting out of this one. It's time to schedule some time with a professional photographer to enact the same plan. Google online dating photographers in your region, and you will find someone. Tell them exactly what you hope to accomplish throughout your shoot and that you'd like to change your clothes at least twice. The shoot will take about sixty to ninety minutes.

STEP 3: On a day when you're feeling pretty good, I want you to put your phone camera against your window and as you face the natural light, take as many photos of yourself as possible while smiling! If you have a tripod or a stack of books to lean your phone on, place it on your coffee table and sit on your couch across from it in your comfiest clothes and snap a few photos of yourself there, too. Use a three-second timer to help you get settled for a non-selfie *selfie*. (Hey, your hands are by your side! For all they know, a friend snapped this photo!)

Once you have some new photos to work with, it's time to choose the best ones.

Do choose photos where

- you look approachable and happy.
- you're enjoying a hobby or another activity you might do with a partner. I had a client who loved tennis, so she hired one of my photographers to snap a few photos of her with her racket at the park. Her now-husband challenged her to a match for their first date.
- you are with *your* pet . . . just one photo, please.
- you can apply a fun prompt that gets the conversation going. My colleague, matchmaker Carmelia Ray, used to have a photo that had her smiling into the camera while she looked like she was cutting a tomato. There was bread, cheese, and turkey right next to the cutting board. Her prompt said, "I'm making a sandwich. Let me know what you want on yours." Presto! This was the best icebreaker ever. I used it when I dated online, too, and can attest to the success. We both had a stream of men sending us their sandwich orders.

- you look wholesome. Pick a photo of you that your parents would love to have on their fridge.

Don't choose photos where

- you're with friends. Unnecessary comparison will naturally arise. Somehow, your friend will always be better looking. It's a phenomenon, really.
- you're in the gym, unless you're a trainer.
- you're with your children, if you have them.
- you're with someone else's children. *Eeeek!*
- you're with someone else's pet.
- you're standing next to your sibling or your best friend of the opposite gender. People will always assume that's your ex. When a man does this, I conclude it's the barometer that he will be judging your looks against.
- it's clearly a headshot from work. It's a dating profile. Not LinkedIn!
- you don't look like you . . . today. If you're showing up to the date and you're thirty pounds heavier or five years older than the photo . . . there will not be a second date.
- you're dressed as a bridesmaid or a groomsman. Men will think you're coming on too strong and women will think it's from your first marriage.

Funny story: I once reviewed a profile of a woman who held a cucumber in every single photo. No explanation offered. I recall her being in front of a historical building, in front of a lake, in her kitchen, and, of course, a deli. I asked her how many men messaged her a day. "At least fifty!" I couldn't stop laughing. She really *pickled* the perfect icebreaker.

If nothing else, remember this: people just want to swipe on people who look like they would be a fun date.

Winning Strategy #2: Get Those Prompts Answered!

Just as important as the photos are the prompts that most online dating sites exhibit. This is the space where you can really shine and tell the singles who come across your profile a little bit more about yourself than what your photos suggest.

Before we dig into the art of prompt writing, we need to really clarify what a dating app truly is, beyond a tool. An online dating app, at its core, is a lifestyle app meant to entertain you. People use them while they're bored on the line at Starbucks or while watching a rerun of *The Big Bang Theory*. And some of you use them while on the toilet. Therefore, please, refrain from turning your online dating profile into a political lawn sign or a long list of abrupt deal-breakers. Nobody cares. People would rather swipe left than have to deal with the ensuing conversation.

If you're telling people to swipe left if they voted a certain way or to talk about anti-gun legislation you support, you're shooting yourself in the foot. (Pun intended!) Even the person who may agree with you is highly likely to swipe left because your profile just isn't a happy profile. People want happy profiles because they're more likely to turn into happy dates, which have the tendency to lead to happy relationships.

ASK MATCHMAKER MARIA

Guy puts "I want someone to call me out on my bullshit" on his dating profile. Is that a red flag?

If I wrote a song, it would be called "Men Don't Know How to Fill Out Online Dating Profiles." They're basically trying to say: "I'm looking for someone who has her own life and passions and enjoys friendly banter." Yeah, I know. Two different sentences. I talk to single men every day. It is what it is. Hopefully this book shows them the light.

If you're mentioning sex or your genitalia in your prompts or messages to a match, and it's not a hookup-seeking app, people are swiping left on you in droves because, regardless of the relationship intent you have, you are coming off as a creep. This includes statements about someone's body ("Wow, those legs go on forever!") or suggestive comments on their possible behavior ("I have a feeling you're not as innocent as your photos suggest").

So, instead, use the dating prompts as a way to communicate your values, likes, and interests so your writing makes the user self-select you because of some perceived commonality.

For instance, one of my favorite prompts I've ever seen on a dating app is: "Typical Sunday . . ."

I would use the prompt for sharing the activities that give me joy on the weekend. The ways I connect with the people I love, and how I enjoy spending my free time.

Do not fill this prompt (or any one like it) by saying something like "Typical Sunday: Finding the bottom of the bottomless mimosas at brunch and telling my parents I went to church." Not only will you seem like a very unserious person at best (and someone with a cavalier drinking problem at worst), you're painting yourself as a liar to countless strangers. Humor is really difficult to understand in a venue as flat as an app—especially between people who have never met. So remember, readers are going to take any "jokes" you make literally and at face value.

ASK MATCHMAKER MARIA

Is it okay to put "hangs out with exes" on red-flag prompts on the dating app?

I just wouldn't select any prompt that would make me want to write something negative in my online dating profile, no matter how valid the request.

Instead, educate the reader about who you actually are: "Typical Sunday: brunch karaoke with my friends, Pilates, dog park (with my dog!), NYTimes Crossword, and catching up with the sibling group chat." It's easy to imagine sharing a day with this person—and actually enjoying it.

Look at how much we just learned with this response. You've managed to tell someone you can care for a living thing, are intellectually curious, and close to your family with a single prompt. What a win. We finally have *message bait*.

Message bait is when prompts or photos provide just enough information to create an icebreaker for a match to message you. We can ask them what their go-to karaoke song is, what kind of dog they have, and where they're located in the order of siblings. We're learning that they enjoy cross-word puzzles (maybe challenge them on the daily Wordle?) and that they like fitness.

Other prompts I enjoy are the ones that force you to be a little competitive, like two truths and a lie. It naturally gets people guessing about you, and wanting to win on their bet. The trick to this prompt is to make the lie be truth-adjacent, because we want to use every opportunity to teach the match about ourselves.[58] For instance, let's say you did a semester abroad in Berlin, you've run one marathon, and you collect monopoly boards. Your "lie" will be that you did a semester in Frankfurt, because it's an opportunity to tell the person about your semester abroad in Germany. Another lie could be "I once got stuck in the elevator with Mark Ruffalo." I like the elevator lie a lot because it can give the person a glimpse at someone who you think is cool. Imagine someone replying, "You shared an elevator with the Hulk? No way!"

Or let's say you just discovered through a DNA heritage website you are 75 percent Peruvian, you're the youngest of three sisters, and you've been to five music festivals in the last three years. Your "lie" is that you visit your cousins in Peru each year.

Heck, you could ask someone in your profile, "Guess my heritage. I'll give you a hint: It's the third largest country in South America. One of its national languages is Quechua. And one of its most famous actresses was on *The Vampire Diaries* (have you watched?)."

You can also think of the perfect response and then choose an open-ended prompt that will allow you to show off your personality. Your response could be anything that you think someone should know if they want to date you, like the movie you've watched a hundred times (for me, that's *Twister*) or a hobby you've recently picked up. There are countless prompts on the more general side that will allow you to put these facts on the marquee of your dating profile. All you need to do is click something like "What if I told you that . . ." or "My current obsession is . . ."

For this strategy, I want you to, say, list your comfort show and any other unique interest or characteristic you may have. For instance, maybe you'd say, "My comfort show is *Seinfeld* and I love improv" or "I loved *Fleabag* (the show!), and I can speak Polish. Cześć!"

I like this format because it can give a glimpse at your sense of humor (without scaring someone off or confusing them) and, depending on the show or unique factoid about you, your core values and sensibility.

For instance, I once reviewed a woman's profile and she told me her comfort show was *The Bear*. I didn't think much of it when I wrote it in her profile, but when I finally saw *The Bear*, a show centered around anxiety, depression, and dysfunctional family dynamics, I began to worry. It's a really great show, but . . . *that's your comfort show?* Ooof.

Refrain from asking people where to find their favorite spicy margarita or the best pizza slice in town. You're not being as unique (or cool) as you think you are. Educate, educate, educate, and let the right person self-select into taking you out.

Once you've rebooted your profile, you must start swiping.

Winning Strategy #3: Open Up Your Radius

Few of my rules or recommendations get more pushback than this one. You—yes, you!—need to open your radius on The Apps. What is it right now? Five miles? Ten miles? What about twenty? Fifty? A hundred? I was willing to hop on a train from New York to Boston to meet a potential match. And guess what happened? I met my soul mate, got married, and now have two beautiful children. Merely *looking* at someone fifteen miles away isn't going to hurt you.

I know, I know. You're already saying, "I would never do that." But whenever someone tells me an "I would never" statement in dating, I say that's exactly what they should do. Once, I heard a woman who lived in Tampa say she would *never* cross a bridge to date. I always urged her to rethink that mindset, as I do with every person near a bridge or tunnel. Tampa isn't unique. I have heard the same protest from people in DC and New York City. They've all confined their dating opportunities to whoever designed their respective metro system in 1969 and 1904. Do you want to leave your love life up to some random civil engineer who was probably distracted by the moon landing?

I challenge you to go on five first dates with people on your "I would never" fifteen-mile-radius geography list (or who possesses any other "never" characteristic, from height to religion). Your best-case scenario is that you meet five nice-enough new people in a new neighborhood, and never see them again. Now you at least have good recommendations for an unexpected part of town. Your worst-case scenario is that you find your soul mate in a slightly inconvenient zip code and fall in love for the rest of your life. It's worth the gamble and gas or transfers on public transportation.

Although we've had more success stories than I can count, I'll tell you about my favorite one. We once had a woman who lived in the Boston suburbs, but traveled into the city every day for her job as a nurse. Let's call her Michelle. Michelle said she wanted to exclusively find a man in the city limits of Boston, because she thought she should date where she worked. She also preferred someone without children. Hoping that she would keep an open mind, we found Michelle a wonderful single dad in her neighborhood (in the suburbs) who wanted to take her out. We reminded her she only had to go on a first date. Remember, that's nothing more than a meetup. So, Michelle hesitantly agreed. She ended up liking him. A lot. They went on a second date, then a third date. Nine months later, they got engaged. By now they've been happily married for years.

Winning Strategy #4: Rework the Age Filter

The most common filter people use online is age, and I get it! Most people want to date around their age. Others have a bias toward an age range, so maybe they'll restrict for more "reproductive opportunities" (men) or they'll scale up, seeking financial, professional, or emotional maturity (women). Whatever ages you're filtering, I want you to add plus two and minus two on both ends. If you were willing to date someone seven years younger or older than you, why would you say no to someone that was, let's say, nine years younger or older? Two years isn't as big of a deal-breaker as you might think it is. Sometimes, those pesky filters keep us away from people hiding in plain sight around us but who are impossible to see if we aren't looking in their direction. All I'm asking is that you be open to another opportunity.

Now, I do have a small asterisk for this, and that's for people under the age of twenty-five.

The brain's frontal lobe, which is in charge of important functions like judgment and emotions, isn't fully mature until around twenty-five.[59] This medical fact is especially true about the prefrontal cortex, which has a lot of jobs that influence our long-term happiness and well-being. Because, you see, the prefrontal cortex is in charge of our executive functions, which dictate so much of how we make decisions. Think: your understanding of consequences, your ability to problem-solve, or your capacity to balance short-term rewards against big-picture goals. You only reach your full capability for all of these life-changing skills when you're in your mid-twenties. You literally cannot make your best choices until then. It's not your fault—it's science.[60]

I always think about how I used to roll up to a Greek island with one hundred euros and a dream when I was twenty. Was there a plan? No. But there was a real "you only live once" sensibility fueling every choice I made over four days. I wasn't thinking about reserving hotels in advance because I knew I'd figure it out at the pier. "There's always a room somewhere." I'd survive on a steady diet of Greek coffee, two-euro gyros, and cheap beer. "I'll hitch a ride or two, no big deal," I told myself. And, technically, I was right. I didn't die. I had a great time. But I also gambled with life and limb more than I ever needed to. Now that my brain is fully developed, I clutch my pearls at the thought of traveling without an itinerary and a predetermined budget. And I certainly would never tell my daughter to follow in my footloose and fancy-free footsteps.

So, considering human psychology, if someone under twenty-five asked me the optimal age range they should be dating in, I'd say: between the ages of eighteen and twenty-five; date up to four years older than you. If you're under eighteen, talk to your parents or a trusted adult about what's best for you at this very tender age. And focus on your schoolwork over dating. You probably have a test you should be studying for right now. Come back to this book in a few years.

Then, once you're twenty-six, I don't care. You want to date sixty-year-old men with yachts and champagne to spare? More power to you. At least your brain can foresee and weigh the possible consequences of your behavior.

And, no matter how old you are, if a notably older person ever says to you, "You're mature for your age," on a date, please remember that you're not. That person is probably deemed immature by their own peers so they're dating much younger. To make you feel comfortable—and themselves feel less guilty—they age you up by scaling your maturity level to meet theirs. However, it's been my personal and professional experience that one day you will be their age and you'll look back, and you will agree with me. You were acting your age. They were being a creep.

ASK MATCHMAKER MARIA

Everyone says I look great for my age. Okay to fudge my age on apps?

No. You don't lie. It's the ultimate turnoff when you have to eventually do the age reveal. Put your real age so you attract the people who want to date your age. If you cannot handle that sort of filtration, maybe online dating isn't right for you. Also, anyone who has ever told me, "I don't look my age," looks their age. I think what you mean is you have more vitality, and good for you.

Winning Strategy #5: Avoid Extreme Dating Fatigue

If you are approaching dating like it's a chore, or if you're losing hope or taking rejection really hard, then you're experiencing dating burnout. Luckily, I have a few tips for you to prevent this.

The 50–5 Rule

Now that you've hopefully started to realign your perspective on dating, we're going to really dig into the strategy here. One of my favorite online dating experts, Erika Ettin, came up with this one.[61] As you dive into The Apps—especially with your new, supercharged profile—you're going to start to get swiping fatigue. It happens to the best of us. So when you're on your preferred app, you're going to count each profile as you go. You either stop once you hit fifty people, or when you get five matches—whichever comes first.

Once you're done swiping for the day, you're going to focus on messaging the people you're matched with. Those people can either be new matches from the day, or *recent* matches. While many of us were raised to believe the man needs to show interest first, it's the twenty-first century and that's nonsense. Approach messaging like playing volleyball during gym class in the seventh grade. There should be a comfortable volley for serve. After about three messages back and forth, you should have a good sense that the person on the end of the phone isn't a creep. Then you must start planning your date ASAP. Do not linger in the app for too long. You are not in the market for a new pen pal, and do not need to live an entire relationship through a phone. Not only will you end up creating a different personality for your match in your mind from the one they actually have, but texting isn't dating. And DMing on an online dating app definitely isn't. Get out there with your match in an IRL experience!

Don't Give Out Your Phone Number—Yet

Think about how many times you've run into an old friend, given them your number, and sworn you would "meet up for drinks soon." And how many times has that actually happened? With someone you already know and like? Now imagine that working out with a complete stranger you've never seen or exchanged real words with. You're more likely to text until the conversation peters out than actually meet up if you give your match your number too soon. Instead, you should . . .

. . . Get off the App Quickly

Once you've messaged back and forth three times, plan something simple yet fun in the next few days with your match. If you're nervous about moving "too fast," this is where you need to remember that you're online dating to get off-line with someone. As matchmaker Louie Felix says, "Stop calling them dating apps and call them meeting-up apps." You're just meeting a new person and hoping for a pleasant time. In the grand scheme of existing, you've met thousands of people in your life. Now you're just adding one more to the list. So there's no need to stress or put pressure on this one meeting.

If you're not sure how to put this plan into motion, I have a hack for getting out of the DMs and into real life. Once your match says something interesting, like "I've been reading a great book," instead of asking questions about it in the moment, put a momentary pin in it and say:

"That sounds really cool. Let's talk about that in real life!" Then share the two immediately upcoming days and times that fit your schedule, and ask if either time works for them as well.

It would look something like this:

> I see in your profile that you studied in Rome.

> Yes! It was wonderful. I really miss going out to this one local spot for tiramisu. Have you ever lived abroad?

> Does going to summer camp in Canada count? I'm kidding. I've done some extended business trips in Germany and Denmark.

> That sounds cool. I'd love to learn more about this in person. Are you free on Tuesday or Thursday of this week?

Their response will tell you if they're worth your time. Spoiler alert: The kind and attentive people who are excited to make a plan to get to know you face-to-face are the ones I want you dating. If they say, "No, those dates don't work for me," without any alternate plan, they're out. Done. Not worth your time. If they give two other days, pick whichever one is actually best for you.

Once you settle on a day and time with someone worthy of you, you could respond by saying which neighborhood or town you live in. No more games. Just pick a venue that's in the middle. It truly, truly doesn't matter who asks whom out. By the end of the conversation, you should be saying, "Great! It's a date!"

> Tuesday works—7:30 okay?

> Oh that's perfect. I've always wanted to try Estella in Downtown Boston. Let's meet there.

> Okay great!

> Great! It's a date!

You can also give out your number once you've actually planned a concrete meetup. If you want to feel extra safe, set up a Google number and give your matches that one. I don't want a graveyard of "Dan-Hinge" or "Emily-Bumble" clogging up your contacts list.

Once you've set a meetup with someone you've deemed worth your while, feel confident in your approach. This isn't a big, stressful date with a stranger. All you're trying to do is see if you vibe in person with someone you're curious about. If this meeting goes well, you can talk about your "real" first date. Yes, it'll technically be your second, but that will be the one where the romantic stops will start to be pulled out. By then, you'll be sitting across the table from someone you already know. And if you're less than enthused by this person, that's fine. You walk past a lot of people you don't have romantic feelings for every day. What's another one?

The reason I love this strategy is that it sort of mimics *in-real-life* dating, which we will talk about in the next chapter.

You get to have your meet-cute in line at a French café with an appealing stranger. Or you bump into someone alluring in front of the fountain at the museum. A dating app might have socially engineered this experience for you, but that's just the details. The feeling of spontaneity—and the lack of pressure that comes with happenstance—is still there.

What matters is that you met. Now they're a very real person you've seen and smelled, and not someone you're imagining a life with because they resemble your celebrity crush in their second photo and know the difference between "their," "they're," and "there."

Winning Strategy #6: Change Up the Apps

One of my favorite modern love stories comes from my dating industry colleague Damona Hoffman. She had been on dating websites (pre-app days) for a couple of years and wasn't meeting tons of people she could vibe with long term. She went to lunch with some work acquaintances and one of them said she had a new boyfriend she met on a different site that she had never thought to join. She felt encouraged because, according to her friends, it was "full of creative people" and it attracted creative, open-minded, intellectual types, the kind of guys she was looking for. Turns out, Damona's experience was terrible the first three weeks. But one day, she received a message in her inbox, just as she was ready to quit. A TV writer named Seth. He was the only person she met off this site. They got on and married three years later. As Damona says, "It only takes one."

So if The App you're on isn't working, it's okay to take a

break. It's also okay to start over on another app, too. You never know . . .

If after reading all these tips and tricks, you still want nothing to do with The Apps (which, I promise you, aren't going away anytime soon), we need to strategize on your alternate approach. Because you need to get in front of those same 125 people the passive swiper is seeing every week. They don't need to be the same kind of people, but they certainly need to be the same number. So you have to supercharge your social opportunities. This might feel difficult, since the world is filled with so many types of people, including the kinds who seem cute on The Apps but feel like demoralizing duds in real life (thus pushing you even further away from wanting to deal with them). There are the people who feel so very mismatched with your lifestyle and the ones who are genuinely less than great. There are even the ones who catch your eye in real life, but you have no idea how to approach. Well, we're leaving no stone unturned when it comes to socializing, because your romantic future isn't one to be trifled with. I'm here to help you with what comes next.

9

HOW DO I ACTUALLY MEET PEOPLE IRL?

HELLO AND WELCOME TO ONE of the topics I discuss the most as a modern matchmaker: IRL dating. The more our society merges with technology, the more people covet the romantic idea of stumbling into their soul mate during the humdrum motions of everyday life. I get it. I watched Meredith Grey turn a messy one-night stand into one of the greatest love stories ever told, too, *Grey's Anatomy* fans.

The interesting catch is that a lot of people dreaming of their rom-com moment don't see IRL dating as something that's merely difficult to achieve. For them, it's almost a sheer impossibility.

There are a lot of adults reading this book who have never experienced a dating landscape without smartphones, or what I like to call analog dating. Heck, they've never experienced *any* landscape without a mini computer in their pocket—and more than likely attached to their hand. Then there's my generation. Elder millennials, rise up! We remember learning how to date through off-line methods . . . and the exact moment when every facet of our social life transitioned into being constantly online. Dating also experienced that evolution, and online dating transitioned from being something we shamefully admitted to participating in, to being the default of how people find dates, at least in the United States.

Up until the time when millennials witnessed the switch from analog flirtations to digital dating, people met off-line. All of our parents met off-line! Many of them dated and mated through what sociologist Ray Oldenburg called a third place,[62] a term that refers to social places outside of our two major social environments, the home (first place) and work (second place). Examples of third places include places of worship, parks, malls, bowling alleys, arcades, and social clubs. There were also the halls and other venues where someone might celebrate a wedding, birthday, or retirement. Ask your parents how they met, and it almost always revolves around them being outside their home. Maybe your parents met at your dad's cousin's wedding or a neighbor's birthday barbeque. They could have been on rival teams at an intramural softball league or at a charity's dance-a-thon. Whatever the case may be, they had the social capital and tacit knowledge to communicate, and connect.

As more facets of modern life become automated, we have ever-fewer interactions with a net total of people. On top of that issue, we're dealing with a loneliness epidemic[63] and the increasingly isolating echo chambers of social media.[64] The social capital our parents and grandparents took for granted is crumbling in front of our eyes. The blame isn't just on dating apps, but on so much more.

Specifically in the US, a lot of that fault can be traced back to our very beginnings. We've always been a country that prizes the individual over the greater group. Never forget: we were founded by a pack of men who were tired of being told what to do. Then, starting in the 1950s, pop culture began to promote the nuclear family. A thriving singular family unit seemed like a good way to encourage security amid the anxieties of a post–World War II nation. The success of just your family—over, say, the other ones on the block—became a point of pride in a country desperate to rebound after fighting two nightmarish wars in less than forty years. Collectivism, which (surprising no one) puts value on the collective society, may have made up the building blocks of other Western nations. But it was deemed un-American.[65]

As the nuclear family has became more important, the role of the family has evolved.[66] The goal of raising children isn't just to exponentially increase the amount of love and connection in the household or to add supportive new members to the wider social fabric. Instead, parents are essentially told their job is to effectively launch the nuclear families of tomorrow and to keep our individualist society spinning. Parents are encouraged to rear independently minded kids who will be self-supporting individuals by early adulthood. Not only should they be going to school and/or getting a "good" job, but also in their own homes and setting themselves up for financial success before their prefrontal cortex is finished settling. During this time, they should also be searching for a life partner to build their own nuclear family with. If someone hasn't "left the nest" by twenty-five, everyone involved is seen as a failure.

So a lot of dating-age people are left feeling like lonely cogs in the machine of life, instead of valued humans who are allowed to ask for connection and empathy. They're putting themselves in shoebox apartments just to prove they've "made it," or living with roommates they may not actually like to pay the bills while asserting their independence. This living situation is different from the multigenerational living that so many collectivist European and Asian-Pacific societies run on, where family members of all ages share their home for whatever financial or emotional reason.[67] A son might live in his parents' house to save money until he finds his life partner and buys a home; his grandparents might live in that same house for eldercare and community in their advanced age.

Many young people in the US, however, avoid this mutually beneficial arrangement just to give the appearance of success—and their parents spur it on. Of course, it's likely that this may have never been presented to them as an option, and their social circle never provided an example. When some people embrace multigenerational living, they feel embarrassment. Every week, a new person asks me if they'll ever be able to find love because they live with their mom. And every week I tell them the right person won't see their very normal living situation as a red flag. Your person will want you to be happy and financially stable.

As access to the family home becomes increasingly restricted, dysfunctional zoning laws[68]—critiqued by Oldenburg— further exacerbate the issue by prohibiting commercial establishments in residential areas, making it nearly impossible for third places to flourish and foster community connections. The demise of the mall, once a hub where groups of young people could roam freely in a bright, open, and welcoming environment, only adds to the problem. Then there's the technology that took vibrant, real-life communities of the past and siloed them into isolating digital spaces; the conversation might be lively online . . . but many of the people talking are sitting alone in their homes instead of, as Ariel from *The Little Mermaid* sang, "where the people are."

Connection is harder than ever, even when we're literally on top of one another. For those adults who have roommates, ask yourselves, how much time do you spend enjoying your lives together versus arguing about who ate what out of the fridge or whose turn it is to buy the darn toilet paper? American malls are requiring an adult chaperone for teenagers, or worse, closing down completely.[69] Religious attendance and affiliation is dwindling, which may improve some people's lives, but also removes them from a traditional pillar of American social life. They may be losing a religion that doesn't fit their lifestyle, but they're also losing the community center that comes with it.[70]

This is all perpetuated by a car-dependent culture where we drive alone, listening to a perfectly curated playlist alone. And if we don't shop online alone, we enter a store wearing headphones alone, complete self-checkout alone, and go back to our homes to log into our work-from-home video call, alone.

Alone, alone, alone.

All of this is to say that the only way to get better at offline dating is to . . . not be alone! You need to know how to undo the many levels of our culture working to make you feel so isolated. The answer is to find or create third places and to have a meaningful conversation where feelings and thoughts can be exchanged. We're going to date like our grandparents (or great-grandparents) once did. I'm going to help you walk this path toward new people, experiences, and, most of all, connection.

This is why I want you to invest in your friendships. I don't think people realize how much better and easier it is to get into a relationship if you really invest in your friendships. The bigger your social circle is, the more likely you are to run into your soul mate. If you're not already, you should be putting effort into your friend groups, asking your boss to send you to more work conferences, and volunteering in your community. Even if you're just manning the registration table at the local golf tournament, that means you're putting your face in front of dozens, if not hundreds, of new people. Your future spouse might not be at that game—but their sister-in-law could be.

ASK MATCHMAKER MARIA

Feeling discouraged about meeting someone great. How do I find The One?

I fundamentally believe there is a lid for every pot. But ask yourself if you're in the right kitchen to find your match. Are you a female pot in a kitchen of exclusively pots? Can you go to a whiskey tasting or join a cornhole league where there might be a few lids? Or, are you a male lid who spends more time talking with other lids about podcasts made by anti-pot lids than making pot friends? If I were still single today, I would get season tickets to my local sports team. And when I say "local" I don't mean something splashy and impersonal like an NFL squad. I'm talking about the minor league baseball team hitting foul balls in your backyard. You'll see the same people regularly and eventually get to know them. Maybe they'll have a single friend who's perfect for you.

I've seen this approach work in real time through one of my closest friends. She became a widow while pregnant with her fourth child. Despite her gargantuan loss, she remained a social person. She went to community-based events. At one of those functions (my annual Easter lamb-on-the-spit cookout), three years after her husband's death, I asked her if she was ready to date. She said yes. And I immediately urged her to introduce herself to my husband's coworker. She agreed he was cute, but the pair didn't talk until about an hour before she and her kids had to leave. It was casual, and they aligned on the fact that they both have children. He asked me for her number before he departed. They went out that week. They've been dating ever since. As I write this, I'm keeping the secret of her impending engagement. My friend didn't go to that Easter dinner expecting to find her person, but she did. So go to the dinner, the party, the conference, or the meetup. The worst thing that can happen is that the love of your life is there (or the person who can introduce you to them).

Now, back to talking about the impact of loneliness on the potential to meet people IRL. It's hard to connect with others when you aren't afforded the basic pillars of connection. If you're at home, engaging in a limiting echo chamber built by companies that want to keep you on their app as long as possible,[71] you're losing out on growth opportunities you don't even realize are being kept from you. Soon enough, you'll have more extreme viewpoints than you ever planned to have, and it will be difficult to interact with people who don't share your exact same beliefs.[72] After all, the words on your screen have been tailored to mirror the ones in your head for who knows how long?

This threat is particularly dangerous for men looking to date women. As certain corners of the internet feed them increasingly more stringent versions of conservatism, the corresponding women in their dating pool are becoming more progressive.[73] If men are unable to tolerate these forward-thinking women, they will end up limiting their own opportunities to connect and, eventually, fall in love and build lasting relationships. They will feel isolated and lonely, and that's dangerous.[74]

Isolation and loneliness are not natural. As a species, we have an instinct to connect with one another. The feeling of loneliness, according to scientists, is an evolutionary phenomenon.[75] Loneliness triggers the release of stress hormones, particularly cortisol,[76] which help isolated humans remain more alert to danger. Stress leads to high blood pressure, increased inflammation, and a weakened immune system.[77] It also makes people susceptible to slipping into unhealthy habits like drug and alcohol abuse, overeating, and not exercising. So the need to be able to appreciate a wide variety of viewpoints may actually be a matter of life and death for the most intolerant among us.

HOW DO I FEEL A LITTLE BIT LESS LONELY?

I often tell my clients that finding a third place is a great way of finding connection in their everyday lives; that connection is what will set them up for success in finding and maintaining a new romantic relationship. You will need to seek out places that promise IRL interaction and create a consistent community that makes you feel welcome. These are the people who will become regular fixtures of your life. This can't be a random occurrence or one-off lark of an event. It has to be a space that routinely fits into your life, and the lives of the people in your greater community.

If you need a role model for this strategy, look no further than my μπαμπά (babá, dad) and my father-in-law. They're so lucky to have been born into a culture and generation that honors a third place. Greek men love a καφενείο (*kafeneio*), or a café. A *kafeneio* can be found on every corner in Greece, from the tiniest village to a sprawling city. Every single neighborhood in all of Greece has one.

You'll know it's a *kafeneio* by the clientele. They're mostly men, who are usually facing in one direction—probably looking at a TV with a soccer game—or people watching. Greek men will play *tavli* (backgammon) and drink coffee or a Greek spirit like raki, tsipouro, or ouzo. They'll talk about the news of the day, gossip, debate, and have heated conversations. I've seen grown men fight with their words at a *kafeneio*. Even if someone shoves a chair, everyone will be back the next day for more.

It's the agora of modern Greece—a gathering place to exchange ideas. There, you're interacting with your neighborhood and getting diverse viewpoints and ideas. Even if you're not a local, you're welcome at any *kafeneio*. There isn't a movie or TV show in Greece that doesn't depict the *kafeneio* as a very public extension of the home.

I mention all this to demonstrate that my father and father-in-law are faced most days with viewpoints other than their own. They've had to navigate maintaining their sacred third place, the *kafeneio*, despite being confronted with differences. Connection, above all else, is the top priority. Social routine is building their resilience. They are not feeling lonely or isolated.

I once had a client, let's call him Patrick, who was starting to feel the pangs of loneliness after attending a friend's wedding. Now that work was letting up, he felt more motivated than ever to find someone special. Asking for advice on how to increase his chances of success, I recalled that during our intake interview he joked that witty banter was his love language. I encouraged Patrick to follow the social media accounts for female authors that exhibited the witty banter he so valued. I just knew that one of those authors' readers would be his match. When one author, Jennifer Ashley Wright, was in his city for her latest book tour, he attended her reading full of curiosity. At one point he texted me, "This is heaven." I believed him. He found someone special on his own at a book reading of pop history.

This naturally brings me to a really fun third-place suggestion: your local library or bookstore. Both venues are hubs for community events, creative writing classes, game nights, and, of course, book readings.

You could also take a class or join a club to find your third place. Here are some activities you can choose from that are easy to find in most major cities or towns:

1. Improv
2. Cooking
3. Foreign language
4. Dance
5. Hiking or kayaking
6. Chess and backgammon

You can even crack open the course listing for your local community college and pick whichever class sounds the most exciting.

The whole point of this exercise is for you to go out, meet

new people, and become more comfortable in places outside your home. This is a workout for your social muscle, and you'll only get stronger at it with more opportunities.

HOW DO I ACTUALLY CONNECT?

I have been told I'm an extroverted, assertive Jersey girl, and I accept that. However, even I have a fear of rejection, and this fear is familiar to all of us. It's what prevents people from approaching others and building a supportive network.

The easiest way to make people feel comfortable is to lean into the expected questions and conversation starters, like "What neighborhood do you live in?" or "What do you do?" or "How long have you been working in that field?" Connecting isn't about entertaining or impressing someone . . . it's about meeting the person's expectations in the initial interaction you're having. Meeting what is expected is the easiest way to connect.

The art of small talk is time sensitive. It's a three-minute vibe check and in that time it's imperative to ask questions. With the answers, you'll try to find a single common thread to bounce from. For instance, maybe someone tells you they live downtown. "Oh, I work downtown! What street are you on?" Now, the conversation can ebb and flow about what you do for a living, what your favorite bars and restaurants are, and other commonalities that might spring from there.

If you're trying to make new connections, I encourage you to block out two days a week and find two local events to attend. Your express purpose at those events is meeting two new people. If after fifteen minutes of meeting these two people, you're just not feeling the event or the conversations, you're free to go. But if you can stay just another fifteen minutes, try! You'll almost never regret it. Don't be afraid to share your phone number (real, or that Google one we talked about in chapter 7) with new acquaintances at the event. And, even more important, don't be afraid to text your new friends about spending more time together soon. Invite them to the next event you're excited to attend; you'll either get a fabulous new plus-one or set up an alternate hangout soon. These tactics will give you the momentum you need to add new people to your social orbit.

HOW DO I FIND SOMEONE TO ASK OUT IRL?

My recommendation is taking on my self-created Five 5s Challenge.

First, you're going to contact five friends on the periphery of your social network and ask them to invite you the next time they go do something fun. These cannot be your closest pals, since going out with them hasn't led to the kind of results you're looking for. Instead, ask friends with hobbies you've never tried or whose partner might know your perfect match. This is the time to hit up your new friends from all the events you've attended. We're looking to update the kinds of people you're meeting and locate your person.

Then, RSVP for five events around you in the next five weeks. That might be a Rotary Club brunch, alumni networking event, a mixer hosted by your favorite podcaster, a salsa dance class, or your closest national park's gala. Yes, nearly all nonprofits have galas and fundraising events; go find them.

Next, attend five services at the house of worship of your choosing, or volunteer five times. You can walk dogs or help out at the local soup kitchen—whatever embeds you as an active member in your community. One of my clients volunteered at a charity's pickleball fundraiser, checking people in. Another client, who doesn't participate in any religion, helped organize a canvas to get out the vote for her community. The point is to see some of the same people who share in your values and build relationships with them.

Next, I want you to go online, and swipe right (or heart, or leave a comment, etc.) on five people that you maybe would have swiped left on in haste before.

Finally, say hello (yes, out loud, to their face) to five people of the gender you want to date. The first time, you will sweat. Then you'll realize . . . that conversation wasn't nearly as stressful as you imagined it would be. It gets so much easier as you practice more. Keep going.

Though it can be way more nerve-racking to ask a person out IRL than it is on The Apps, the tips we talked about there are still relevant here.

Just remember, every person is an opportunity. Maybe when you're volunteering, you meet someone who has a fantastic ring on her finger. Matchmaker Louie Felix says to exclaim how beautiful that ring is, and ask them how they met their spouse. Then, pivot the conversation and tell them you're hoping for your own love story soon. Who knows! Maybe she has a friend who has a son who is single. You never know . . . but you have to believe!

Here's a nifty matrix to keep track.

Once you start to implement some of the tips in this chapter, you'll notice your social capital beginning to skyrocket.

Matchmaker Maria's Five 5s Challenge

Reach out to 5 friends	Register for 5 events in your region in the next 5 weeks	Volunteer 5 times	Attend house of worship or community-based event 5 times	Say hello to 5 people

Whether you meet the love of your life tomorrow or simply make some new friends along the way, you'll see just how much better you feel. Your confidence will be undeniable, as will your ability to connect with just about anyone. So on the day you just might go to the local bakery for the same pastry as a cute stranger, you'll be ready to say "hello."

And every great love story starts with just one word.

10

HOW DO I ACTUALLY DATE?

I'VE ANSWERED THOUSANDS AND THOUSANDS of dating-related questions. A lot of those questions have to do with the first blush of dating—the panicky tiptoes that take two people from strangers at a bar to partners at a family holiday party. All these questions ooze anxiety and confusion. Which makes sense. Putting yourself out there to fall in love can feel like trying to reel in a good fish in a pond of piranhas or taking a step on that scary bridge in *Squid Game*.

In fact, dating can be daunting, no matter how prepared you feel. The thrill of sitting across from a new person can feel a lot like anxiety, even when you know a first date can (and should) just be a low-pressure meetup. Then, once real feelings get involved, the stress can skyrocket. You may start to wonder "How often is too often to text?" or "When am I allowed to define the relationship?" or "Is there ever a time that's too early to say 'I love you?'" Now that you're holding this book, the answers to those questions don't need to be a mystery. As you start to get to know people, I'm here to reveal the exact steps you should take to lock down the relationship you've always wanted. All you need to keep in mind is—much like the 12-Date Rule—not everyone deserves to complete this journey with you and enter a long-term relationship or marriage. If someone falls off by date five or you decide to call it quits after a year of dating, we're going to call that a win. They weren't your person, and you'll be one step closer to finding the one who is.

Before we dig into your date-by-date game plan, we need to set up some ground rules.

YOU'RE SINGLE, AND THEY'RE SINGLE, UNTIL YOU'RE BOTH NOT SINGLE

Justine, a coaching client of mine, was elated after her first date. She told me they had a second date planned for the next day. However, a few hours before the date, she told me that she went on the app and noticed he had updated his photos. *What does this mean?*

Comedian Jared Freid has made a job out of talking about the pitfalls of modern dating. Naturally, he has the perfect reply to this dilemma: "No one likes to know how the sausage is made." I've adopted this outlook in my own dating advice toolkit. What Jared means is that we all want to ignore the steps necessary to actually end up in a relationship. There's a lot of swiping, and nodding, and asking about people's favorite colors. Yes, your date is doing this with you. They're also probably doing it with other people, in the effort to find *someone* they actually click with. If that person happens to be you— great. On the road to you a lot of other stuff had to happen, maybe even including that little "active" button lighting up their profile after a great first date.

You're not helping yourself by wondering what's in the metaphorical breakfast meat casing. If you met through a friend, or in some other, more IRL, manner, you would have never known someone had updated their profile. You wouldn't have access to that information. You would only know if they called you when they said they would or if they showed up to your third date on time. Now that you do know, you need to remember their app activities might not mean anything. It's just them, being single, doing single things. You're *also* on the app checking up on them. Should they hold your "active" green light against you?

It's okay to panic. But try not to.

I need you to accept that you are dating. That means you're single until you're not. The same goes for everyone else you're dating. You could have an amazing first date with someone and feel an instant connection (notice that I didn't use the word "spark"?). Let's call that individual person A. And person A could go on a different first date the very next day with someone else. This isn't cheating or a betrayal. It's dating. After all, you, too, could have a third date planned with someone else, person B, after your magical first date with person A. But that's a commitment you've made and it's only fair to honor it. You need to give your plans with person B as much energy as you gave person A the evening prior. After all your planned dates, you can start making decisions.

Even if person A updates their photos—one of The Apps' most stress-inducing post-date moves around—you have to accept it's part of this process. It's entirely possible person A thought you were out of their league, and wants to shore up future prospects before you break *their* heart. You might not be the only person anxious about securing a match in this equation.

ASK MATCHMAKER MARIA

Why do they say they want a second date but then disappear?

I think people say things on a first date that are easy. A lot of people dislike confrontation. A lot of people are people pleasers. So it's much easier to say, "Let's do this again," than the more honest, "I had a good time but I just didn't feel a connection. Bye forever." I don't think they're trying to hurt you. They're just trying not to say the mean thing. Remember, the stakes are very low one date in. Don't sweat it.

If the idea of dating even a handful of people at once gives you anxiety, I'm going to let you in on a little secret. I know this method works because it's how I eventually settled into a loving and committed relationship with George. I met my husband on a Friday in December in Boston, and as I've already mentioned, we spent the weekend having multiple dates together, both solo and with our mutual friends. We went on a walking date through the Freedom Trail. He took me out for cocktails. All of our friends went to brunch together. That's at least six dates in Matchmaker Maria date math conversion. On a roll!

Monday morning, I left for NYC. George flew out to Greece for Christmas break to visit his parents. I was sure I'd see him again, just not sure when.

Now, a few days prior to my trip to Boston, I went on a different first date with a longtime acquaintance whom we'll call Mike. We had interned together years earlier for a US senator's reelection campaign, and when our paths crossed as adults, ironically at an event for his own election campaign (he was running for office), he asked me out.

Our date was at a cocktail spot in Brooklyn and it was a nice first date. We shared a lot of the same values and passion for politics. Before I even left for Boston, I had agreed to go on a second date with Mike the Wednesday after I returned.

So much had happened in that one weekend, and as elated and infatuated as I was, George wasn't my boyfriend. I couldn't have predicted the future, but I knew in the reality I was living, I had a second date coming up with Mike, so I planned for that.

We went to country karaoke in Manhattan, which is always such a good recipe for a second date as watching people croon to Garth and Shania is a very specific love language. However, within two minutes of being with Mike again it was clear to me that he wasn't the guy for me. Nothing went wrong. There was no catastrophe. I simply didn't feel the same way with Mike that I had with George. George was the guy.

If I had canceled my plans with Mike, I wouldn't have been able to experience the undeniable contrast between two perfectly good men. It gave me the opportunity for a gut check that allowed me to enter a partnership with George—who also had crushes of his own at the time—without hesitation. I also learned I would be dating someone who respected my freedom. He never tried to tell me who I could or couldn't see, now that he was interested in me. His confidence in himself and his trust in me only made my attraction stronger. So as you're getting to know people, you're going to hold this story in your heart. It might not totally beat back the anxiety of the unknown as you fall for different people and begin to imagine a future with them. But it will make you know that the right person will choose you, no matter how many first dates either of you go on.

YOU SHOULD KNOW YOUR
ATTACHMENT STYLE

One of my clients, let's call him Arjun, hired me as his matchmaker in 2015. He was thirty-five years old and had moved to Manhattan for his PhD in mathematics at Columbia six years earlier. He loved the city so much, he stayed. Arjun worked in investment banking, clocking in fifty-five-hour weeks, but still tried to prioritize dating. On weekends, he'd go rockclimbing or play tennis. Despite his jam-packed schedule, he managed to swipe himself into a few relationships.

I asked Arjun how he was currently meeting matches. "The Apps, mostly," he said.

I asked him about his last three relationships.

Anytime I ask a client about their past relationships, I learn what I need to know about the psyche of the dater. What do they consider a relationship to be? Do we learn about a three-month situationship? A four-year, on-and-off relationship that started in college? Have they ever had a longer-term relationship? Are they an adult virgin with no relationship history? (Which is much more common than pop culture will have you believe.)

In this dating audit, as I like to call it, I ask for:

1. What is the name of the last person you dated?
2. How long did the relationship last?

3. What did you feel during the relationship?
4. Why did you break up?

I essentially want to uncover the dating patterns, if they have any. I encourage you to go through the above process with yourself.

Some people will recognize a dating pattern, and they will typically fall into the below types:

1. **Dating the same person with a different name**

   You'll fall under this dating pattern if you struggle to spot any differences in the personalities of your past partners. It's likely that all your past partners were emotionally unavailable, controlling, or exhibited narcissist traits. You may have noticed your relationships fail for the same reason.

2. **Forming codependent relationships**

   You'll fall under this dating pattern if you are a people-pleasing sort of person. You never want to say "no" to your partners. You have weak or no boundaries within your relationships and may make excuses for your partner's immature or bad behavior. You put your partner's happiness above your own.

3. **Dating people for the sake of trying to change them**

   You'll fall under this dating pattern if you date for potential versus the reality of an individual. You enjoy feeling like a savior and the idea of changing people sounds romantic and exciting to you. All of your exes are "projects" and you have found yourself dating people who exhibit various kinds of destructive behavior.

4. **Dating people with the fear of being alone**

You'll fall under this dating pattern if you give the benefit of time to relationships that you might be unsure about because you hope issues will correct themselves—even if there's no evidence of growth or change. You may say things like, "Things will just be better in three months . . ." Your partner may have also convinced you that you'll never meet someone "who loves you like I do." This is not true.

Breaking these harmful dating patterns will take acknowledgment that they exist and some introspection. For instance, how did you behave in the relationship? Were you controlling? Enabling? Codependent? Did you feel victimized? Confused? And do your relationships now mirror the relationships you witnessed as a child? So much of how we date is a reflection of how our parents modeled our understanding of what a relationship is. If you want someone to help you understand these questions, you can turn to a professional. Therapy can always be so beneficial, but it's particularly helpful when you have romantic questions that can't be solved over a ninety-minute brunch with your friends.

Which brings me to . . . attachment theory.[78]

My client Arjun was a great catch! I had no problem sending him out on dates. His dates would write back that they had a wonderful time and wanted to see him again. This is a major goal of mine as a matchmaker!

But the feedback that Arjun provided lacked a little self-awareness. For one, he always thought the date went terribly, even though I had evidence from both his match and him that they had an enjoyable conversation, found each other attractive, and shared so many things in common. However, he focused on small imperfections and put up walls where vulnerability was required for a truly successful first date.

And what's worse was that he pined over his very first match, a short relationship that ended after three dates. She wasn't coming back, and somehow every woman I set him up with was being measured against a person who wasn't interested in him.

The writing was on the wall, so I purchased him the book *Attached* by Dr. Amir Levine and Rachel S. F. Heller.[79] "You're not going on another date until you read this."

A few days later, Arjun met up with me at Union Square for a walk and talk.

"Maria, I'm avoidant."

I looked at him without reacting even though my mind was screaming, *I KNOW!*

"I don't want to be like this. I want to lean into my person."

Attachment theory is an explanation for the emotional bonds between infants and caregivers, and in dating, it explains how our early childhood attachments affect our adult relationships.

The first attachment theorist was psychologist John Bowlby. Born in London in 1907, he was deeply interested in child development and the anxiety and distress a child may experience when separated from their primary caregivers. While other child development theorists believed attachment was a learned process, Bowlby believed attachment was part of the evolutionary process—that children are born with a drive to form attachment to their caregivers to receive comfort and security.

And now that I write this, having kids, I'll tell ya . . . babies are born wanting connection.

In the 1970s, psychologist Mary Ainsworth pioneered research with babies in her Strange Situation study.[80] This study involved observing children ages twelve to eighteen months responding to a situation where the young child was left alone and then reunited with their mother.

Picture a child left in a new day care by its parent. Upon the mother leaving the young child, would the child begin to cry? Would the child self-soothe and begin interacting with the toys in the room? Or would they continue to cry? When the parent returns, say, twenty minutes later, does the child acknowledge the parent and come running to perhaps show off a new toy? Or do they ignore the parent at the doorway? Or maybe they never stopped crying.

When Ainsworth conducted her study, she followed a very similar procedure in a basic sequence that involved a day care worker (aka a total stranger) in the room. She did this experiment with about a hundred American infants and mothers. Each child was observed for twenty minutes as their mother and stranger entered and left the room in three-minute intervals.

Some children were very distraught while others were very indifferent. Ainsworth observed three main attachment styles: secure, anxious, and avoidant.

Each style can be defined by the level of avoidance and anxiety in the child.

Infants that exhibited a secure attachment style trusted their caregivers. They didn't avoid their mothers and exhibited low anxiety when she was present. They felt comfortable exploring the unfamiliar room when the mother was nearby. They became a little upset when she left but relaxed and continued playing when she returned.

Infants that exhibited an avoidant attachment style had no preference between the mother and the caregiver (a stranger). They avoided closeness with anyone and rarely felt anxiety due to the absence or presence of any particular person. They didn't appear upset about the separation nor did they acknowledge the parent when she returned.

The significance of these behavioral patterns has consistently shown association between early childhood, adolescents, and adult romantic relationships. The attachment theory of love proposes that the type of romantic relationship one has as an adult is determined by the type of relationship one had with one's primary caregiver as a child.[81]

I needed Arjun to learn about attachment styles so that he could get out of his own way. And now, I need you to do the same thing. Having even a cursory understanding of where you fall on the spectrum of secure, avoidant, and anxious attachment will help you find compatible partners, improve your existing relationships, and stop cycles you may not even realize you've been running through for decades.

Essentially, Ainsworth and her team theorized that children who have a secure attachment style as infants have the healthiest and most enduring adult relationships. Their adults are consistent and responsive to their needs. As a result, they're able to develop trusting relationships and communicate their needs directly. They will care for a partner in the way they want to be cared for.

If you watched *Sex and the City* (and forgive me if you haven't), I want you to picture Samantha, Charlotte, Harry, and Steve. These are our secure characters. Most, if not all, of their plotlines involve them communicating directly, being flexible in their relationships, and providing a sense of clarity if anyone around them seems confused or anxious. I know some readers are shocked right now. A lot of people assume Samantha could never be secure since she is unabashedly independent and has cultivated a deep stable of lovers. But she has never led anyone on. She is always communicating her expectations. When she chooses someone to commit to, she doesn't leave until her needs or boundaries aren't being met.

Charlotte, on the other hand, is often thought of having an anxious attachment style, but really, she's just an anxious *person*. In terms of her relationship and attachment style, she is quite secure. She isn't someone who often initiates conflict to be acknowledged or sacrifices her own boundaries to make someone stay. In fact, she's willing to say the difficult or honest thing, even if that means someone could lose interest. Charlotte proves as much in an early season 1 episode, after her latest beau, Bryant, flatly reveals he wants to have anal sex the next night after dinner. When the day comes, she gathers her friends and debates the issue. By the time Charlotte is in bed with her guy, she tells him honestly—she has no interest in being "Up the Butt" Girl. Bryant understands, and asks if they can just do it the old-fashioned way. Charlotte is very, very, very into that idea. Yeah, she was anxious about how Bryant would react, but never let that feeling stop her from speaking her mind. Surprise—you, like Charlotte, can be anxious without an anxious attachment style.

Anxiously attached adults are defined by their desire to be very close to their partners, and seeking high levels of approval and responsiveness. They may exhibit high levels of distrust, worry, and impulsiveness in their relationships. They experience extreme distress when they feel distance, and will do anything to alleviate that sentiment. When speaking to clients with an anxious attachment style, I try to highlight something that might be a trigger, and show them how to work around that trigger. I help them to understand that they are drawn to the rush that comes with the neurotransmitter dopamine. Therefore, the anxiety of chasing someone with an avoidant attachment—who, as the name suggests, tends to avoid intense intimate relationships—is very addictive to them. That kind of relationship is a natural dopamine train.

So if you are an anxious attachment, I want you to find a new source for your dopamine. That way, you're not looking for a partner to play into your anxiety cycle. I want you to become a weekly regular at a comedy club, or go see a jaw-dropping action film every month. Once a season, I want you to hop on the wildest roller coaster at the nearby amusement park or pick up a hobby that provides physical activity, like pickleball. Really, anything else that will give you a rush. Soon enough your anxiety will be sated and you'll be swimming in dopamine.

With avoidant attached adults, my advice is a little different. First, I would say maybe it's time for therapy. Avoidant attached people are focused on independence and self-reliance, which makes it very difficult for them to settle into the intimacy of a close relationship. By protecting your autonomy, you may miss out on the comfort of being known and loved by the right person. As you date, you should question why you're attempting to disassociate in the relationship or why your partner's interest creates stress.

In Dr. Levine and Heller's book, they discuss the anxious-avoidant trap, and I will be the first to tell you, as someone with a secure attachment, you can easily find yourself victim to this. You see, it's a catch-22! The avoidant may hold back acknowledgment of the reality you're both in for fear of being intimate. You, a secure or anxious person, might not pick up on the cues that they're being avoidant and may think it's just a matter of you being patient.

I have witnessed anxious and secure people give the avoidant unprompted compliments as a way to show the avoidant admiration and recognition. The avoidant loves the ego boost, and their attachment system may be temporarily quieted, which results in extreme closeness that will not last. Suddenly, the avoidant's ego is boosted and the anxious or secure person is experiencing the high of emotional intimacy. But that very closeness quickly sets alarms off for the avoidant, leading them to push their partner away. The partner then feels anxious and confused, setting the entire sequence into motion once again. You or a friend have probably experienced this confusing trap. Some of you might be in the midst of it right now, and I'm very excited to get you out of it.

This vicious cycle is addictive. And it's why a show like *Sex and the City* was (and remains) so popular. Our protagonist, Carrie Bradshaw, had an anxious attachment style. Mr. Big was avoidant. Shocking, I know. Nearly every single plotline between these two characters involves Mr. Big keeping Carrie at arm's length. And every time Carrie goes to leave . . . be it Paris with the Russian or after bashing Mr. Big over the head with her bouquet *after he left her at the altar*, he always comes running back. Ahh!

I was once told by my mentor, relationship scientist Dr. Terri Orbuch, that 25 percent of men and women are avoidant. I remember hearing that and thinking . . . great. Now, I know—25 percent of men in NYC are undatable unless they seek help. However, someone who displays an avoidant attachment can absolutely be in a relationship. They just need to understand and follow a few things in order to enter and maintain a long-term relationship:

1. Being strongly motivated to be less avoidant can actually help someone acquire more of a secure attachment style.[82]

2. A fun and supportive partner can help someone be less cautious about intimacy.[83]

3. Entering a relationship doesn't diminish someone's own identity, and they're still allowed "me" time when they have a partner.

4. Everyone deserves to be happy. And if a relationship will make someone happy, they shouldn't deny themselves that joy.

Having this knowledge equipped me with the ability to recognize someone with an avoidant attachment, and whether they were trying to make themselves ready for a relationship. I also needed to acknowledge when that person didn't want to commit. It wasn't their fault—one in four men possess this attachment style. Our incompatibility was just part of the tricky randomness of probability.

So a few months later, I did just that.

I met a guy through OkCupid. Let's call him Theodore. We talked on the phone first before meeting, and we vibed . . . although there was a bit of a heated debate about gun control. Theodore asked me out for our first date and we met in downtown Manhattan a couple of days later. Theodore and I had great chemistry, and he even pulled me in for a kiss as we left the venue.

As we were walking, he asked me about my job as a matchmaker. I told him about how I recruit and vet matches on behalf of my clients, how I coordinate first and second dates, and how I collect feedback after each and every date.

He was curious. He asked, "Do you think you could send me the feedback form? I'd love to fill it out for this date." I nervously laughed, but thought, why not? I forwarded him the link we usually send to our clients.

He put me in a cab, and I went home. An hour later, I had an email in my inbox. It was the results.

Was there chemistry?	Quite a lot!
What did you like about your match?	Physical attractiveness
	Sense of humor
	Dressed appropriately
	Personality
	Conversation skills
	Eye contact
	Manners/politeness
	Personal hygiene
	Attentiveness
Was the venue appropriate?	Yes
Did you enjoy the date?	Yes
Would you like to continue to get to know your match?	I think there is potential with my match. I would like to continue to get to know him/her.
Comments:	I did pick out a pretty awesome restaurant, after all. The only reservation is that Maria and I are looking for different things. I can tell she's looking for something serious. I'm not there yet. I really did enjoy my time with her, and I do want to see her again.

And there it is. The 25 percent.

Theodore is telling me he wants a second date, and in his own words, he's also telling me "I'm not there yet."

And I know what Young Maria would have done before she learned about attachment theory or had that illuminating conversation with Dr. Orbuch. She would have read this and said, "Well, of course! It's just a first date! I'm not there yet either!" He checked off that he wants to see me again . . . of course I will see him again.

And in the dark corner of my brain, I would have also convinced myself that if we kept dating, he'd see how smart I am, how cool I am, how funny I am, how fun I am, what kind of a cook I am, that I'm great in bed, too. He'd see all these things, and then . . . then he'd be convinced to date me seriously.

But you know what, I didn't.

This was the best first date I had ever been on, and only a crazy person would not have wanted a second date with me. But he did want a second date. So he's not crazy . . . he was just going to drive *me* crazy.

You see, I have been on this roller coaster before and so have all my friends. So have many single people. A month from now, I would be in love with him. I would try to define our relationship, and he'd say something like "I don't believe in titles" or "Let's just keep dating and go with the flow."

And I would have believed him, thinking he just needed more time. Maybe I would have convinced myself that I needed more time.

And then six months later, we would have one of those conversations that frustrates you over dinner, where the tears stream down your face, and you look away as your cheeks grow hot because you've realized you've fantasized a relationship with a person who is incapable of leaning into their own vulnerability.

And they'd try to reassure you, but also reclaim their innocence in the matter by saying something asinine like "Remember I told you I'm just not there yet."

So I never replied to his feedback form which was his "creative" way of asking me out on a second date. I forwarded his form answers to one of my closest friends, fellow matchmaker Laurie Berzack. "What a shame. This was such a fun first date," as a way to just hold myself accountable. Laurie was super encouraging. "Who else is on the horizon?" she asked.

I told her, "Oh, I have a first date coming up with a guy I know running for state senate." That was the last man I would date before I met George.

As you start to unravel dating with your own (or dealing with a partner's) attachment style, it's important to remember that none are bad, and they are no one's fault. There's no shame here—only pragmatic solutions to universal issues. As Ainsworth's research first found, the roots of one's attachment style stem all the way back to their initial relationships with their caregivers as babies and toddlers. You can't blame one person for emotions that were decades, and generations, in the making. After all, the treatment one's childhood caregivers dole out is based on their own attachment style . . . which was solidified by the behavior of *their* childhood caregivers, and so on, back through the annals of history.

Arjun, using the work of Dr. Levine and Heller, found himself a therapist. I, true to my word, started setting him up again. His very next match, Anika, was a highly ambitious and goal-oriented dermatologist in the city. Everything aligned, and I was not nervous for their first date. I didn't want him to lean out. I wanted him to finally latch.

The feedback form was positive on both ends. There was a second date. And a third. And a fourth. And now they're married, living in New England, running a vegan restaurant together.

I've studied relationship science extensively, but if you were to ask me which theory changed my life, it's attachment theory. My clients use it, I've used it in my own relationships, and I even utilize it in my professional relationships. It's that powerful.

BE OPEN TO MIXED-COLLAR DATING

Meet one of the final true taboos in modern dating. Everyone is all for mixing things up in relationships now—until you start talking about college and tax brackets. Many straight women tell me they would "never" (that word again) date someone who doesn't have the same level of degree as them, or makes less than they do. They've been socialized by generations of hypergamy, or the act of marrying "up" for social and financial benefits. Once upon a time, as we've talked about, women were chattel to cement monetary safety for themselves and their families. While most Western cultures have done away with this formalized approach to dating, women are often still raised to feel embarrassed if their men aren't footing the bill and bringing home the bigger percentage of the bacon. This societal trick has these women missing out on a lot of great guys. Straight men, on the other hand, were never raised with such expectations for their future spouse. So they are now free to date "down" (and look like a traditionally masculine provider); on the "same" level (and be seen as a respectable modern feminist); or even "up" (and be lauded as a confident and forward-thinking man).

In most Western societies, women have been socialized for over three thousand years to seek a partner who will provide. Of course, in the past, women needed men for survival, whether it was physical or financial. They couldn't buy property, have a bank account, or vote.[84]

While we have progressed as a society, hypergamy continues to exist.[85] I hope this book proves once and for all that, yes, education and money certainly matter. But happy relationships are built on so much more than those old-fashioned expectations.

Thought leaders like *Date-onomics* author Jon Birger are trying to encourage women to give themselves more opportunities to find a compatible match. They recommend opening up to what Birger calls "mixed-collar dating."[86] There are more women currently enrolled in college than men.[87] As a result, all genders are going to need to get more comfortable with dating people from separate financial and educational strata. It's a Hallmark Christmas movie's dream: white-collar woman meets blue-collar guy.

However, this reality doesn't mean you need to date just anyone from a different collar. This is where all the work we did in chapter 4 around your compatibility pillars comes in, along with using the knowledge of the dream partner that you began to manifest in chapter 5. You *can* be compatible with someone outside of your educational background or salary band. You just need to find someone who shares the same values and reality as you.

One of my clients, let's call her Nicole, is an in-house law-yer for a tech start-up with a salary in the $300,000s. She always pictured herself with someone with an advanced de-gree. After we did her matrix together (see chapter 5), we recentered the values that she hoped to share with someone she trusted. To expand her horizons, I challenged her to re-move her two no-nos as she swiped: be open to dating some-one over fifteen miles away and be open to dating someone who isn't a lawyer or a doctor. Enter Richard. He was a high school teacher and lived twenty miles away. She had never thought to date a teacher. And she had never dated someone who lived a whole bridge away. Yet, here he was, commuting to her, courting her, and providing her the emotional secu-rity she had always looked for. Plus, he had access to a better healthcare plan and a good pension! She couldn't believe her luck. I told her, he's lucky to have met *you*.

I also want to tell you about my friend Alex. He's such a catch! After high school, he went to trade school to be-come an HVAC technician. From there, with zero student loan debt, he began to work. He saved enough money to buy a multifamily home, of which he rents out the first floor to help pay off the mortgage. He works at a big pharmaceutical company, repairing air vents, and receives solid health insur-ance. He reads the *New York Times*, listens to murder mystery podcasts, and has a strong group of loyal friends. The idea that someone would pass on him because he does not have a bachelor's degree feels like a missed opportunity to meet someone with a big heart and a strong work ethic.

I have so many stories like this, and so do you. Maybe this is (or will be) your story, too.

HOW DO I MASTER THE ART OF CONVERSATION?

A core part of dating is simply being able to speak—to share your perspective and being actively interested in someone else's. To accomplish that goal, you need to get used to showing empathy and vulnerability, and often with someone you don't know very well. As I personally learned from Brené Brown's *Daring Greatly*, to build your vulnerability, you must give yourself permission to be open and authentic. You're tasked to talk about your experiences and your feelings. This cue lets people know you're open to connection. By practicing empathy, you open yourself for connection by understanding others' perspectives and feelings, creating space for more meaningful relationships.[88]

You're showing a potential partner what it would be like to spend a lot of time around you, and you want to put your best foot forward.

The hack I most recommend is starting a date conversation like you're already in the middle of it. Instead of making panicky small talk, say something like, "Hi, Megan! It's so good to meet you, I was just in this neighborhood a week ago and wanted to check out this bar. I feel like I manifested it." Now instead of awkwardly staring at the menu, there is a plethora of topics on the table. You can chat about why you were recently in the neighborhood, what you like to do with your loved ones, what interested you about the restaurant specifically, or even whether you believe in manifesting. Suddenly, you're not talking to a stranger, but relating to a new friend who could become more.

If you need a conversation igniter for a first date or a singles mixer, I encourage you to do the below 3–2–1 date prep. You do this *right* before you go out so it's top of mind.

- Write down three things that made you laugh or gave you happy and joyful feelings this week. It could be a scene from your new favorite show or a podcast you listened to or a conversation you had with a sibling.
- Write down two things that make you unique and interesting, like maybe you're the oldest of three (older-sibling energy) or you collect comic books or you're always game for a music festival.
- Write this one call to action to yourself: You're there to have fun, so have fun and give people grace. Everyone is trying.

You don't need to ask what someone is looking for or reveal your exact timeline for marriage and children. All you need to do is have fun and get to know the person in front of you. This is the time to talk about the pop culture you love, the great vacation you just went on, and the parts of your career that you're most passionate about—and remember to get the same information from your date. The best dates are a volley between two equal partners.

WHAT SHOULD I DO ON A FIRST DATE?

Eventually, after reading all this, you're going to go on a first date. I'm so happy for you. You know some of the main ground rules that will make your dating experiences all the more successful, and now it's time to get into the nitty-gritty of an actual *date*. Wherever you go, I hope it's a location that lets you stand or sit next to each other instead of across from each other.

I also advise that first dates should be no longer than ninety minutes. If you want it to be longer, call it a night and plan your next date ASAP. The last thing I want for you is to experience an entire relationship over a single evening. That's how you end up not getting a second date. You've already given someone the girlfriend or boyfriend experience. Maybe they're full and do not want any more servings.

Look down at your wrist. Is there a smartwatch? Okay, take it off or turn off the notifications. One of the biggest complaints I hear after dates is that they kept looking at their watch, when I know the real truth: The watch has notifications enabled and every call, text, and water reminder slightly nudges the wearer every few minutes. You can't help but look, but you're also giving the worst first impression. If you're someone whose profession demands they're reachable by phone 24/7, let your date know immediately with a little bit of charm. Explain that you know it's not typical, but you need your phone on the table—and it has nothing to do with their sparkling personality and dazzling looks. You're sorry, and that's why the meal is on you tonight.

WHAT DO I DO AFTER A FIRST DATE?

Once you're done with your date, you only have to ask yourself two questions: "Did I enjoy myself?" and "Am I still curious about this person?" And that's *it*. You don't need to decide if you could see yourself spending the rest of your life with them. Or if there was "a spark." You don't even need to decide if you're attracted to your date. All of those questions (and every other one you probably have) can be figured out on a future date. If you had a nice time and would like to know more about this person, schedule a second date.

In the wake of your first date—and I so apologize for being heteronormative in what I'm about to say, but it's The Straights that are the most confused—both genders need to keep one thing in mind: If a second date was not agreed upon before the end of the first date, it's the guy's job to ask the woman out for a second date. And he has three days to do it.

I rarely believe in separate expectations for the genders, but this is one of the exceptions. I promise. I've set up thousands of first dates, and that's just the truth of the ritual that is straight dating. A woman can ask a man on a first date, a third date, and a thousandth date. But when it comes to the second date, it's on the man.

There are some truths to consider as women wait for a man to ask for a second date. The ultimate rule is that if a man is really excited about a woman, he will trip over himself to ask to see her again. My husband could barely wait the two hours until I got on my train to ask when he could take me out next. In fact, at least 80 percent of the dates I have set up over time have had second dates scheduled by the following morning. "I'm enjoying myself. When can we see each other again?"

If a man seems to be interested in you but isn't tripping over himself to set up a second date, one of two outcomes are possible:

First, you sadly might not be a priority, and dating, in general, might not be a priority for him. It's not personal.

Second, he might be trying to subconsciously prepare you to have very low expectations in a relationship (or, more likely, a situationship). So if a man asks you for a second date five days after your first one, directly ask him why if he doesn't offer up an explanation. Because someone looking for a real relationship won't try to string you along.

Should a man wait ten days or more to ask you on a second date . . . turn him down. This is a person who doesn't care about leaving you confused or making you feel embarrassed. Particularly since that means you're not seeing them ten days after a first date. It could take ten more days to plan another outing. If this person really needed a week and a half before his next date, they easily could have shared that immediately after a first date and promptly planned accordingly. And they didn't do that. This is not the kind of person who deserves to have you as a partner.

If after your first date you're texting back and forth but he's yet to ask you out, call it out. "Hey, it's fun texting you, but when is our next date?" Texting isn't dating, remember? Nip it and set the expectations that you're looking for someone to go out with, not someone to distract you during work hours or while laying on your couch.

HOW DO I APPROACH SECOND AND THIRD DATES?

Second and third dates are the perfect time for a date that centers around an activity. Think of some of your local bars and find out which one has live music for a night. Boom, you're on an activity date. There are endless activities happening in your area: trivia night, pasta-making class, arcade tournament, culinary tour, etc. Maybe a bar in your area has shuffleboard or some ax throwing. Most of these activities will cost what a typical meal at a sit-down date would. The difference, of course, is you get to connect with your date in a different way. It's exciting and, ultimately, the goal is to get the dopamine flowing.

A common issue I find particularly interesting is when new daters, especially straight women, complain about having to *sometimes* be the one to plan the dates. I empathize, but I also have to tell you, in the long run, it doesn't matter, and wouldn't you rather do the fun stuff you've always wanted to do here? Have a list of activity dates in mind and fire them off. Even a walking date over some gelato is preferred over a sit-down dinner.

One place you're absolutely not going for a date during this period is to the other person's home—or having them over to your place. Especially if this is someone you've met from the internet. You can take that very personal step after three dates. This recommendation isn't about the possibility of physical intimacy. We've already talked about the 12-Date Rule. Instead, I just want you to be safe. You should really only consider a home visit before the third date if you have friends in common and there are active stakeholders in how you treat each other. Then, and only then, can you make the exception.

By the end of the third date, you should know if you're attracted to the person you're dating. If you gave it these three shots and the feeling just isn't there, it's okay. Let them go, no matter how much you align on other values. You gave your heart three chances to catch up to your brain and it didn't work. You need to be attracted to your partner, plain and simple. So, on to the next.

HOW SHOULD I APPROACH
THE DATING PERIOD?

You've enjoyed someone's company enough to get past three dates with them. You're utilizing the 12-Date Rule (or saving sex for whatever boundary makes you feel comfortable). You like this person. Amazing! You need to hold one adage in your mind at all times: you shouldn't feel confused.

You should never feel confused. If you feel confused at any moment, ask the person you're dating to clear that up. Unsure when you'll see them again? Ask. "What are your plans for this week? I'd love to coordinate when we're seeing each other again." Are you the kind of person who needs to be communicated with each day? Ask. "I know I'm more of a texter, and I see you're not. Could we call or video-call each other each day instead?" I'd also ask them what *they* need from me so as not to feel confused and/or acknowledged in a relationship.

It's at this point that you should be sharing your vision for the future. You don't need to quiz the other person on what they want. Instead, declare your dreams and see how they react. You can be honest and say, if it's true, "I'm dating right now, but I would like my next relationship to lead to marriage if they are the right person." (I just know you raised your eyebrows, but hear me out!) Someone who isn't interested in marriage or children—if either of those milestones is in your life plan—will make their feelings pretty clear pretty quickly when those subjects arise. And, in equal measure, someone who also wants those things will light up over your frankness and readiness.

This is the perfect time to let your date meet your friends, or get to know theirs. Is someone having a birthday party? Bring them along. Do your friends get together once a week to watch the game? Well, I hope your date likes wings. You'll be able to learn much faster whether you really like this person. And you can ask your friends if they think this person complements you. Rather than asking your pals what they think of your date, ask if you seemed at ease or if they believe this new person brings out your best qualities.

While you should be exploring each other's worlds at this time, there's one group of people who shouldn't be involved in this part of the process: family. There's no tapping in your siblings for a once-over, or making your parents meet someone who isn't a boyfriend or girlfriend. That scenario is unnecessarily stressful for all involved.

WHEN SHOULD I DEFINE THE RELATIONSHIP? (AKA HOW TO AVOID THE DREADED SITUATIONSHIP)

There's no need to worry about getting to this part of the relationship before, at least, the three-week mark. I have milk in my fridge older than your relationship. Yes, your anxiety may be rising as you start to fall for a new person, but you probably still don't know enough about them to make an informed decision. So just take a deep breath and give yourself a little more time. By now, as we discussed the importance of in chapter 7, you should know how your date is on a good day and on a bad day, as well as how they treat you on each. You should have also met at least one of their friends by now, and vice versa. Only when you have all this information, and it feels compatible with your life goals, should you approach defining your relationship.

As with many dating conversations, you should approach defining the relationship (or DTRing) as a statement of what you want, rather than a question of someone else's desires. This is your life, and you're in charge of its direction. So somewhere between about week three and week six, you're going to state in very clear terms what you're looking for from this person. If you want a script, you can say, "I really like you and when I like someone this much, I feel like I want a relationship with them." The other person might ask what a "relationship" means to you. And you'll say, "You're my boyfriend and I'm your girlfriend. We would be in an exclusive relationship, building toward a future together." It's up to them to respond with what they want. If you two match up, woohoo—you've got a new boyfriend or girlfriend, partner, or significant other. Now it's time to continue to date and determine if you are emotionally compatible and if your lifestyles are compatible enough to be a fit for marriage, if that is ultimately your goal. And if you don't align, that's great news. You're one step closer to finding the right person for you.

As you work to figure out where you may—or may not—align, one step you're not going to take is letting another person leave you confused. I bring up confusion again because it is so common that people remain dating someone despite not knowing where they stand. That is how you end up in the dreaded situationship. This is why it is necessary to set expectations and boundaries by six weeks. Anything longer leaves you open to something murky, where you're giving girlfriend or boyfriend privileges to someone who refuses to commit to you. Do not agree to be exclusive with someone who won't say directly if they want to be in a long-term relationship with you. Do not buy birthday gifts and holiday presents for someone who isn't your boyfriend or girlfriend. (Okay, maybe those large Hershey Kisses that they sell at convenience stores. That's kinda cute.) Don't take them to your friend's wedding or let them meet your parents. That's not your partner, and if they don't try to commit to you by the three-month mark, they likely never will be. Avoid these people at all costs. This is a win—you're free.

HOW DO I KEEP MY MANIFEST IN MIND?

As you get to know your matches, please remember you have your manifest tucked into your metaphorical pocket. Once you're several dates in, why don't you glance at your spiritual dating guide? Remember: this person doesn't need to match every single line of your manifest. You might not hit every one of their dream list items either. But ask yourself if your current relationship is reflective of what you imagined for yourself. If you're seeing an 80 percent satisfaction rate, keep going. You're on the right path.

11

WHAT'S MY RELATIONSHIP ROAD MAP?

WHEN I DO ask a Matchmaker Wednesdays on my Instagram, there are a few questions I often receive that I tend to avoid answering, and they usually revolve around timelines. I can help people get into a relationship, but from there, it can feel out of bounds to advise people when to get engaged and married with zero context of their ages, their relationship, their personalities and backgrounds, and their overall compatibility.

When I get a timeline question, I often worry that the person asking is sixteen. I remember dating as a teen, and it mostly revolved around hand-holding at a matinee showing of a movie or walking around the mall. I also remember, at sixteen, watching American TV shows that followed a very specific formula:

1. Introduce a family that has an unprecedented number of teenage hijinks.

2. A teen has a long-term relationship with someone throughout high school.

3. Said teenager goes to college; a plotline will involve them giving up a spot at an Ivy League university to keep their teenage relationship going.

4. ???

5. Series finale: a college student will marry their high school sweetheart a few years into college.

Shows and movies that I watched as a child and teenager that have followed this formula include:

1. *Saved by the Bell*
2. *Full House*
3. *Boy Meets World*
4. *Family Matters*
5. *That 70s Show*
6. *A Walk to Remember*

This formula left a lasting impression on me . . . and on everyone around me. Of course I called into the local radio station to dedicate "All My Life" by K-Ci & JoJo to my high school sweetheart. We were fed a diet of dating formulas from producers who wanted *Saved by the Bell* wedding ratings. After all, Zack and Kelly were the ultimate American royal couple of the nineties.

I moved to Athens when I was eighteen, and the following spring, I met my next boyfriend. I was on spring break and my girlfriends and I went to Mykonos in April, like many college students did in Greece. Off season . . . with off-season prices. (This was back in 2004. I cannot imagine the prices now that

Americans have discovered Mykonos.) I met another college student who turned out to be a local. He was pursuing his studies in a different city in Northern Greece and had decided to visit his parents on his college spring break. We were at a daytime beach bar, and we got to talking and instantly hit it off. We exchanged numbers, and a couple of hours later he invited me out with his friends.

We went for cocktails at a local bar followed by sweet crepes at 1 A.M. right as the shop closed. As we were walking up, a sudden rainstorm began, the kind that included heavy lightning and required finding shelter.

A Volkswagen Beetle was on the side of the street. I don't know whose idea it was, but someone opened the door, and somehow six of us crammed inside. (None of us owned this car, by the way.) I don't know how this became romantic, but I was suddenly living in an episode of *Saved by the Bell*. We were face-to-face and all of our friends were cheering for us to kiss, and so we did. It was bashful and funny and fun. I was Kelly Kapowski and I had just survived a Greek Zack attack!

Greek Zack made plans for the following day. We spent the whole day together, but I knew I'd be leaving to go back to Athens in the early evening by ferry. He was also supposed to return to college a few days later. We kissed a little more, but there was never really any conversation about the future. It was truly a PG-13 Greek fling, of what all Saturday specials are made of.

Until, I finally arrive home, and there he is . . . my Greek Zack, at my doorstep, holding flowers. He flew into Athens, and surprise! Now I have a boyfriend.

My first Greek boyfriend.

My first Greek boyfriend who did not grow up on a diet of

Saved by the Bell, Full House, and *Boy Meets World.* I entered a relationship with someone who wasn't aware of the fast-paced and long-lasting relationship trajectory that I was reminded of each and every time I turned on the TV.

So how we talked about our future was . . . lopsided. I was big-picture, and he just wanted to know what we were doing on Saturday.

One day, we were in a disagreement about something. I don't even remember. I only remember his response to me: "Maria, we're nineteen. We're never getting married to each other. Can't we just have fun?"

Oh my God. He was right. How come I didn't think like he did? It shook me awake from the timeline haze. In hindsight, I now realize that none of my friends or family who had grown up in Greece were bombarded with images of young marriage unless it was a film from the 1950s or 1960s. All the shows on TV were basically about best friends having marriage issues in their forties or workplace-oriented shows with people over twenty-five. Throw in some reruns of *Friends* and *MacGyver.*

I had to learn to rewire my brain and unlearn timelines. This took a couple of years, and mistakes, *terrible mistakes,* were made along the way. I won't tell you about those missteps here, but maybe we'll talk about them in my next book.

A few months later, my boyfriend and I broke up. Not because of our differing upbringings and understanding of timelines, but because both our stays had expired in the respective timelines of our lives. It just wasn't meant to be. No series finale wedding for us.

Do you ever reflect back on your high school or college years and cringe? Or maybe you sometimes get hit with an overwhelming sense of awe? The benefit of time allows our brains to fully develop. Hindsight allows us a more nuanced understanding of the social dynamics that were at play and our own personal identity; it's so much easier to see the bigger picture from a distance. We can thank our frontal lobe—and its handy prefrontal cortex—for all the self-awareness that arrives somewhere around twenty-five. It's responsible for decision-making, planning, impulse control, and social behavior, and only ends up maturing well after we're out of high school cafeterias or college dorms. Or even our first adult job. It's taken me years to understand and forgive myself for the mistakes I made during young adulthood. But I was literally immature and rolling in the wake of experiencing intense emotions—the kind of feelings that cannot be biologically avoided at this time in life. I needed to learn and acknowledge my deal-breakers. I had to find out behaviors I was no longer willing to accept. I needed to build my instincts and learn to trust them to help me figure out when it was time to walk away from someone or when someone was worth committing to for the long run. Hopefully this book helps you capture this knowledge for yourself.

I never want to be the person telling a sixteen-year-old exactly how their life should go. But I already said in chapter 8—if you're under eighteen, come back to this book later. Go read the Bill of Rights or practice a new hobby. For the rest of you, I do have some overall guidelines that will take you from swiping to relationship to wedding cake . . . or at the very least, a celebration cake!

STEP 1: DATING

We've talked about dating a lot. But let's do a quick refresher and break this process down by time and numbers:

- Only attempt online dating when you can meet up with a new person within **seventy-two hours**. Anything longer, like, say, a week or even ten days, and you'll end up getting a pen pal instead of a partner. You will inevitably build this person up in your head, and the expectations will be too high. Then, once you do meet them, the real person will seem lackluster in comparison to the fantasy.
- Your first-date meetup should only last the length of **two drinks**. Anything else, and you need a secondary location, like grabbing gelato or a walk to the subway to end the night. Any more cocktails, and things start getting hazy.
- About to go heteronormative on this one, but if a man goes on a date with a woman and he doesn't contact them within **three days**, he's not interested in a second date. The one thing every man I've ever helped get married has in common? Each one has tripped over themselves to get a second date with someone they're actually interested in, usually before the date they are on is over. No one is waiting more than three days if they're interested.
- If they're not asking you out but keep texting you, you have permission from me to throw out an "I'm confused" text. "Hey. I'm really enjoying our

conversations, but when is our next date?" Just say it and see what happens. You'll receive one of two texts: either "Oh yes! How about tomorrow?" or "Hmm, let me get back to you." The second guy . . . is a time thief. Abort!

So How Do I Get That Date?

As we've talked about, you want to meet up with someone you're interested in as soon as possible. If you've had about three volleys on an app—or a perfectly lovely conversation IRL—ask to set up a one-on-one hang. Check back into chapter 8 for a quick and painless reminder of how to ask someone out. One of two answers is acceptable for someone worth the honor of going on a date with you: a "yes," or a "no" with an alternate plan in the near future.

However, there's one response that might *seem* acceptable in this era of modern dating—but it actually isn't. It's sneaky. After trying to set up a meetup, a person might say, "I'm not ready to meet. Let's talk a little more." This is a person revealing they're not serious about dating and might be fishing for instant validation from a stranger. As I keep telling you, you're not in the market for a pen pal. Because before you start defending this kind of evasive behavior, remember that they would be falling over themselves to see someone they're genuinely excited about. If Natalie Portman, Pedro Pascal, or Jenna Ortega were on Hinge trying to take someone out on a Wednesday . . . that person would be seated at the bar on Wednesday in their best duds. No questions asked. And they're certainly not telling those people, "I'm not ready to meet."

As you prepare to meet up with the person who has their priorities in order, you might feel the urge to check in before your date. You don't need to do this. You're going on a date! You're not this person's personal assistant checking in for a scheduled Zoom call.

Some dating commentators will go so far as to say you shouldn't even get ready for a date if the other person doesn't confirm by 2 P.M. on the dot the day of. Ooof! I disagree here. Instead of making a snap decision, assume the best about your match. If you're feeling stressed, reach out with an affirmative message. At around 11 A.M. the day of your meetup, say something like, "I'm wearing a green dress tonight. Let's see who spots who first!" Or, for men, you can say, "I'm so looking forward to seeing you tonight. What color outfit will you be wearing so I can look out for you?" Now you can quell your anxiety while also putting your best foot forward.

Podcaster Ilana Dunn not only followed up with a message from a guy that matched with her months before, but she told him how she was looking forward to meeting up just one hour before their date. She assumed the best, and he met those expectations when they finally met up. Now they're married!

Once your meetup goes well, and your second drink ends up being more ice than margarita, it's time to start putting the brakes on your date. But good news! You can start planning your second date right then and there. Matchmaker Louie Felix has a foolproof hack for subtly pulling off this level of planning. Once there's a lull in the conversation, bring up a fun activity that you know the other person would love. Like, say, a cooking class at the restaurant down the block or mini golf at the local course. If you're aggressive, like Louie, you can pull up the details right then and there and make a concrete plan. Or, if you want to take things a little bit slower, you can promise to text them the information tomorrow. Either way, you've scheduled a date and are well on your way to spending more time with a great prospect.

STEP 2: ENTERING A RELATIONSHIP

The getting-into-a-relationship period is different for everyone. But . . .

- It's perfectly fine to decide to enter a relationship after **twelve dates**, if you utilize Matchmaker Maria math.
- You should never give someone over **three months** to decide they want a committed relationship with you. This is how you end up in a situationship, giving someone the privileges of being in a relationship with you . . . without actually being in a relationship. It's an experience that will erode your self-confidence, dignity, and sanity, for someone who is not worth the effort, by definition of their treatment of you.

ASK MATCHMAKER MARIA

Six dates in three weeks. He asked me to be exclusive. I feel rushed. Isn't it too soon?

It's pretty average for people serious about being in a serious relationship to ask for exclusivity by week three to four. That being said, if you feel rushed, that's valid! Just say you need a few more weeks of dating to get there. That's all. And after those few weeks—let's say three more—if you still don't feel ready to commit to this person, it might be time to let them go. That's okay! There's no villain here. Just two people who might not be a perfect fit.

During this time, you should obviously be having fun. As we talked about in chapter 7, it's normal to spend your first few dates enjoying your city, going to great restaurants, and drinking sexy cocktails. Please do that. But in between all the laughs and—hopefully—make-outs, you need to be sharing your values and learning if the person across the table aligns with you. Connecting on your values is the only way to determine if longtime partnership is possible—or if you would even want that from your date.

Dating is a practice. It's meant to help you figure out what you want and which types of people work best for you. Sometimes, as you learn more about a person, you realize that you might have a crush on them, but they're not actually the best fit. For example, when I was dating, I was excited to hear someone call themselves spontaneous. As a single woman in NYC, I loved it when my friends would call me and say, "Get ready. We're going out!" So I figured I, too, was spontaneous. But when I finally dated someone who really was spontaneous, I struggled. As I dated this person, I felt like I was lacking the structure I valued in the community I had built for myself. It wasn't sustainable *for me*.

STEP 3: SAYING "I LOVE YOU"

Getting to the L-word can vary. My DMs are filled with people who have arrived at the "I love you" stage after following the 12-Date Rule. But on average, I've heard anywhere between **four and twelve weeks** is where the word tends to pop up—and some people wait up to **seven months**. Beyond that, it might be time to have some serious conversations with your partner on where they see your relationship going and what you both want out of it.

But while we're on the topic, let's talk about love. Did you know Sanskrit has ninety-six words for love? Farsi has eighty and Greek has five. The English language is limited to just one word. No wonder so many of my US-, Canadian-, and UK-based followers are confused about their feelings in the various stages of a relationship.

I'm going to clear up "love" for you using the Greek words because, well, there are only five! And, also, I have felt each type of love. So I can tell you all about them!

1. **Eros:** *lust love.* You meet someone special, and now you can't stop thinking about them. You have to talk to them again, see them again, kiss them. It's the rose-colored glasses. The honeymoon. The lovey-dovey stage. This is the first love you experience when you start to date someone.

2. **Philia:** *platonic love.* This is a respect for friendship and cooperation. It's enjoying someone else's company and feeling secure and accepted with those at the highest level of relation to you.

3. **Storge:** *natural and instinctual love.* Storge is the love

a parent has for a child and vice versa, even the furry kind.

4. **Agape:** *love love.* In addition to it being a soul's recognition of another soul, *agape* is used in ancient texts to denote unconditional love. It's a love of mutual respect and partnership. It's the type of love you have to choose, and it's not based solely on instant connection or attraction.

5. **Mania:** *obsessive love.* Mania is unhealthy love that reaches the point of madness. It describes what one feels when they have a harmful obsession (and sometimes delusion) with their perceived partner. The Greek *mania* is the source of the English word "mania" and similar words like "maniac" and "manic."

When you're dating someone, you start with *eros* love. *Eros* will eventually plateau. Then you and your partner will have to either choose *agape* love *together* or separate.

In *Why We Love*, Helen Fisher explains that the first stage of love—what I call *eros*—is driven by intense attraction, thanks to a rush of dopamine and other neurotransmitters fueling that sense of excitement and passion. This "romantic love" phase is exhilarating, full of emotional highs, but it eventually gives way to what Fisher refers to as attachment.[89] This stage is marked by feelings of security, calm, and deep affection—what sounds a lot like *agape* love to me. That's when you're no longer just riding the highs; you're building something real, something lasting.[90]

If you feel like you need to say "I love you" after several weeks, that's fine, and honestly . . . really average based on research[91] and my professional experience. Now, if you were Greek, you'd say «Είμαι ερωτευμένος/η μαζί σου.» This loosely translates to "I'm in lust with you," and the person receiving it would understand what you mean. But in English, it's just "I love you."

And if you kept dating and built on your initial chemistry and connection, you'd say «Σ'αγαπώ.» In English, you're just saying "I love you."

So it's not your fault you're confused. The language you're using isn't exactly differentiating the vast spectrum of human emotion. Sorry.

STEP 4: INTRODUCING YOUR PARTNER TO FAMILY

Whatever you do, do not introduce your partner to your family the way my husband did . . . which is that he didn't. His cousins, in their mid-thirties, took it upon themselves to go through my Facebook profile and print photos of me from college and send them to my future mother-in-law. If you're an elder millennial, think about the kinds of photos we took and posted on Facebook between 2005 to 2010. Yeah . . . it was a lot of business-casual club wear and eyeliner. And weird facial expressions. And props!

Despite being Greek and sharing the same faith as George, my in-laws deemed me too different from them. They didn't like that I wasn't from their tiny village in Crete. They didn't like that I was a business owner. (Too risky in their eyes!) And they finally had someone to blame for George staying in the States. Despite the fact that we met in 2013. And he moved here to start pursuing his PhD in 2001. I cannot tell you how shattered, anxious, and confused I felt. So did George.

A couple of months after the Facebook photo fiasco, I was in Greece for my sister's wedding. George invited me down to Crete to meet his parents and his sister right after. He was really proud of me, but the stress and anxiety had hit a peak. His mother wanted this relationship to be over. I just wanted her to like me. George was trying to appease all sides with his instinctual diplomacy. I was certainly not going to put an ultimatum between my boyfriend and his mother. I decided I had overstayed my welcome in Crete, and I needed to depart early. I didn't want us to break up. I just wanted to not be there. George pleaded. There were lots of tears between us. And then he promised to advocate for our relationship. It was okay that his mom didn't like me. Neither of us could control her feelings. I could only control how I felt, and I felt supported by my boyfriend. I felt like he had my back. I knew who I was and what I stood for. I knew she'd eventually see that her son was happy. I knew she'd finally grow to like me . . . even love me.

. . . And seven years later, she did! After I had two babies. Plus, she grew to miss us during the pandemic. We couldn't fly to George's family in Crete while the world was in lockdown—and you know about what they say about absence and making the heart grow fonder. Once we were able to finally visit, she was fine! It's a dream come true!

So when should you introduce your partner to your parents? You know your parents. *You tell me.* Just remember this: You have to live your life with your partner. Not them. You have to advocate for your relationship and each other. Being together means you're a team.

If your parents are telling you they don't like your partner, ask questions! Is it because your partner is *different*? Well, even if they're different, there's no guarantee they'd like your next partner if they were the same! Even if I had never stepped foot in the US, George's mother could have still thought I was too different. I could have been born in Crete, and she still wouldn't have liked that I hadn't taken my first breaths in their specific village. When a parent is just looking for something to pick at to prove that a perfectly lovely new person isn't good enough for their little prince or princess, they'll find it. It doesn't mean you're bad. Or that your "difference" is an actual deal-breaker. Most of the time, it's because parents struggle to let go of the vision they have for their child's life. But sometimes, parents have very founded concerns about their child's new partner.

If your parents are scared for your safety in a relationship, self-reflect. Talk to a friend or a sibling to get their perspective. It's possible you're blind to a partner's bad behavior.

Now that you know what not to do, let's talk about what *to* do. The best way to introduce your partner to your parents is to follow in my footsteps. I took George and my parents bowling. I utilized the noisy atmosphere that comes with free-flowing food and beer as an active distraction. Before my parents met George, I told them a few things about him and I also let them know that I felt happy and supported in my relationship. They were delighted. The whole afternoon was fun. Although George was stressed out on making a great first impression, he didn't show it. They fell in love with him just like I had. I knew they would.

STEP 5: MARRIAGE IS ON THE TABLE

I know this is maybe the point in the timeline you want to know more than anything. So I'll give you the easy answer first. If getting married is one of your goals in life, and you are in a relationship, the possibility of marriage should come up within **six months**, if you're with the right person. In the spirit of generosity, I'll give you **eight months** in case you're shy. But don't be shy; we're talking about one of the most important decisions of your life. Be bold when choosing who to spend your life next to. Once, when my son was six, I asked him what he thought someone needed to know before marrying someone. His rules were: "You need to like each other. The other person needs to love you. They need to have a job. And together, you need to have money." He's not exactly wrong.

By the time I was with George for six months, we had laid everything out on the table. We had shared our deepest secrets and felt at peace. We agreed, "This is it—now we know." After those conversations, a switch flipped for both of us. We weren't dating just to have fun. We were dating to eventually marry. That kind of commitment and intent can still be there if you have questions about the other person or your relationship. At six months I still needed to meet George's parents, who lived five thousand miles away. We wanted to go on more vacations together and have silly, sexy dates. But our intent was to start learning how to build a world together. We were learning to compromise in the way husband and wife do. The time to simply "hang out" and "see what happens" was over.

At seven months, we went to an engagement party together for a childhood friend in New Jersey, and George gave me a look I hadn't seen before. "I'm moving here one day. I don't know when," he told me—and I knew he wasn't kidding. It was a matter of fact we would share our lives here eventually. He proposed eighteen months later. If we weren't long-distance at the time, it probably would have been even sooner. Now, thirteen years later, I'm writing this in our home in Central Jersey where we live with our two beautiful kids.

Although George is a great guy, I didn't decide he was spouse-worthy just *because* he's a wonderful person. There are a lot of wonderful people in the world. You need to know more than someone's general likability to properly conclude they're the right fit for lifetime emotional, financial, and romantic partnership. So let's talk about the questions to ask yourself to figure out if the person in front of you should even get to this point with you.

Are They a Kind and Attentive Person?

Are they kind to you and the people around them, whether they know them or not? Are they giving? Are they engaging in your relationship to understand and support you? And, equally important, do they make requests to connect?

Does This Person Exhibit Emotional Resilience?

Emotional resilience is the ability to adapt to stressful situations, and to cope with life's ups and downs.[92] Exhibiting emotional resilience doesn't make stress magically disappear, but it allows a person to acknowledge problems and manage adversity. It also requires a strong sense of self-awareness.

Someone being able to name their feelings and adopt helpful strategies to manage their emotions is a lifelong exercise. Maintaining a positive outlook and gratitude for life are key components.

Another key component is having a strong support network. One of my favorite prompts to ask people on dates used to be "Tell me more about your friends." Friendships can provide a sense of community that in turn strengthens resilience by providing perspective and feedback.

ASK MATCHMAKER MARIA

I worry about my own resilience after surviving narcissistic abuse in a previous relationship. How can I work on that for myself?

I've seen how heartbreakingly common this journey is, and I want you to know that you're not alone in this. Many have walked this path and emerged stronger—including me. You can, too, now.

According to clinical psychologist and narcissism expert Dr. Ramani Durvasula, it is possible to build resilience after narcissistic abuse, which is rooted in grandiosity, a lack of empathy, a chronic sense of entitlement, and a chronic need to seek out admiration and validation from other people.

That person's hurtful behavior had everything to do with them, and nothing to do with you, your actions, or your value. You're an amazing person who deserves kind love. Dr. Durvasula emphasizes the need for radical acceptance for survivors. Recognize that the narcissist won't change—and reclaim your identity. Remove your ex from all parts of your life, and surround yourself with a strong support system. Prioritize healthy relationships and confidently embrace the nonlinear journey of healing.

Do You Share the Same Reality and Moral Compass?

We've spoken a lot about sharing the same reality as your partner. This goes hand in hand with sharing a moral compass. Your moral compass is your personal set of beliefs and values regarding right and wrong. Morals are dynamic and will change throughout your life as you gain knowledge, meet new people with different experiences from your own, and cope with adversity.

When it comes to, say, politics, do you believe in the same essential truths—even if your solutions or opinions on those truths differ? We talked about this way back in chapter 3: It's really hard to build a life with someone who doesn't live in the same reality. Someone who believes the 2020 election was stolen will have a hard time partnering with someone who doesn't. Not only because of disagreements, but because they'll constantly be rolling their eyes at each other.

Are Your Conflict-Resolution Styles Compatible?

When they speak to you, are they speaking to you in a constructive manner? Or is it a more demeaning or criticizing manner?

According to Dr. John Gottman of the Gottman Institute, the biggest indicator of a couple's success is not whether they argue, it's how they argue.[93] Conflict is inevitable in relationships, which means a couple's ability to find their way through disagreements will determine their long-term success. Employing strategies like active listening, taking responsibility, and working on solutions together will only strengthen a relationship.

Are They Reliable?

Only commit to the rest of your life with someone who is dependable—and proves that through actions over words. Maybe they're not the best texter. Every generation before managed to build decades-long, strong marriages without the ability to text. It's not the bedrock of a good marriage. But maybe they video-chat with you every day? Or you get a phone call every night that you're not together. That is worth more than any "LOL" blue bubble.

Have You Discussed What You Need to Unlearn?

No matter how great your upbringing was, there is more than likely *something* you need to unlearn from your parents. One friend of mine had a picture-perfect childhood and her parents have been married for nearly four decades. But even she needed to unlearn the idea that one's romantic relationship should be the only important relationship in one's life, as her parents modeled for her. So ask your partner what they're trying to unlearn from their upbringing—and share what you're working on from your own life. So much of long-term incompatibility comes from the core triggers that were—often unconsciously—seeded in us as children, from our caregivers. Unearthing those now and talking through them will only bring you closer.

Do Your Future Goals Match Up?

Do you two have the same milestones you're expecting and are excited about? Have you talked about how you'll react to the financial curveballs that inevitably come with time? What happens when your kid, if you choose to have one, gets sick? Tackling inevitable questions like this early in the relationship helps stamp out resentment at the root.

For instance, if you are indeed considering having children, do you agree on childcare plans, education, and extracurricular plans? What about saving to pay for their college education one day? What lifestyle are you living when you know the answers to the above?

How about eldercare? Most of us have parents that will need someone to care for them as they become less independent. Does that responsibility fall on you? A sibling? An eldercare facility? Can you afford an eldercare facility? How much is your lifestyle affected when your emotional bandwidth is spent caring for someone?

Do you want to buy a house? Do you envision combining or splitting your finances? How do either of those options make you feel? How do you envision money and its role in your relationship? My favorite example of sharing financial values comes from an Anthony Bourdain clip from 2018. No, this moment doesn't revolve around a romantic relationship, but I still hold it close to my heart—and a similar conversation could easily occur between two people on a date. In the episode of the late celebrity chef's food and travel show, *Anthony Bourdain: Parts Unknown*, Bourdain could be seen eating with three locals in Singapore and talking to them about how many people in the country have maids.[94]

"Everybody's got a maid, looking after their child at home," one woman said. It "frees them up to join the workforce." However, she also noted the downsides of having a maid, as she claimed that her husband didn't "know how to serve himself water." As she went on to explain that her husband also couldn't do his own laundry, and the rest of her friends agreed that they didn't know how to do laundry either, one of the men in the group asked Bourdain when the last time was that he did laundry, in a tone that sounded like "Come on . . . Like *you* do your laundry?" In response, the chef expressed how much he liked doing the chore.

"I enjoy throwing my clothes into the washer and removing them to the dryer," Bourdain said. "It's a process that makes you feel very satisfied with yourself."

The mood shifted almost immediately. Bourdain and the young locals valued their time and money in very different ways. Quickly, one of the world's most comfortable travelers felt very uncomfortable with a pack of strangers. (Or maybe they felt uncomfortable with him!) Their interaction wasn't the same after that. So are you paired with someone who lives in your laundry world? Because it's going to be very difficult to mix your lights and darks otherwise.

STEP 6: MOVING IN TOGETHER

If you want to get married one day, you should wait to move in with your partner until **after you get engaged**. Yes, I know not everyone does this. And yes, I know some people who don't follow this rule live happy lives over decades of marriage. But this is still my advice to you. I know you will still have some familiar responses, like . . .

"But I want to test-drive this before I commit." You're talking about a human being, not a car. I encourage you to do a monthlong sleepover at each other's houses. Whatever it is that you think you need to learn about someone, you can learn in that time period. Bonus points if your AC goes out on a hot summer day. I promise the honeymoon period will be over by then, and you'll get an honest look at what your lives would look like together. For similar results, go on a vacation together that lasts over a week. Complicated travel or large-scale packing should be included.

"But my lease is up in a month!" Talk to your landlord. Tell them you want to go month to month while you're determining the future of your relationship. The last thing I want you to do is decide who the potential parent of your child is based on the same criteria you would use for a roommate you found on Craigslist. The person you live with (and eventually marry) will have the greatest effect out of *anyone* on your financial, mental, and emotional well-being. You need to choose this person wisely.

"What if they don't clean up after themselves? I don't want to wait till we're engaged to find this out." If this is a partner you're considering moving in with one day, you're going to need to learn how to have conversations about house management and your expectations and theirs. This can be hard at first, and it gets easier.

"Screw it! I'm going to move in with my partner!" Cool! I get it. The financial burden of living on a single income and not wanting to live with a stranger or friend is completely valid. All I'm asking is that you have a crystal-clear conversation about your relationship expectations before you pick up your keys. You should ensure that moving in together isn't being used to stall other relationship milestones. If you're looking to get married and/or have children, talk about your goals for the next three years. Do your intentions match up? Or is someone saying, "We're going to live together, why do we need a wedding?" or "It's still way too early to talk about babies." This isn't a person you should sign a lease or get a mortgage with. You could be legally joining yourself to a time thief, or simply someone who lacks long-term compatibility with you.

But if you both agree on what the future holds for you as a team, by all means—it's time to start planning that housewarming!

STEP 7: PLANNING THE WEDDING

Once you've gotten a ring on your finger—or gotten down on one knee, depending—and feel ready to jump into the wedding-planning trenches, I've got some good news. The total time it takes to plan a wedding shouldn't take **more than a month**. But the process of preparing, finding a venue, and finalizing guest lists obviously takes a lot more time. So you should be in this stage for about **six months to a year**. If you're two years engaged and you haven't seen any active movement toward marriage, you should start asking questions about the timeline. Something is amiss.

My husband proposed in February 2015. We had our civil wedding in New York City by December 2015. We wanted our life to begin. (I also wanted his health insurance!) Then, in July 2016, we had our big wedding in Athens. I always consider our New York wedding the one that was for us, and our Greek wedding the one that was for everyone else. And I love both of them with my whole heart.

Now that you're equipped to understand a generally fair timeline for your next relationship, you can decide what parts of my advice work for you—and what parts you want to adjust for your own love story. I don't care that you follow my rules to the letter. I care that my rules help you create the greatest romance of your life. Each of us is on our own journey to meet our special someone, and your steps, whether they look just like mine or not, are valid. As long as you're considering where you've been in a relationship and where you hope to go, I'm happy. What matters is that you understand what an initial *eros* love looks like, and what it takes to transition to an *agape* kind of love. The love that I wish for all my clients and friends—and the kind of love I'm willing to tell people to hold out for if they haven't found it yet.

12

I'M HEARTBROKEN. WILL I EVER GET OVER MY LAST BREAKUP?

A WOMAN CALLED ME RECENTLY. She wanted to get my perspective on her most recent breakup. She told me all about the guy she was just dating. "He checked off all the boxes," she lamented. I asked her what those boxes were. He lived near her in Philadelphia. His place was in the city, and she was a mere twenty minutes away in a suburb. He was just six months older than her. He worked as an accountant. A month into dating, he asked her to be his girlfriend. I didn't have the heart—yet—to tell her those were all surface-level details. A lot of men, in fact, lived within a twenty-mile and one-year-age radius. And many of those men worked in some field related to numbers.

And then she took a deep breath to tell me the rest, the stuff that really gave me an inside look into the relationship. "Well, he always had to control how we spent time together," she began. "In the six months we dated, he only visited my apartment five times. I was always taking Ubers into the city." I asked why he couldn't come to her in the burbs. "He has a dog and said he doesn't ride well," she quickly replied. So how often was she trekking to the heart of Philly? Were there sleepovers? How did the guy make her feel? "I would come in three times a week, and I'd sleep over most Saturdays. But once it was Sunday morning, I felt the pressure to get out," she said. "He'd urge me to get ready because he wanted to drive me home before he went to the gym."

I exclaimed, "Wait . . . he drives, but you paid for Ubers three times a week?!"

"Yes, and most dates we went on, we paid fifty-fifty."

She continued telling me about her relationship history with this man. Most dates revolved around his neighborhood and what he wanted to do. But he had brought her to meet his parents, and he had met hers. They had made plans to go to Italy for a wedding in four months. Yet when she wanted to go away for a weekend with him, he dragged his feet. He didn't want to reveal which days he would be available for a romantic little jaunt. Finally, once they finally did schedule a trip to New York, he decided to torpedo the relationship. In the middle of packing their bags for what should have been a dreamy excursion to the Big Apple, he broke up with her. Apparently, he didn't see a future.

As she told me this story, I started to map where they individually fell across the five pillars of compatibility. I could picture where they were a match, and where there was a yawning chasm between them. She felt physically attracted to him and they were on the same wavelength. Their dates were enjoyable and they could hold lengthy conversations.

However, at no point in our conversation did she ever mention their emotional connection, or how they supported each other. She definitely didn't give any examples of feeling supported *by* him. It also became clear that they lacked mutual respect. She could easily explain away his cold behavior, but it didn't sound like he recognized all the effort she was putting into their connection. The Uber payments alone!

I assured her that the breakup was a blessing. I explained that her person would have been enthusiastic to spend the "day" portion of Sun*day* with her. She wouldn't feel rushed to exit that person's life just so they could get on with the parts of it they actually valued (in her ex's case, getting to the gym). He would maybe even ask if she wanted to join his gym, so they could work out together. The right person would want to drive over to her neighborhood for dates. They would look forward to a weekend away. They wouldn't avoid revealing when they would be free for such a trip—they would enthusiastically want to plan one with her as soon as their schedule allowed. They would also prioritize that quality time as much as any other valued portion of their world.

Sadly, she had ended up dating someone who was looking for what I like to call the girlfriend experience—the luxury of sex with romantic exclusivity and companionship on their own (often selfish) terms. Someone who receives the girlfriend experience gets to avoid the emotional duty, compromise, and general responsibility of a relationship . . . while getting all the perks. In this guy's case, he was awarded wonderful company at all the best bars and restaurants in his neighborhood. He even had the possibility of securing a travel buddy to subsidize half the costs of a European vacation for a friend's wedding. Although he ultimately passed on that part of the equation, the attractive offer initially was on the table.

My caller thought her list of checked boxes described a catch. I told her that list was actually incomplete. I leaned into helping her identify what kind of person deserved her time. Some people, like her ex, wanted to keep her around as a useful placeholder. Other people wanted to invest in her as a partner. Those were the people I wanted her to pursue. And everyone else? They could go right in the bin.

There's a good chance you picked up this book feeling a lot like my caller. You might be in desperate need of a full dating-mindset reboot, just like she was. And that desire tends to arise after a big breakup. Sometimes I feel like this chapter should have been chapter 1, but I placed it here rather than at the beginning because I thought it needed to come after you've learned everything you need to know to get into a Matchmaker Maria–approved relationship. Sometimes people do all the right things, take all the right steps . . . and things still don't work out. Your partner isn't actually *your person*.

And that's okay. In fact, it just might be a good thing. Whether you've recently broken up with someone, are the one who's been broken up with, or are simply still smarting after a long-ago heartbreak, I want you to know all these feelings are valid. I'm here to help you get through whichever period you're in and come out the other side a happier and more healed person. The kind of person who is ready to build a great life with the right partner.

Each time I speak to someone looking for dating help, I ask them about their last relationship. How long did it last? How did you feel? How did you break up—and why did you break up? Their answer usually starts out really positively. And then it'll turn. They'll say something like "Well, the warning signs were there and in hindsight I can see that I ignored them." Or "I always felt really anxious." There are almost always red flags beforehand, and people who break up almost always ignore them until it's too late.

Sound familiar?

During an episode of my podcast, a woman called in to talk about her relationship woes. Let's call her Sarah. Sarah's bartender boyfriend had been saying he wanted to get a new job and move out of his parents' house. But he wasn't actually applying for jobs or apartments. In response, Sarah had been sending him listings for both, and watching him let those opportunities pass him by. She asked me if she should give him another chance.

For whatever reason, this triggered a memory I had from college. Back then I was dating a guy who loved to talk about his ambitions. He swore that one day he would get additional degrees and a slew of high-paying jobs. The potential for greatness. I was hooked.

A few weeks later, I wanted to go to a big party. He said he couldn't because he had to write a paper. I don't know how, but suddenly I was writing his paper for him. *I also* had a paper due for the exact same class. Did we go to the party? No. Throughout our relationship, I found myself constantly trying to help him reach his potential so his high ambition could meet mine. The problem was, of course, that he was all talk. So when my hard work ethic would be rewarded with a job opportunity or an early graduate school acceptance, he would grow upset or downplay my achievements. We would end up fighting. It was so exhausting! (And in hindsight, I recognize that I was likely dating a narcissist, but I digress.)

So I asked Sarah if she had ever wrote her friends' papers during college. Of course she had. It quickly became clear: Sarah loved dating people who were projects. Many, many of my clients—especially my women clients—deal with some form of "I can fix them!"-ism. So many of us are raised to be caretakers and put others' needs far above our own. So it's only natural that socialization would color how we date and what we think our role should be in a romantic relationship. But Sarah shouldn't have been dating a project (nor should you). She should have been dating a full and complete person.

They broke up shortly after the episode aired.

There is no shame in wanting to show care through service. We just want to make sure it's not a one-way road. This is why I always tell people it's important to audit a relationship while you're in it—and particularly once you're out of one. You might be able to work on this yourself, or you could turn to a therapist for help. But you need to ask yourself some tough questions. At the top of the list? Why weren't you happy in your relationship? What was the true cause of the split? If you want to say, "I don't know," that's probably not exactly true. You do know. Or at least have an inkling of what went wrong. It's time to consider what patterns you may have continued in this situation and want to break going forward. Because once you get to the root of the problem, it's easier to prevent it in the future.

I had to learn that hard lesson myself. In the relationship where I dated a man for his potential, I was deeply unhappy. Yet I didn't know how to get out. I was young and the emotional ups and downs of the relationship had become so complicated that it felt hard to break up. One day, I wrote myself an email and scheduled it to arrive in my mailbox five years later. I asked my future self if I was happy, and begged her, "If you're not happy, you need to get happy. Don't still be in this." Now, years and years later, I know I should have broken up with that man right then and there when I hit "send" on that email. But I couldn't. I wasn't ready. I had to wait six more months until I found the courage and strength to leave. It helped that I did it while visiting my parents.

I snapped out of it, broke up, and vowed I'd never date the potential of a man again. I bet this resonates with many of you.

After that relationship, I decided I would never date someone who didn't think the sun shines out of my butt. And I needed to feel the same way about them. I realized I needed someone who admired the hell out of my personality, temperament, and the manner in which I carried myself. I found that feeling in George. A few weekends ago we went to a club. I heard someone say, "Oh, that's Matchmaker Maria's husband." In fact, that happens to him a lot. At the grocery store. In his Instagram comments. One time in the courtyard of the US embassy in Athens, someone yelled at him from across the courtyard—"You're George! Matchmaker Maria's husband!" It can happen anywhere, really. And he loves it. He smiles and says, "Yeah, that's me!" He knows who I am doesn't take away from the wonderful person he is. My ex-boyfriend, on the other hand, would have gotten angry or offended, and felt wildly emasculated. He would have insisted he wasn't "Matchmaker Maria's boyfriend," but instead, that I had the honor of being *his* girlfriend.

So in many cases, breakups are good, ultimately. They're

natural. Yes, I successfully got into a relationship with my ex-boyfriend. But it was right for me to leave. Because if I had stayed, I never would have been able to build a life with George. And I'm so proud of that life. We're not all meant to go the distance with every person we go on a date with. A lot of breakups are just recognizing that an initial attraction or flicker of possibility doesn't translate into interest in a lifetime commitment.

Now you don't need to break up the moment you feel dissatisfied. Sometimes a rough patch is just a rough patch. Here are some questions to help you decide whether you need to come up with an exit plan. And if you're someone currently processing a breakup, these questions can also help you recognize some important truths about your past relationship.

HOW HAPPY ARE YOU?

I don't believe in absolutes, but you should be about 80 percent happy in your relationship. I know some people might want to be happy 100 percent of the time in a relationship, but that's not possible. The ordinary issues of a bad day at work or a terrible commute will dim your happiness when you walk through the door. Then there are the big things that influence a relationship, like ailing parents or true financial difficulties. And the COVID-19 pandemic showed us we can't even predict the curveballs the world can throw at a couple—ask all the people who realized their relationship was over before lockdown was.

So about an 80 percent happiness rate is realistic, and even good. The remaining 20 percent you can figure out together and supplement the places that might be rocky. That's why you need a vast bank of happy memories, strong communication, and loving support to fall back upon during the difficult times.

If you start to realize you're misaligned on, say, 30 percent of your relationship, it's time to start asking questions. Your outlook on growing a family cannot be part of that 30 percent. If you want to be a parent, this is a core deal-breaker. In fact, if you want to have children and your partner does not, and you still end up having them, it will most likely not be the happy family situation you're imagining. Instead, you may end up raising those kids alone. You may stay together for your children, but it will be difficult to avoid resentment coming from both sides of the marriage, should you wed. On one side will be resentment for having to have kids in the first place; on the other will be resentment for shouldering the core responsibilities of parenting alone.

To start working on that 30 percent—or 40 percent, 50 percent, or wherever you are on the unhappiness scale—you need to start communicating with your partner. I know approaching difficult conversations might be hard. Some people are afraid of what they perceive as conflict. But your conversation may not be "conflict" at all, with all its negative connotations. It may actually be something else entirely: sticking up for your boundaries. To start feeling happier, you should share your expectations and see how your partner responds.

This might be a good time to turn to a couples therapist for guidance. If you feel reticence or even shame about needing to turn to a professional, I'm here to help assuage those feelings. A couples therapist's job is literally just to help you learn how to communicate with your partner. That's an amazing thing.

You would never judge someone for going to a personal trainer to improve their health or a kid for having a Little League softball coach. So why beat yourself up for needing the same kind of help?

DO YOU SHARE THE SAME VALUES?

We talk about values a lot. But misalignment in values is what often leads to long-term incompatibility. It's possible one's heritage, religion, or parental expectations might be impacting those values. But those factors might also turn into issues someone needs to unlearn before they can be a fully present and equitable partner. To understand core values, look at how someone shows respect—and how they accept it. Do you agree on how you perceive justice in the world, or how you understand community? How involved are you in your community and why? Do you both demonstrate kindness the same way? What are your expectations on accountability and integrity? These are the atoms that build up the day-to-day pillars that maintain our lives. You may not think about them often, yet they dictate so much of what you feel and believe. If you have core disagreements with someone on these factors it's very difficult to share a content life with them.

In the early 2010s, OkCupid did so well helping users figure out whether someone shared their values.[95] It inquired into your outlook on children (of course) and drugs (less expected, equally important). You would share how open you were to meeting someone off the app, which is actually an integral way of depicting your intent—are you swiping to date IRL or just looking for the dopamine rush that comes with a new match?

It would even ask you moral questions to determine if you saw the world's problems in an absolute way or a relative way. For instance, it would ask, "In a certain light, would nuclear war be exciting?" An absolutist would say, "Absolutely not." Someone who sees the world in a relative coloring could think, "Well, sure, it would be exciting in a really loose definition of the word, but it would also be terrifying!"

What I'm saying here is that an absolutist may be a good match for someone who also shares their worldview (or at least admires it) and vice versa. The same goes for someone who views things in a more relative light, too.

Misalignment in core values can show up in many ways. The ones I hear about the most as a matchmaker usually are communication and finances. Someone might not feel acknowledged or appreciated. And due to basic outlooks on values, that's naturally a very shaky bridge to cross. Or, when it comes to money, two people might completely disagree on how they value money and the experiences they want to spend it on. It's grueling work trying to plan a life with someone who categorically doesn't agree on where the funds should go.

It's necessary to remember you can share values across cultures. You don't need to have the same religion or ethnic background to align. That's why *My Big Fat Greek Wedding* was so successful in 2002. Yes, Greek American people finally felt represented on-screen when they met Toula Portokalos, played in all her curly-haired glory by writer Nia Vardalos. But the movie also appealed to Latin American, South Asian, and Middle Eastern viewers, along with every other culture that is defined by dedication to big, supportive communities that offer love even when they are far away from their ancestral homelands.

This might sound harsh, but if you realize your core values and your partner's core values are severely misaligned—it's time to break up. I know you may have put time, effort, and love into this relationship. You might be deeply enmeshed in each other's lives and maybe even have met each other's loved ones. A lot of the couples I've seen who get married and divorced quickly ignored the warning signs of misalignment of core values and still threw the wedding. I don't want you to be the next person to deal with this painful—and expensive—experience. So you *and* your partner need to save yourself from a lot of heartache and end the relationship now. In the long run, you'll be freeing yourself up for much happier lives with more compatible people.

ARE YOU CONFUSED?

People sow confusion in a relationship for a few reasons. You will likely need to be direct with your partner about why they are being confusing, and to ask them to stop. You can even be vulnerable and share the anxiety that confusion in a relationship makes you feel. During that conversation, you might realize you're dealing with an avoidant, who is maintaining confusion to avoid emotional intimacy. You might find out you're dating a time thief who is keeping you on the hook out of selfishness. As a worst-case scenario—and I would never wish this upon anyone—you might be dealing with a narcissist or emotional abuser. Or you could be dating someone who doesn't realize they're confusing you and immediately adjusts their behavior to be a better partner.

The only way to learn the truth—and possibly exit the situation—is to start asking questions. This approach is particularly integral in cutting off situations, which are built and sustained on confusion. If someone doesn't want to demystify the relationship status at six months, or claims they still don't know enough about you after literally half a year, it's time to let go.

ASK MATCHMAKER MARIA

Every time we disagree, he ends it. The next day he is back. How do I discuss these issues and end this cycle?

First, you both have to acknowledge that this isn't healthy conflict resolution. At the very least, it's hurtful. At the most, it could be abusive. Frankly, I think you should break up. The person you're dating needs to grow up and go to therapy.

DO YOU WANT TO BREAK UP?

This is really the question to ask yourself. Because if you truly don't want to be with someone, there's no one and nothing that should talk you out of ending a relationship. All other reasons aside, you might just know that this is not the relationship for you. There's no "bad" reason to break up. In fact, I think some people should break up faster. When you talk to people in happy relationships and ask them about previous ones that failed, a lot of them will say something along the lines of "When I dated my ex, we should have broken up six months in, but we kept dating for two years." As soon as you realize your relationship is leading you toward a future you don't want, and nothing can correct that anymore, it's time to say goodbye.

I once had a client who decided he couldn't date a vegan. You might think that's silly—who cares what someone else eats? But, while dating a vegan, he learned their lifestyles didn't actually match up. Veganism, more so than vegetarianism, will impact many facets of your life. It dictates what's in your fridge and what kind of restaurants you frequent— along with the kinds of eateries you never go to again. My client considered himself a foodie. He wanted to experience adventurous eating dates and trips with his partner. Dating someone who had chosen not only to avoid meat, but also milk, eggs, butter, cheese, and even honey, wouldn't fit his life plans.

Eventually, he told me, "We have really different values." He felt stupid in the moment, but relieved in the long run.

***

Once you've decided to break up with someone, I recommend you only do it in a public place* or via phone call. Not only will it keep you from immediately having breakup sex and unnecessarily prolonging the relationship for three months,

---

* This advice does not apply to people who find themselves in an abusive relationship. In that case, you should feel confident in choosing to just disappear. Contact the Rape, Abuse, and Incest National Network (RAINN) and feel empowered to call their hotline at 1-800-656-4673.

but you'll feel safer. You'll also be able to regulate your own emotions, along with the ones of the person you're breaking up with. If you need a script for how to end a relationship with kindness and closure, I've figured that out for you.

All you need to say is, "I don't think, based on my long-term goals and your long-term goals, that we're on the same page. So I think it's time to break up. What questions do you have that I can answer for you right now?" Then, answer as much as you can for them. If they ask, share the ways your core beliefs mismatch, the way your communications styles don't mesh, or the manners in which your life plans diverge. Giving someone the clearest picture of why a relationship isn't working—while still keeping their feelings in consideration—is the best and most compassionate way to help them understand this really is over. You're not going to change your mind or come crawling back in two weeks, or two months, or two years. If they ask to remain friends, be honest. Say, "That's going to confuse me— *and you*." These are very reasonable answers to expected questions. Ask if there are any further ways you can offer closure during a really stressful time.

If someone truly isn't accepting the situation, you might get questions like "Why?!" If you need to, you can be blunt. You can say, "Just because." Or, if you want to give more context, "I don't see this working. I don't want to waste my time or yours, and we should both be committed to finding the right person. We might care about each other, but we're not each other's person." Should they ask if there's someone else, you could answer them honestly. Yet, in the end, that doesn't really matter. You could recenter yourself and remind them, "Other people are irrelevant in our relationship. This is not working for me. It's nobody else's fault." This is your decision.

IS "RIGHT PERSON, WRONG TIME" REAL—OR JUST A PLOT DEVICE FROM ROM-COMS?

As you settle into a breakup, you need to disillusion yourself from the popular narratives that come with heartbreak. Because even if you were the one to do the breaking up, your feelings will be bruised, too. A popular problem I encounter as a matchmaker is the right-person, wrong-time fallacy. You've probably experienced this trap, or someone close to you has. As the name suggests, it's the incorrect assumption that someone you like, but cannot maintain a healthy relationship with, might not be a good fit *now* . . . but could become one at some mysterious, shadowy later date. This is a lie we tell ourselves.

We all live in a four-dimensional world. That includes length, width, and depth in the physical world. Still, there's one more dimension we forget, because we can't see it: time.[96] That's the dimension you're not factoring into your right-person, wrong-time assumption. Let's use New York City streets as an analogy for this line of thinking. In this scenario, you are at Thirty-Fourth Street and Fifth Avenue, sitting pretty at the Empire State Building. The person you're breaking up with (but are convinced could be the Right Person eventually) is all the way uptown, by the American Museum of Natural History on Seventy-Ninth Street and Columbus Avenue. It's Sunday, December 21, at 7 P.M.

Let's jump a year into the future. It's *Monday*, December 21, at 7 P.M. Even if your ex is now at the Empire State Building, who is to say either of you is the same person you were 365 days earlier? Who knows what they experienced on their trek from the Museum of Natural History to the Empire State Building? Even the neighborhood itself could have changed. Did the Dunkin on the corner become a Chopt? Did the arcade across the street shut down? And we're not even accounting for *you* in these questions. Who is to say that you waited that entire year at the entrance to the Empire State Building? At this point, you could be across the river in Williamsburg. You could have taken a taxi to John F. Kennedy Airport and hopped on a flight to Los Angeles. Hell, you could be wearing a bathing suit on the beaches of Paros, Greece, by now. (In December? I doubt it.)

When you break up with someone, you invite the possibility of both of you becoming entirely new people. And it's because you've seen different things, met different people, and felt different things. Even if you haven't fallen in love or dated a new person, you will have grown in ways you could never imagine or maybe haven't considered. Your professional outlook has changed. You've watched new shows and listened to new music. You've both faced different adversaries and come out with new perspectives. Even if you think you'll always be the same person with the same feelings, I promise you that you won't.

And even if the person who broke your heart does decide they want you back four years later, you need to ask yourself if you want them. You might say something like "Well, they're finally going to therapy." Okay, but if someone had to break up with you to better themselves, there might be more cracks in this relationship than you're admitting. Life is long and full of problems. Your partner should be the person you turn to in order to weather the difficult times. It is, in fact, a key part of successful long-term partnership. If someone needs to leave you to better themselves, excel in their career, or whatever else they might say, there's a fatal compatibility problem. This person doesn't want to lean on you. And if they're able to lean on other people like friends, family, or a mental health professional before you, they're probably not your person. Therapy likely won't change that.

Still, people often point to certain celebrities or news stories to "prove" that the right-person, wrong-time phenomenon is real. When I started writing this book, the epic love story of Jennifer Lopez and Ben Affleck was a popular example. Back in the early aughts they were one of the hottest—and most complicated—Hollywood power couples. They broke off their first engagement in 2004, only to rekindle their romance in 2021, after marriages, kids, and public scandals. They wed in 2022, eighteen years after their initial split.

I'm here to remind you each step of this romance made international news. As does every time a pair of high school sweethearts reunites in their sixties. Do you know why? Because it's rare. So don't bank on it becoming your story. "Bennifer" couldn't even bet on it being *their* story. By the time I finished writing this book, they had announced their divorce in August 2024. At least one of my friends left work early to mourn the second death of their celebrity romance. You'll miss a lot of great opportunities with more compatible people if you're waiting for your phone to light up with just the right text message from just The Right Person at The Right Time.

Still, even if you understand that ending your relationship is the best thing for you, that doesn't mean you won't be in pain. Breakups are very, very painful. It's perfectly normal to experience a breakup, feel like you can breathe again, and then be crying into your pillow forty-eight hours later from missing your ex. Depending on the length of the relationship, you probably imagined an entire future with this person—if you didn't already fully share a life together. You're going to experience grief for what could have been and what was. You might experience triggers from the most basic stimuli. Like, if you went to the same bagel shop every Saturday, seeing that place might make you sad. *Bagels* could even bring a tear to your eye.

I once dated someone who was Irish. I was so charmed by his accent and his heritage. But once we broke up, anything that reminded me of Ireland hurt. Living in Manhattan, a city riddled with Irish pubs, was a nightmare. Particularly since men love going on dates in said Irish pubs. I didn't even want to see a pint of Guinness, no matter where I was. Even though I knew we weren't meant to be together, everything that reminded me of him was a painfully negative trigger. It's okay that your pragmatic brain understands the need for a breakup while your heart mourns.

HOW DO I KNOW IF I'M BEING GHOSTED?

There are a few ways of being broken up with. One of them is ghosting. One of my biggest goals as a matchmaker is to reframe the way we talk about ghosting in modern dating. We use the phrase too much—it's lost its true meaning. These days, "ghosting" is used when someone disappears after a few messages on The Apps or following a small handful of dates. That's not ghosting. That's losing interest in someone who is a relative stranger. You do not owe anyone anything if you're gone on two dates with them, and they don't owe you a lengthy breakup text. The lack of communication is the message. It's not the most mature way of ending things with a new person, but it's not ghosting.

Ghosting is when you've established a relationship with someone and they vanish. I'm talking about a lot of dates. Maybe you're consistently casually seeing this person. Maybe they're your boyfriend, girlfriend, or partner. One day you text them . . . and nothing. They're gone, baby, gone. That's ghosting. I would know. I've been ghosted. This was before "ghosting" was a part of the dating lexicon, but looking back, this was a prototypical case. Way back when, I was dating someone for several weeks. We spent a lot of time together. We went on two trips together, and I met one of his friends on one trip. He gave me a lot of verbal affirmation, which made me feel great. We texted, we called, we went on great dates. It was very, very real.

But I also knew he wasn't totally letting me into his world. If this guy's personality was an onion, I was only getting just past the skin. While I was getting more and more vulnerable, he wasn't budging. Like, he wouldn't even tell me his birthday. And I was the one who felt silly for asking.

One Friday, this man went on a business trip to Italy. As he left, he kissed me and told me he would see me the following week, on Tuesday. So when the day came along, I texted him asking when I should pick him up from the airport (yes, I was that good of a semi-girlfriend!). The message was never delivered. When I phoned, the call immediately went to voicemail. Again, ghosting wasn't in the dating conversation yet. I couldn't even fathom the possibility that someone I had been dating so consistently would just delete me from their life less than one hundred hours after they had last seen me—and made plans with me. So I was terrified. I worried his phone had been stolen or that he had been gravely injured. I started calling hospitals in Southern Italy and using what little Italian I knew to figure out if he was hooked up to some IV, dying. No one knew where he was, and none of my calls or texts were going through to him.

Amid my tears and panic, I finally realized I had his email address. Eureka! If he responded to an email, at least, I would know for sure if he was still breathing—or if I needed to send a search party to a foreign country. I told you, I'm a problem solver. I sent him a message, asking him to just let me know what was going on. If he were alive and well, I would appreciate a confirmation for my peace of mind. And if I didn't hear back, I would call his mom to let her know something horrible had happened to her boy. A mere thirty minutes later, I got a two-word email back.

"I'm alive."

The pain of trying to give myself closure was unimaginable. Or, actually, you might be able to conceptualize it. So many of us have gone through this kind of pain, or some related slight. It's devastating. I felt like I shouldn't trust another person again. Heck, I didn't even know if my ex—someone I cared enough about to go to JFK Airport for!—had actually gone to Italy. How could I believe anything another person ever told me? I could feel my heart forming a callus around itself to protect me from all the monsters lurking around the corner. The only thing that stopped that shell from calcifying around me is realizing my ex had done me a favor. He was someone who was always going to hurt me. Ghosting me at such a grand scale proved that fact. But by ending things when he did, I realized he had saved me from so much more future pain.

HOW DO I DEAL WITH A BREAKUP?

I truly feel for anyone in this situation. Whether you've suffered the indignity of a true ghosting, received a lengthy and unexpected farewell text, or had your favorite restaurant ruined with an ambush breakup from someone you're in a committed relationship with—it's all so painful. I'll never forget that feeling of realizing I was being broken up with—the unwelcome rush of hearing your heartbeat in your own ears. That awful moment when it feels like you've been doused with freezing cold water. And by someone you may like (or love), no less. Even if you're unhappy in the relationship—or have suspected something was amiss for a while—it's still an undeniably brutal experience.

However, in this agonizing instant, I want you to feel something else: gratitude. You are being gifted the time to process this loss with the other person. This is your chance to ask the questions that will help you sleep during the difficult nights ahead. Ask anything. Ask everything. All your questions may not be answered, but at least you won't be kicking yourself saying, "Why didn't I think of that!" It's okay to feel angry and sad. This is an upsetting and hurtful experience. But it's also, ultimately, a blessing. You don't want to be with someone who doesn't want to be with you. You're amazing, and your now-ex is only giving you the opportunity to go find someone who sees you in all of your splendor.

As you process your breakup, let's go over some dos and don'ts for this delicate time.

Don't . . .
- call them. That will just reopen the wound. Anytime you communicate with your ex, you'll raise

more questions. The well is endless and you'll never find the bottom.

- expect them to give you closure, if you were the one who was broken up with. They can never give it to you—it must come from inside. Like I said earlier, you can ask questions that will lead to future closure during the breakup (not for weeks and months after). But you're the only one who can ultimately make yourself feel at peace with what has happened. So either that will take time, or you'll learn to live with it never happening. Either is okay.
- get bangs. You'll regret it eventually, if not immediately. You can get a haircut, though.
- be embarrassed if you change your mind. Sometimes we tell our friends, "I'm going to break up with them." And then we don't. Rather than icing out your friends, and isolating yourself into a floundering relationship further, accept that this is your unwavering support system. Let them be there for you now, hold you accountable always, and pick you up when you do finally leave.
- listen to that one Alicia Keys song, "Fallin'." Ever since Alicia crooned that first syllable over twenty years ago, I cannot imagine how many people she has inadvertently convinced to stay in crumbling relationships. (Guilty!)

Do . . .

- acknowledge your feelings, whatever they are. Cry. Feel angry! Particularly if you are the person who was broken up with. That's natural. You might feel like someone else has decided your fate, which is upsetting. But that's proof your ex isn't your person. In the best relationships, decisions are team-based. A big choice was made without you, so you're not a team.

- write a letter getting all your feelings out. Don't send it to them, though. You can share it with a friend or talk it to death with a mental health professional.
- know you might be hurting for a while. It could be a few days, a couple of months, or even years. Sometimes shorter relationships, where you were able to build a fantasy around a person without experiencing the hard, incompatible truths that come with long-term partnership, sting the longest. Sometimes you never shake the heartbreak. But you can manage the pain while also enjoying your life and rediscovering yourself.
- download a dating app when you're ready. For some people that's on the subway ride home from the breakup. No one should tell you it's too soon. Maybe you'll be ready then for a casual relationship over a more long-term one. Either way, wait until you're no longer going to take your baggage out on someone else. That doesn't mean the baggage has disappeared. Just that you're able to balance your very justified emotions with the ability to thrive beside them. And you can meet people whenever, without having to decide the next important romantic fixture in your life.
- get those endorphins flowing. Go dancing. Join a

running club. Go to a comedy club. Try skydiving! Do anything that will get you around people and flooded with happy hormones. You're going to feel a lot better.

- block them. No further explanation needed.

ASK MATCHMAKER MARIA

How do I get over the lost potential of a three monther?

Remind yourself and acknowledge that what you're currently mourning is a fantasy that you made up about how that relationship would look like over time. You probably envisioned couples' costumes at Halloween and meeting your family at Thanksgiving. You probably imagined going on vacation with him over New Year's. All that has been stripped away and you can't get over it. The truth is that short relationships hurt more because we feel paralyzed in our thoughts by the fantasy. Eventually, time will heal.

Breakups are a part of dating. The possibility of them, essentially, is the ticket to the ride of love. It's okay if you need to take a rest from dating after a breakup, or turn to a professional to help you perform a full romantic reboot. More than anything, I hope you know that you're not a failure for going through this. Every relationship is a learning experience, and now you're even more prepared to meet the real love of your life.

You're one person closer to your person.

13

HOW DO I MAKE IT WORK
WHEN I MEET MY PERSON?

THE NEW WORLD OF SOCIAL opportunities you've cultivated throughout this book will probably open you up to an endless array of possible dating options. You're no longer limited to your zip code, and the love of your lifetime can take root anywhere. You're being invited to breast cancer awareness walks in new cities and supper club get-togethers across the US. As I keep telling you, the larger your social circle, the closer you are to finding the metaphorical lid for your pot.

Just the other day, I was looking at a message I received from a graduate of my Agape Intensive course, Fatima. Since classmates tend to maintain lively chats, Fatima wrote to me and all her friends that she had just been proposed to by her wonderful boyfriend. On a trip to Paris. Before she was in a relationship, Fatima had slept with her manifest next to her bed every night, and her now-fiancé checked every box.

On Fatima's first date, she was honest (No games! Be direct!). She told her now fiancé, Colin, what she saw for her future. It just so happened that a lot of Fatima and Colin's vision overlapped. Before meeting Colin, Fatima was worried she would scare a man off due to her living situation. You see, she lived just next door to her widowed mother who needed her attention every day. But she followed my rules and felt confident setting her boundaries. She knew the right man would understand her very understandable family situation. Colin did. Now Fatima was engaged and her mother adored her future son-in-law. Mission accomplished.

I woke up to Fatima's message and had a spring in my step for the rest of the day. Just because I open my eyes to stories like that every day, it never makes it less special. In fact, I screenshot every single one and save them to my phone. My storage is screwed, but my device is literally bursting with love. I wouldn't change a thing. I hope your love story is the next one in my inbox.

But the work isn't done now that you know how to find your match. Maybe, since you opened up this book, you've found your person. Or maybe you're still swiping and socializing until you find them. But either way, I want this final chapter to be our most hopeful. I really want us to visualize what your life is going to feel like once you find the right person. Because merely getting into a relationship isn't the end of your story. It's just beginning. So we're going to talk now like you've just entered the relationship we've been working on creating.

HOW DO I SUSTAIN A LONG-TERM RELATIONSHIP?

What comes next is maintaining and growing that relationship. Great relationships are like group school projects. You will both be putting in effort, and wanting to ace the class, right? Only now, the class will be life, and an A-plus is enjoying a happy one. Thankfully, the work doesn't have to actually *feel* like labor. You'll just need to start implementing certain habits and outlooks to keep your dream relationship a dream relationship.

In my own marriage, we stick to the principle that maintaining perfect equality isn't the goal. A word like "equality" doesn't take into the wider context of living, and the complications that come with it. Nothing is ever perfectly fifty-fifty. Instead, we try to have an *equitable* life that factors in fairness and the ever-changing scales of both our experiences as individuals. So you need to expect that sometimes you'll be the rock and your partner will lean on you, and sometimes they'll be the rock and you'll be the one holding on for dear life. Someone could lose their job. Someone could be going through grief. Eldercare could become a sudden problem. You could become new parents. Hormonal imbalances could turn someone's mental health upside down during postpartum or menopause, or any of the countless other changes that come with being alive. There is always something happening. You should feel safe sharing when you need some extra support.

Even the mundane could trigger a change in the rock/leaner dynamics. When I get my period now I know I'm going to be a lot less sunny than my usual self. So I tell George, "I just got my period. I'm going to be mean today. It's not personal. I cannot control it." Now he knows, up front, that if he notices I'm cranky, there's nothing wrong with our marriage. I still love him. I'm just dealing with the biological stressors that come with being a cis woman. And he's my rock all the way through it.

Although we all deal with down times, there will also be a lot to feel excited about when you find yourself in the new, settled stage of a relationship. You will have a partner for all the fun stuff you've always wanted to do or accomplish in your city. When you've found the right person, you'll have a cheerleader for your exhilarating moments and a shoulder to cry on for your worst ones. You'll be sitting next to the person who brings you the calm I want everyone to have. When I go to bed every night next to my husband, I thank the universe—or whatever magic brought me George—for the serene, grateful feeling of peace that fills my body. It's the same feeling one of my clients once told me she felt the first time she slept with her now-husband. She had spent years covering up after sex. But with him, she finally felt comfortable enough to walk to the bathroom in the nude.

Your life will feel significantly easier.

And you'll have so many milestones ahead to share. There are the ones that may be obvious, like the day you decide to move in together or the moment you both say, "I do." But then there are the less expected ones that are unique to every couple. The silly moments that become years-long inside jokes, and the routines that will only ever be yours.

ASK MATCHMAKER MARIA

I've been with my partner for a while. How do we keep the romance alive?

One of the best parts of a committed relationship is the comfort that comes with it. However, you will also need to make sure you don't get too comfortable. You have to be really passionate and persistent in remembering that dating doesn't stop just because you're committed. Please keep dating. You could do something as simple as a weekly movie night or as extravagant as weekend getaways every four months. George and I swear by our Marvel Monday dates, which have kept us so close over the past few years. We put our phones away. We make popcorn (I'm a jalapeno cheese girl). We hold hands on the couch. If we want to get out of our home, we also go to Topgolf or see a Broadway show as often as we can. Concerts and comedy clubs are a regular part of our social calendar. Once you have a built-in best friend you also like making out with, the possibilities for fun are endless. It ultimately doesn't matter what kind of dates you choose—just that you're going on them. This is the best way to remember you're not roommates or organization partners, tasked with holding up the ever-increasing puzzle that is a complete life. You're also two people in love, filled with the love chemicals that remind you of that truth.

Speaking of fun, it's time to talk about sex (baby). Hopefully, once you find yourself in the right relationship, you will be having a lot of it. Whether you're hitting the sheets regularly or find yourself in a bit of a rough patch, I'm going to pitch something very near and dear to my heart: Schedule sex. Please schedule sex, particularly if you find you have busy lives or start raising children.

I've been scheduling sex since 2020, and it changed my

marriage. Our sex day is on . . . *I'm not telling you!* But, whenever it is, it's one of my favorite days of the week. I spend the day knowing I'm going to get lucky with my husband. We send each other sexy texts, and think about each other all day. Honestly, it gets you going, even when you're miles apart. Then, once we're both home, we prepare for the main event. We both take showers. We light some candles. I press "play" on Maria's Sexy Time playlist, which is—shocking no one who's read this book—mostly nineties R&B. What will surprise you about scheduling sex is the ripple effect it has on the rest of your week. Because the next day is bathed in the afterglow of the night prior. My husband and I are still sending each other hot texts. Only now we're talking about the very real things we've done to each other, instead of the possibility of what could come. And, soon enough, we're only a few days away from our next scheduled rendezvous.

The best part of this equation? You can also have sex outside of your scheduled day or days. In fact, all the hot feelings that come from scheduling sex will end up encouraging you to spend some *quality time* together any day of the week. But no matter what, with scheduled sex, you know you're connecting to your person one day out of the busy, stressful, packed week. You'll be shocked to realize how scheduled sex improves everything else. For George and I, it makes us happier spouses, which in turn makes us better parents.

If you don't feel like you're having the amount of sex you prefer (or even just the moves you like or the level of kink), talk about it! You should be able to discuss intimacy with the person you're going to spend your life with—life is going to send way bigger issues than the kind that arise in the bedroom. And if you realize your issues might be rooted in a physical problem, talk to your healthcare provider. There's no shame in needing help.

As I lovingly look at my husband doing experiments at the kitchen table with my son or watch our daughter dance around the house, I feel so thankful we've put this much effort into maintaining our joy as a couple. By keeping ourselves happy, we're giving a gift to our children that we as a society don't think about enough—happy-parent privilege. When kids have two happy parents, they're set up to succeed, not only in relationships, but more generally in life. They grow up understanding what good conflict resolution looks like and the idea that not all confrontation is a bad thing that should induce stress. They know that talking through the hard stuff can actually improve a situation. They see accountability and what it looks like to truly follow through in a situation, and how those things make everything better for the people around them.

HOW DO I MAINTAIN MY SENSE OF SELF IN A RELATIONSHIP?

My husband can't be everything to me. To be in a happy marriage, I've needed to keep my emotional world ever-growing and diverse. This is the same advice I give to the Greek theater kids at my church (and now, you). If you follow me on Instagram you know one of my great passions in life is coaching them in competition. Although I met many of them when they were in the eighth grade—and continued to coach them through high school—a lot of my so-called kids are now fully grown adults, many with college degrees.

Since they're so new to dating, the advice of a matchmaker like me could change their lives—and save them years of therapy. I'll tell you what I tell them. You need hobbies once you fall in love. Your career may pay for the food on the table, but it's everything *else* that will keep you balanced. An empty calendar leaves a vacuum for anything else to occupy it. It's easy for that hole to be filled with an all-consuming relationship. Especially now that you've learned how to find someone worth partnering with.

But your new crush—or partner—cannot be your hobby. Because what happens when your walking, talking hobby is busy with their own life? What if your hobby has to go on a business trip? I saw this with my own life when I went to college in Athens. When I look back on my big relationship during that era, I realize my boyfriend only had one real interest: running. Traditionally, that's a great form of exercise and diversion. But for him, his hobby ended after about an hour. And it was a very individual practice. So he felt entitled to *my* time for the other twenty-three hours in a day. I was his hobby.

The issue was, he wasn't my hobby. I was in the debate club, which took up a lot of my day. Not only did we have three-hour-long practices each Friday, but I also spent a lot of time preparing and reading up on my debates. I was going to tournaments around Europe for my debates and hanging out with my many friends—from both debate club and *other* extracurricular activities. Debating gave me a bustling social circle to explore. In response, my boyfriend showed a lot of hostility and insecurity around my very reasonable passion and admirably full life. He even told me to quit when I was elected president of my college. Today, I would have told him to buzz off (in much more colorful language). Yet at the time, I didn't know how to respond to being someone's entire world. Being on either side of that coin is painful. At this point, you hopefully know too much to fall into this kind of relationship, but love can always take us to unexpected places.

To figure out if you're susceptible to falling into this tendency, I recommend asking yourself a few questions. You can even apply these to past relationships, should you have them, to consider your usual behavior when partnered. Ask yourself, how often do you talk to your platonic friends? How often do you make time to see them? If your answer is "not that often" to both questions, it's time to shake things up. As an adult, I've ensured I have brunch with best girlfriends every three weeks. In case you were wondering, I'm a huevos rancheros kind of girl. When I'm not downing a chai latte with my girls, we're going to dance clubs and volunteering in our community together.

Should you realize you tend not to prioritize relationships outside of your romantic one, don't fret. And certainly don't emotionally beat yourself up. It's natural when you meet someone you really like that you'll want them to reciprocate those feelings. The easiest way to accomplish that goal often appears to be sharing their temperaments, behaviors, or interests. That's simple mirroring and has been a key component of successful human interactions since we started walking upright. But just because you may suddenly be open to hearing a lot more about Dungeons & Dragons than you ever expected, you shouldn't rearrange your entire personality.

One way to maintain your own life is figuring out what makes you happy now. If being a homebody falls into that category, that's totally okay. You don't need to hike up a mountain or go rock-climbing every weekend to qualify as "someone with hobbies." All you need to do is find something that delights your indoor-kid sensibilities. Why not learn to crochet while you watch your favorite sitcom? Or get really into reading manga, which might also introduce you to a culture outside of your own. You can even play video games, which could probably introduce you to a vast new group of people who share your interest. You could become a regular at your farmers market, or pick up a paint brush and learn your way through the color wheel. When you have hobbies you're excited about, it becomes easier to be curious about a date or future partner's interest . . . without feeling the need to adopt them for yourself.

ASK MATCHMAKER MARIA

I never get to just talk to my partner anymore—there's just so much to accomplish every day. What strategy do you use in your relationship when you feel like this?

Since I've gotten married, I've learned that building your own world can only strengthen your relationship. Dr. Terri Or-buch's *How to Get Your Marriage From Good to Great* inspired this epiphany in my relationship, but you don't need to be married to read it. George and I now follow the book's ten-minute rule, which says that you need to have ten minutes of non-maintenance conversation every single day. As you settle into a long-term relationship you might notice how easy it is to ex-clusively talk about the points that keep a life on track: your job, the apartment or house, the bills, the chores, your upcoming commitments and plans, the kids, if you have them. What you'll notice is missing is either of the people in the relationship—their thoughts, their feelings, what excites them, or what is making them sad.

As a way to live by the ten-minute rule, George and I have been leaning into our hobbies and interests—the things that make us who we are. My husband is an avid comic book collector and fan, so he'll tell me what he's watching on eBay that day. If he wins something, we're both invested in the success. He also loves pop culture podcasts, so we listen to those together and discuss them. On the other hand I'm a political junkie who loves Eurovision, the European singing competition. (In fact, I love it so much, I wrote my master's thesis about it.) So there's a lot to talk about! Should you even share an interest with your partner, you still might manifest it in your lives differently. That's okay! Maybe one of you is constantly reading about the hot new restaurant openings in your city, while the other is perfecting their homemade pizza recipe. Whatever your differences, they'll add excitement to your relationship. Remember, you don't need to be the same person to be compatible. When I consider the couples I really admire, they align on their lifestyle, but not their entire personalities. As we talked about earlier, lifestyle is made up of how you value spending your time and your money. If you can respect and encourage your partner to pursue the topics they love, you're on the right road. When I look at my *theia* Aida (aunt) and *theio* Vasili (uncle), I feel so much joy seeing how fond they are of each other and their interests. My aunt loves taking photos, and my uncle doesn't roll his eyes. He brags about her talent and shows anyone he can how beautiful her work is.

My husband and I approach spirituality in the same way. While we both value that pillar in our lives, it manifests in completely different manners, despite the fact that we share the same religion. There was a time when I would go to church every Sunday and George didn't. For him, as a man who was born and raised in Greece, being Greek Orthodox is part of who he is all the time. In Greece, there's a different holiday or observance every day. So religion feels as much like an identity as it is a practice. There's less of a need to go to a physical church each week to show one's piety. It's baked into the air. However, for me, attending my church is how I find my community—and I always have since I was a little girl. It's the church I was raised in, and now help lead. That's where I go to see my friends, and my parents' friends, who watched me grow up in the church's pews. That space is as much of a home to me as the one I grew up in. That's why I take my own children with me every week. George, witnessing his own children being raised in a Greek American experience, has also become more involved with our community.

Despite our different approaches to our faith, I have never shamed him for not experiencing spirituality in the same way I do. When he doesn't want to come to church, that's his business. Even in marriage, I can't make him behave the way I behave or feel the way I feel—and that's good. That's respect. At most, I can encourage him to follow his interests in whatever way feels right to him. I'll ask him if he thinks he's going to go to service this week, and accept whatever his answer is. Lately, he's been joining more, as my community feels more like our entire family's community. Plus, he gets to dress snazzy on a Sunday morning. It's a win for all of us.

One of the best ways to maintain your own interests is by traveling solo—or, at least, with people other than your partner. As I write this right now, my husband is in Crete on a boys' trip, and I'm in New Jersey with the kids. In return, when I go to Greece on one of my girls' trips that I organize through Agape Escapes, a spin-off of my matchmaking business that facilitates new friendships through adventure, George is the one to take the lead with our family. We allow the other person to enjoy their trip, and text minimal updates. Maybe we'll share a two-minute FaceTime, and wait to get the full voyage recap when we're reunited at home. It's wonderful.

WHAT PITFALLS MIGHT COME UP IN A RELATIONSHIP?

Once you find a relationship worth committing to, and enjoy your own passions, you will start to see your love flourish. So I have another hack for keeping your relationship on the happy track: watching out for what the Gottman Institute, which researches relationships, calls the Four Horsemen.[97] These markers are the first signals that something could be awry in your relationship. The earlier you notice them, the easier it is to maintain a healthy partnership. Let's go over these Four Horsemen and how you can keep them at bay in your own life.

Criticism

Criticizing your partner is different from offering (possibly negative) feedback or voicing a complaint. For example, a complaint would be "I was scared when you were running late and didn't call me. I thought something bad had happened to you. I hope going forward, we keep each other updated on our timing." That would be a very understandable pain point to share with a partner. A criticism, however, would go along the lines of "You don't care about how your behaviors affect other people. I don't believe you're that forgetful. You're just selfish. You never think of others and you definitely never think of me." Do you see the contrast and how differently each might hit a partner? In my marriage, I've noticed my husband might drive a little fast sometimes. Rather than saying, "God, you're always driving so fast, you're not thinking about the safety of our kids," I share a vulnerability and a request and say, "Hey, babe, I get worried when you drive this fast. Could you slow down a little bit?"

Instead of jumping to criticism, slow down. Using personal "I" statements and speaking from the heart help. Still, you're probably going to criticize your partner *sometimes*. It's inevitable. We are only human. But you should try to keep criticism to a minimal level—and acknowledge when you do it with an apology.

Contempt

Contempt arises when someone doesn't feel appreciated or acknowledged in their relationship, according to the Gottman Institute—it also says that it's the top predictor for divorce. When I think of contempt, I picture someone sneering. You're not just expressing your displeasure about something to your partner. You want to make them feel worthless and despised. You want them to feel shame and to know how little you think of them. This is a disastrous approach toward the one person in the world who is supposed to be your teammate. No wonder contempt is one of the single biggest factors in divorce.

Think about a relationship like a tennis match. You're doubles partners and the problems of the world are your opponents. That opposing team could be something small, like housework that's piling up, or huge, like a family crisis. Sometimes your partner in the doubles game is going to miss the ball. It happens. But who is going to stick out a difficult game when their partner makes them feel worthless? That worthless feeling arises from the contempt.

Something people don't realize about showing contempt is that it hurts them, too. In the moment, it might make them feel in control. Especially if someone feels like they're minimized or not respected in the relationship. Exerting control over their partner by making them feel a certain way (in this case, *bad*) could give them a fleeting taste of power. But as contempt erodes a relationship, it hurts both parties.[98] In the tennis analogy, you don't win because you've broken your teammate's spirit. The opposing pair is the one with the trophy. You lose and there's a chance you won't play another game together. That doesn't sound like fun, does it?

I learned this lesson myself after I had my first child. George wasn't able to move from Boston down to New Jersey full-time, so we weren't only in a long-distance marriage—we were long-distance first-time co-parents. I was filled with contempt. I was angry at the situation, but ended up turning that feeling toward George. The stress of the postpartum period (and the wave of hormones that came with it) did not help the situation. When he would come home, he would see me looking frazzled with the baby. And out of kindness and care, he would ask, "How was your day?" That question made me livid.

"Really?" I asked. "You're asking how my day was? How do you think my day was? I'm exhausted."

Maybe you've been in these sorts of situations, too. Your

partner's driving above the speed limit, and you say, "Are you insane?! Why are you driving like a lunatic?" Or maybe you told them they loaded the dishwasher wrong, so they exclaim, "You're so mean. You must really get off on making people feel small so you can feel big."

These statements arise from contempt. And now that we've identified a few, I am so pleased to tell you that there is an antidote to this sort of speech pattern.

When there are difficult emotions, you must make:

1. a clear statement of how you're feeling (I'm tired. I'm scared. I'm sad.);
2. then a request (I'd like for you to spend more time with me. I'd like for you to slow down. I'd like for you to use different words.);
3. and finally an invitation. (Please tell your boss you need a more flexible schedule. Could you go the speed limit? Can we talk in a few minutes after we have had time to cool off?)

This takes practice, but when you're more mindful of how you express your words, you'll get to the core of what the real issue is. Earnest honesty can be the antidote of contempt.

I'll be honest with you, it took us four months to get through that rough patch. I'm still so thankful George gave me the grace to see I wasn't defined by the contempt I was feeling.

Defensiveness

There are a lot of ways to respond to criticism. Defensiveness is the only one that's one of the Four Horsemen of a relationship in trouble.[99] You will know it's afoot when you—or your partner—begins reacting in a way that assumes you're being accused unfairly of something. And rather than trying to fix the problem, you look for an excuse and play the victim.

While scrolling on TikTok the other day, I saw a crystal-clear example of defensiveness. In the video, a mom returns home to her husband and kids from a birthday brunch for her sister. Let's say everyone woke up at 9 A.M. and she left at 10 A.M. When she got back at 3 P.M. . . . nothing had changed. The kids were still in their pajamas and hadn't even eaten yet. The house was a mess. The woman was understandably upset. But her husband didn't apologize. He blamed her. He told her that everything was her fault—she knew he didn't know how to parent the kids on his own, and that was her job. He works all day and should have been able to rest, he claimed. In fact, she should have fed the children before brunch and taken them with her to the event.

None of that should have happened.

In a perfect world, the husband would have taken care of his own children in the five-hour span of his wife's absence. But if that was never going to happen, he could have taken accountability for his actions. He could have apologized. He could have told her she was right—and to leave for an hour. Maybe go get her nails done. He should have promised that once she came back, everything would be fixed.

Rather than giving your partner excuses—or trying to convince them *they're* the problem—you should try to consider whether your defensiveness is only adding to the issue. In that case, go toward the compromise and focus on solutions-based responses over protecting your own ego.

Stonewalling

If someone doesn't show contempt during a disagreement, they may exhibit stonewalling instead. That occurs when someone completely withdraws from the interaction at hand. Maybe they're feeling attacked. Maybe they're feeling unheard. But instead of responding, they turn away. They might start to engage in distracting behaviors like cleaning the house, biting their nails, or picking at their skin. This reaction makes them feel like they have some sort of control over what seems to them like an uncontrollable situation.

I don't know if she's aware of this, but the TikToker Reesa Teesa illustrated stonewalling with her spellbinding tale of marriage with a serial liar.[100] In a series of videos, Teesa described her relationship with a man who faked phone calls with family members, fabricated his job and financial situation, and evaded his wife's questions at every turn. Anytime Teesa seemed to be catching on to the truth of her husband, he had a new lie ready to keep her on the hook. Toward the end of her story, Teesa detailed the exhaustion she felt speaking to someone who refused to be honest with her. Rather than call her husband out or defend herself against the lies, she gave up. She said nothing. She was just trying to get to the end of the day with as little conflict as possible.

But even in the most mundane circumstances (which is certainly not what Teesa experienced), it's important to remember you cannot avoid conflict in a relationship. If you ever feel overwhelmed in a conflict, ask for what you need to feel secure, rather than shutting down. If you ever find yourself in a relationship where you feel like you can't ask for basic emotional safety, go back to chapter 12 and consider whether it's time to leave. But if you do feel okay requesting what you need, I want you to set the boundaries you require for good communication. Ask for a twenty-minute time-out, or whatever feels good to you. Then return to the conflict when you're ready to dig in.

WHAT DO WE DO IF I THINK WE NEED HELP?

If you ever start to notice that the Four Horsemen are at your door, it might be time to go to a couples therapist. I often recommend them to people at the very beginning of their love story, even before they start to notice issues. There's no shame in turning to a professional for help. As we've spoken about before, a therapist will simply teach you how to communicate more effectively as the couple that you are. That's great. Needing guidance doesn't spell doom for any relationship. Instead, should you ever find yourself on a therapist's couch, look at it as proof that you want to do better in your relationship.

One truth to realize as you start to take stock of your relationship is that the only people who ever really taught you how to be in one are your parents. Most of us repeat the mistakes of our parents without even realizing it. So if your father often isolated himself during times of discomfort, it's likely you may also avoid tough conversations in favor of alone time. Or if your mother tended to apologize with bowls of cut fruit versus actual verbal communication, you might think acts of service are the same as saying "I'm sorry." They're not. As we talked about in chapter 12, it's necessary to unlearn certain behaviors that our parents incorrectly modeled as perfectly healthy.

You might think that putting in all of this effort is hard work. It is, but it shouldn't feel painful at all. With the right person, it will feel rewarding. That being said, I'm not going to lie to you, some moments might be stickier than others. For instance, once you become truly serious with someone, the first time you sit down and really talk about your finances might be intense. It might take weeks to get on the same page about what sharing a checking account really means for both of you. That's perfectly normal. Turning two separate lives into one takes a little bit of time and elbow grease. But if you continue to look at your partner with admiration and appreciation, it will make everything feel so much smoother.

After all, improving the communication in a relationship doesn't have to be macro-level work all the time. Instead, you could make it fun and use these conversations as ways to get to know the most important person in your life. Have a night where you just ask each other open-ended questions. Here are some questions I think could really get the conversation flowing:

1. How do you feel in our relationship?
2. What makes you feel loved?
3. What do you need from me to feel like you're being acknowledged and heard?
4. What kind of gifts do you like to receive? And when do you want to receive those gifts?
5. When it's your birthday or a holiday, would you rather get a gift like a memento, or would you prefer to share an experience?

6. Considering your attachment style, what's the best way I can support you?
7. For important topics, is there one best way to communicate information to you?

Whenever you have these chats, really listen to the responses. At this point, you should keep in mind that you will want to be acknowledged by your partner—just as they will want to be acknowledged by you. Try to remember their words as best you can. Because after having a deep heart-to-heart like this, it will hurt your partner so much more if you act against the desires they've communicated to you in a really vulnerable and optimistic way. Treasure what they have to say.

After more than ten years and countless thoughtful conversations with him, I've realized George is a visual learner. Therefore, while we were trying to buy a house, I was not just going to send him a Zillow link and hope he got everything he needed from there. He is a person who likes knowing every variable there is before making a decision. So I made him a PowerPoint presentation to get all of my points across. I took into account what we could afford, the location, the pros, and the cons. It all worked out. I finished writing this book from our perfect house; I love our fireplace and all the space our kids have to play. And in return for my consideration, my husband takes my perspective into account. I'm the kind of person who doesn't just want to hear, "I like this." That kind of phrasing feels very meaningless to me. If I do something and George likes it, I need him to explain what he liked about it. That's the only way I'll fully appreciate the words.

WHAT ARE BIDS?

One of the other small ways I keep my own relationship on track is by keeping something called bids in mind. Bids are the basic request to connect and, according to Gottman, "the fundamental unit of emotional communication."[101] Romcoms are filled with the grand-gesture bid—someone running through an airport to profess their love or stop a doomed wedding. But the bids that tend to fill your relationship will be small. They're asking someone about their day or even showing them the meme that made you laugh out loud over lunch. Relationship scientist Logan Ury pointed out that bids are often subtle since it's actually very vulnerable to ask someone you're in love with to pay attention to you.[102] You could be accused of being needy or annoying. While that would never be the case with the right person, anxious minds can twist anything. So you should look out for bids in your relationship in order to make your partner feel seen and special.

Traditionally, there are three ways you can respond to a bid, according to Gottman:

1. Turning toward (acknowledging the bid).
2. Turning away (ignoring or missing the bid).
3. Turning against (rejecting the bid in an argumentative or belligerent way).

To illustrate the differences between bid responses, let's pretend I just got off the phone with my best friend, Arete, as George entered the kitchen. I tell him, "I just had the most interesting conversation with Arete." If George was turning toward, he'd respond by saying, "Oh yeah? How's she doing?" If he was turning away, he'd likely not say a thing as he walked over to open the fridge. If he was turning against, he'd reply, "All you ever do is talk to Arete."

Always try to turn toward the bid. Again, you rarely need to do anything extravagant to successfully accept a bid. It could be as easy as hearing your partner say "Show me!" after you tell them you saw a funny meme. Or "Thank you. Just what I needed!" after they bring you a coffee. Your partner's day could instantly be improved by just a few words. And that's way better than ignoring them as you try to pour *yourself* a cup of coffee.

The Gottman Institute found that couples in the healthiest relationships turned toward a bid 86 percent of the time; so-called disaster couples only turned toward each other 33 percent.[103]

It's turning toward bids regularly that improves communication and connection in the long run. They're the bedrock of making each other feel seen and loved. When bids tend to be turned down or even rejected over time, partners begin to notice. Then, those Four Horsemen will start to manifest in all parts of a relationship. And soon enough, the negative feelings of a rejected bid from Tuesday night will pop up during a Saturday night dinner party. Once this kind of resentment and frustration becomes the norm, a breakup isn't far away.

If you ever realize you have been rejecting bids, or even attacking them, it's likely you will also notice a higher frequency of arguments in a relationship. One trick George and I have implemented to deflate any escalating argument is having a safe word or phrase to instantly add some levity. For us, it's "simple as this." It's a ridiculous line from an adult film—that we never watched, I swear!—that always made us burst out laughing. So if either of us hear it during a disagreement, we have to separate and calm down before returning to the discussion. You can make this totally your own. One couple I saw on TikTok wears party hats when their arguments get too heated. It's impossible to stay quite so mad when you look like you're at a five-year-old's birthday party.

WHAT'S NEXT?

Should you follow all of my advice once you're in a relationship, you're going to start looking—and, more important, *feeling*—very happy. With outward happiness comes the questions. If you've started dating you might hear "Are you two planning to move in together?" or the even more loaded "When do you think you're getting engaged?" Once you get engaged you'll immediately hear "When's the wedding?" and once you've said "I do," nosy people might start asking, "When are you having kids?"

These are inevitably stressful questions. But you don't have to get stressed. You will have gotten into the relationship you want by moving with confidence and using direct communication. Never let anyone take that from you—and don't give away your own power. Instead, direct the conversation exactly where you want it. Start talking about how happy you are. If someone asks, "So, where's the ring?" just say, "I'm really enjoying dating them right now, and I'm excited for our future."

And you really should be excited for whatever is next for you—and I can't wait to see where it takes you.

Because, ultimately, you're on your way to being one half

of the greatest team of your life. You will no longer be a single person. Instead, you're two players converging their lives to become one unstoppable force. That's how I look at my marriage. George and I are on Team Penguin. We have little penguin details all over the house—the kids even have penguin-patterned clothes. If you ever happen to choose a mascot with your partner, please let me know what it is. I'm already so curious.

But being on a team isn't all glory and cute tchotchkes. Teams can never be stagnant. They have to keep growing and improving so they can keep winning their games. Think about the NBA—or WNBA, which I think deserves far more love and admiration. Those athletes never stop, even if they just won a championship and easily could coast into the off-season. They're still working on themselves, trying to be their best. In fact, there *is* no off-season for good relationships. If you keep growing, your love will also continue to grow.

You'll know all of this effort is worth it if you can look at your manifest and confidently, honestly, say the person in front of you matches the words on this page. At this point, I know almost anything you've asked for on that piece of paper is reasonable—if not the very least you deserve. Do you feel comfortable? Do you feel acknowledged? Can you be vulnerable and speak from your deepest truths? Are they kind and emotionally stable? Do you feel hopeful about the future and at peace when you close your eyes every night? If so, congrats, you're really side by side with the person worthy of being called your teammate in life.

As you maintain your team, you'll learn when your teammate needs a check-in. Or when they need you to cover the part of the court (aka the responsibilities of daily life) that they usually manage. That's okay. You will have both built a team together for this exact reason—so neither of you will ever have to shoulder it all alone ever again.

And I'll be rooting for you from the sidelines.

CONCLUSION

WHAT COULD MY HAPPILY EVER AFTER REALLY LOOK LIKE?

NOW THAT YOU'VE ALMOST FINISHED this book, you probably think I'm done surprising you. But I have one last story for you, as a treat for getting here. Did you know I'm heavily inspired by the sitcom *Parks and Recreation*? It really speaks to who I am at my core. Because of course I'm moved by really hardworking people trying to do their best at their jobs, while being kind and thoughtful to the people around them—the people they love. That's the exact attitude I hope to bring to everyone in my own life, including you.

Parks and Rec came out in 2009, which was the same year I became a professional matchmaker. In February 2013, the episode "Leslie and Ben" debuted. Guess what? I fell in love with George in January 2013. At that time, I told him, "I love you and I like you." As I watched Leslie Knope, played by ball of sunshine Amy Poehler, marry her perfect match, Adam Scott's witty, calzone-loving Ben Wyatt, I heard my words reflected back at me. During her vows, Leslie tells Ben she loves him and she likes him[104]—and the rest of the world cries happy tears. I felt like our couple goals were so in sync and I felt so pleased.

This is the feeling I want for you. I hope this book helps you find someone you love, but more important, someone you like. I hope you're pleased with them and with what your life looks like together.

Because it's easy to fall in love. You could fall in love with a great piece of music or a slice of cheesecake tomorrow. A lot of people think they're in love with Andrew Garfield. But they don't know that man! They just think they love him based off of interviews and well-lit red-carpet photography. You can even love someone you actually know, based on a few perfect interactions. But people don't divorce for lack of love. In my experience, they call divorce lawyers due to a lack of like.

Hopefully you know by now what you like, and what is likable about you. To be the kind of person who is likable enough to warrant another person wanting to hitch their life to you for decades is to do likable things. It means listening and engaging in meaningful conversations. To want to laugh with another person—and not make them the joke. To respect opinions and boundaries, but also to know and share your own honestly. To consider other people's feelings and know how your own are influencing your behavior. To be dependable and trustworthy, the kind of person someone can count on.

Like is what keeps relationships together. I hope I've taught you enough for your next one to maintain the ebbs and flows of what the world will inevitably throw at you.

As a professional matchmaker, I have dedicated my career to understanding the intricacies of human connection, the art of pairing people, and the ever-evolving landscape of modern dating. In these pages, I have shared the rich history of matchmaking, not just from my personal experience but also through the lens of my family heritage and Greek mythology. I've delved into how pop culture and contemporary dating trends have shaped our behaviors, influencing the way we approach relationships today. You know more about me, and the way I see the world, than some of my closest friends.

Together, we have explored the red flags that can signal potential pitfalls and how to avoid them. It feels like we went on an archaeological dig through the most treacherous of emotional jungles together.

As you navigate the world of dating after reading this book, my hope is that you find the confidence to embrace new opportunities and the wisdom to make meaningful connections. I believe in the power of love and the beauty of finding someone who complements your life.

I hope this book continues to be a companion on your journey to discovering love, and may you feel the same pleasure in meeting each new person as I have felt in sharing this journey with you.

Because it's been a pleasure to meet you through the pages of this book. I don't know if you're aware of this, but when Greek people meet one another for the first time, they say, "*Harika poly.*" That's also what you say the first time you tell them goodbye. It translates to "Pleased to meet you." It conveys a sense of politeness, friendliness, and a positive attitude toward the encounter. This phrase is commonly used in social and professional settings to express goodwill and a welcoming demeanor. You should try it in your own life.

After all, *Harika poly* is, actually, one of the most important phrases in my own life.

When I met George during that famed trip to Boston, that was the first thing we ever said to each other. We might have been in a tequila bar 4,917 miles from his hometown in Crete—but we were still Greek. *Harika poly* was a must. As I shared in the book, what followed those words were two whirlwind mega-dates in thirty-six hours (technically, using Matchmaker Maria date math, they were five dates). At the end of those "two" dates, I had to go back to New York City. I was staying with my friend Maria, but George came along to take me to the train station.

Together, the three of us walked to the platform where my train would be. I was hoping Maria would hang back and give me a moment alone with George. I really wanted to kiss him again before I left. He was so cute and I was so excited about him. She was oblivious. God love her.

So we all stood there together, finishing up some awkward conversation. I have no idea what we talked about, but I remember in vivid detail how much I wished I was smooching George instead. *Blah, blah, blah,* awkward pause. The conductor yelled out, "All aboard!" I wasn't going to kiss some new guy in front of Maria. She was also my employee. This was it—I had to go. So I stuck out my hand to George and said . . . "*Harika poly.*" Firm and polite. What else could I have done?

And I was gone. As I sped back to New York, I popped on some music and looked out the window. I felt happy. I had butterflies, and none of them were born from anxiety. If George and I were a weekend romance, so be it. It was a beautiful weekend romance. But I sincerely hoped it wasn't. One hundred weekends together sounded pretty nice instead.

So I patiently waited for George to text me back. Show me a sign this could be something. I was buzzing . . .

. . . George was not. Back in Boston, he was so disappointed. "*Harika poly?* Did I just get friend-zoned?" he asked himself. He was convinced that I had given him the kindest brush-off of all time. "Was this *just* a weekend romance?" he thought. "Fine—I'm not going to text her."

Now don't worry. This is a love story, remember? His strike lasted two hours. In that time, he joined Maria for a little shopping. She asked George to help her pick a dress and he took a photo of her with his phone. When he got home, he used that photo as an excuse to text me. "Look at what Maria bought for that event you're going to."

I responded right away. One text became endless texts, back and forth. Those texts converted to video-chatting. He went to Crete the next day, and we video-chatted while he was there. I remember he was in his village, where there is limited Wi-Fi. He didn't let the gods of technology stop him. He would contort himself on the balcony to use the neighbors' Wi-Fi, just so he could see my face over video chat for at least an hour each day.

Soon enough, as you know, we started dating.

What you don't know is that two years later, just a few days before Valentine's Day, I hosted one of my Love Lockdown parties. You know, the one I mentioned back in the intro—where all the women get locks and the men get keys. Find your match! This time, Boston Maria and *another* Maria—the same two Marias I had once tasked with helping find my husband—were now helping me host this singles mixer.

I didn't know this, but George was coming.

He managed to hop on the last train out of Boston before a snowstorm effectively shut down the city. When he entered the party midway, I was genuinely so surprised. And then the even bigger surprise hit. He proposed, in front of the Marias and a bunch of strangers. And I said yes, obviously.

Sadly, I have no video or photographic evidence of this major milestone because one Maria was in the bathroom and the other Maria was encouraging the singles to get to mingling. In their defense, George never told them when he was going to do it. Even now, he continues to surprise me.

Fast forward to July 30, 2016, my wedding day. The scene is the church in Voulgiameni, a coastal suburb of Athens. In our religion, the wedding ceremony isn't what you've seen in American rom-coms. First, the guests arrive. They stand outside the church because, as custom dictates, the first people to enter the church for a wedding must be the bride and groom. Then George arrives, and everyone claps upon his arrival. Because, in Greek culture, George simply showing up *is* his "I do." He doesn't need to say it. As I pull up to the church, decked out in all my wedding finery in the Mediterranean heat, I see George from inside the car. He's holding my bouquet. Again, another custom. The groom gives the bride her bouquet as his offering.

Once I emerge, everyone starts to clap again. Me showing up is *my* "I do." My dad is standing to my left, and my mom to my right, and they both walk me to my groom. I'm smiling ear to ear and George is, too. I try to take a picture in my mind, to hold on to it in preparation for whatever comes in the ensuing years. "This," I tell myself, "this is the happiest day of your life. Don't forget it."

George hands me my bouquet, and I lean in to give him a kiss.

George takes two steps back.

He sticks out his hand.

And he says, "Harika poly."

And now I say to you, *Harika poly.*

ACKNOWLEDGMENTS

As I reflect on the journey of writing this book, I'm reminded of the strength and generosity of my circle—the people who championed every page and draft alongside me. Your support has been my foundation, and without you, this book would not be here.

To my editor at St. Martin's, Sallie Lotz: You are my lighthouse. From our very first meeting, I knew you would hold a special place in my life. In many ways, we're the perfect match—just like the couples in this book. You saw the potential in these pages and believed I could bring them to life. That's why I chose you as my dream editor, hoping you'd choose me back. Thankfully, you did, and these pages are proof of our book-love story.

To the entire SMP team who worked on this book, Anne Marie Tallberg, Joel Fotinos, Amelia Beckerman, Brant Janeway, Sophia Lauriello, Danielle Christopher, Sara Thwaite, and Jill Schuck: Your enthusiasm and encouragement mean everything to me. I am beyond grateful for each quick reply, every encouraging word, and the shared excitement for bringing this book into readers' hands.

To my agent at WME, Haley Heidemann: You are a friend for life. Your straightforwardness, pragmatism, and honesty mirror my own, and I value your insight and partnership immensely. I believe in you as much as you believe in me. I hope this book lives up to your expectations of Matchmaker Maria. Thank you for finding my dream publisher. When I say we wouldn't be here without you, I mean that literally.

To Ariana Romero: I still remember the evening we met, introduced by a friend whose love story I had a hand in. Your warmth is infectious; you're the happiest person I know, and I couldn't have written this without a little of that joy. You've helped me turn *Ask a Matchmaker* into a heartfelt narrative about finding love. Sometimes, I think you're in my mind—but stay as long as you'd like. I'm so glad you're here.

To my husband: You're mentioned in this book at least seventy times, so maybe, you're my favorite. Words like "thank you" could never express what you mean to me, even in Greek. You've been my steadfast support, my biggest fan, and the reason I could tackle this project. Whether you're helping with our kids or simply cheering me on, you love both me and the persona of "Matchmaker Maria." For a lifetime of feeling "too much," I could never explain how much your love has meant. I love you, and I like you, George.

To my sister: Siblings share a history, but as adults, we choose our relationship. Chrisoula, I'm so grateful we chose this closeness. You're my collaborator and friend, the biggest cheerleader in *Ask a Matchmaker* success. Thank you for making me feel unstoppable. I couldn't have done this without you.

To my parents: You've shown me that love is a journey. This book was written during one of the toughest chapters of your own lives together, and I'm grateful for the values you instilled in me. Those values led me to George and our family. I could write an entire book about how much I cherish you both.

To my children: You're young now, and may not fully grasp what I do, but I know you understand I help people find love. I love the way you call me Matchmaker Maria when I'm wearing hearts! I hope your father and I are giving you the example of love that will inspire your own. Until then, stay curious and keep reading. It will only expand your minds and your hearts.

To the Agape team, Louie Felix, Chrisoula Mavrianos (again), Lucinda Luttrell, and Anna Maria Tavanli: Your support throughout this process has been invaluable. Every love story in this book is a testament to our shared commitment. The confidence you have in my dating philosophy gives me faith that the world will believe in it, too.

To my colleagues and mentors, Lisa Clampitt, Laurie Berzack, Michelle Jacoby, April Beyer, Rachel Greenwald, Paul Brunson, Dr. Terri Orbuch, and Dr. Ramani Durvasula: Each of you has advanced the understanding of relationship dynamics and transformed the field of dating. Starting out, I was unsure of my next step, but you made this journey less lonely. I am proud to stand beside you and excited to see the conversations this book will inspire.

To my friends who lent an ear or looked over pages, sharing your real-life experiences, Chrissy Rutherford, Teresa Triantafillidis, Daniel W. Dick, Moschoula Kramvousanou, Erin Maher, Alana M. Variano, Amierah Ismail, Katie Morse, Kristin Gosweski, Amalia Kalogridakis, Mark Greene, Diana Santaguida, Damona Hoffman, Arete Bouhlas, and the

Koufis sisters: Thank you for always picking up the phone when I was stuck, reading over pages, and trusting me with your stories.

To my followers: I still can't believe we're here. Looking back to 2018, when I first started #AskAMatchmaker, I could never have imagined my Matchmaker Maria-isms making it to *The New York Times, CBS Mornings,* and now, this book. Your enthusiasm has empowered me to be honest, bold, and fully myself. Great relationships aren't built on games, and because of you, I've found my voice. Now, go spread the word and help others find the love they deserve!

NOTES

1. Homer. *The Iliad*. Translated by Robert Fagles. New York: Penguin Books, 1990.

2. Homer. *The Odyssey*. Translated by Robert Fagles. New York: Penguin Books, 1996.

3. Coontz, Stephanie. *Marriage, a History: How Love Conquered Marriage*. New York: Penguin Books, 2005.

4. Hodgson, Nichi. *The Curious History of Dating: From Jane Austen to Tinder*. London: Little, Brown, 2017.

5. Bailey, Beth L. *From Front Porch to Back Seat: Courtship in Twentieth-Century America*. Baltimore: Johns Hopkins University Press, 1988.

6. Smithsonian Institution. "The 19th-Century Bicycle Craze." Accessed September 11, 2024, https://www.si.edu/stories/19th-century-bicycle-craze.

7. Susan B. Anthony, interview by *The New York World*, February 2, 1896.

8. Kitts, Thomas M. *The Hollywood Surf and Beach Movies: The First Wave, 1959–1969*. Jefferson, NC: McFarland, 2005.

9. "History of Oral Contraception and Its Impact on Dating." *American Medical Association Journal of Ethics*. Accessed September 1, 2024, https://journalofethics.ama-assn.org/article/history-oral-contraception-and-its-impact-dating/2012-06.

10. Romano, Aja. "The Forgotten History of Video Dating." Vox, February 1, 2021, https://www.vox.com/22262353/great-expectations-history-video-dating-vcr-apps.

11. "How the Internet Has Changed Dating." *The Economist*. Accessed September 1, 2024, https://www.economist.com/briefing/2018/08/18/how-the-internet-has-changed-dating.

12. Khazan, Olga. "How Match.com Digitized Dating." *The Atlantic*, April 25, 2019, https://www.theatlantic.com/technology/archive/2019/04/how-matchcom-digitized-dating/586603/.

13. Doyle, Jack. "In the 25 Years Since Its Launch, AOL Instant Messenger Has Never Really Gone Away." *Smithsonian Magazine*, May 18, 2023, https://www.smithsonianmag.com/innovation/in-25-years-since-its-launch-aol-instant-messenger-has-never-been-away-180980086/.

14. Kennedy, Kate. *One in a Millennial: On Friendship, Feelings, Fangirls, and Fitting In*. New York: Macmillan Audio, 2024: 63.

15. Ansari, Aziz, and Eric Klinenberg. *Modern Romance: An Investigation*. New York: Penguin Publishing Group, 2015.

16. *The King of Staten Island*. Directed by Judd Apatow. Universal Pictures, 2020.

17. Schwartz, Barry. *The Paradox of Choice: Why More Is Less*. New York: Ecco, 2016.

18. Dixit, Avinash K., and Barry J. Nalebuff. *The Art of Strategy: A Game Theorist's Guide to Success in Business and Life*. New York: W.W.Norton & Company, 2008.

19. Fisher, Helen. *Anatomy of Love: A Natural History of Mating, Marriage, and Why We Stray*. Revised Edition. New York: W.W. Norton & Company, 2016.

20. Lembke, Anna. *Dopamine Nation: Finding Balance in the Age of Indulgence*. New York: Dutton, 2021.

21. Cox, David. "Coronavirus: Why Dating Feels so Different Now." BBC News, February 25, 2022, https://www.bbc.com/worklife/article/20201116-how-the-pandemic-has-changed-our-romantic-relationships.

22. Law, Tara. "More People Got Mental-Health Treatment during the Pandemic." *Time*, September 8, 2022, https://time.com/6211734/mental-health-treatment-pandemic-young-people/.

23. Emba, Christine. "Men Are Lost. Here's a Map out of the Wilderness." *The Washington Post*. Accessed September 11, 2024, https://www.washingtonpost.com/opinions/2023/07/10/christine-emba-masculinity-new-model/.

24. "Debating Fresh & Fit—Off The Rails." YouTube, uploaded by H3 Podcast, March 13, 2024, https://www.youtube.com/watch?v=lPlIXTHQsHA.

25. Kahloon, Idrees. "What's the Matter with Men?" *The New Yorker,* January 23, 2023, https://www.newyorker.com/magazine/2023/01/30/whats-the-matter-with-men.

26. Miller, Zeke. "A New Reason to Swipe Right? Dating Apps Adding Vax Badges." AP News, May 21, 2021, https://apnews.com/article/politics-coronavirus-pandemic-technology-health-lifestyle-39e59dc1f6e475fa98a27b115c05b48d.

27. "'I Couldn't Date a Climate Change Denier!' The Couples Who Bond—and Split—over Love for the Planet." *The Guardian,* September 5, 2022, https://www.theguardian.com/lifeandstyle/2022/sep/05/i-couldnt-date-a-climate-change-denier-the-couples-who-bond-and-split-over-love-for-the-planet.

28. "Cosmopolitan Greece Covers." Gallery. Accessed September 1, 2024, https://coversarchive.wixsite.com/gallery/cosmopolitan-greece.

29. Anastasakis, Othon, and Katerina Lagos. *The Greek Military Dictatorship: Revisiting a Troubled Past, 1967–1974.* New York: Berghahn Books, 2024.

30. "The Policy on Gender Equality in Greece-European Parliament." Accessed September 13, 2024, https://www.europarl.europa.eu/RegData/etudes/note/join/2013/493028/IPOL-FEMM_NT(2013)493028_EN.pdf.

31. Fisher, Helen. *Why Him? Why Her?: Finding Real Love by Understanding Your Personality Type.* New York: Henry Holt and Co., 2009.

32. Tiffany, Kaitlyn. "The Woman Who Made Online Dating into a 'Science.'" *The Atlantic,* October 27, 2023, https://www.theatlantic.com/technology/archive/2022/12/helen-fisher-science-online-dating-apps-tinder/672419/.

33. Coontz, Stephanie. *Marriage, a History: How Love Conquered Marriage.* New York: Penguin Books, 2005.

34. Janega, Eleanor. *The Once and Future Sex: Going Medieval on Women's Roles in Society.* New York: W. W. Norton & Company, 2024.

35. Porter, Tony. *Breaking Out of the Man Box: The Next Generation of Manhood.* New York: Skyhorse Publishing, 2016.

36. Greene, Mark. *The Little #MeToo Book for Men.* New York: ThinkPlay Partners, 2018.

37. Mulvey, Laura. "Visual Pleasure and Narrative Cinema." *Feminisms,* 1975, 438–48. https://doi.org/10.1007/978-1-349-14428-0_27.

38. "Victoria's Secret, the Hypersexualized Iconic Millennial Brand, Tried to Remake Itself as Feminist—and Gen Z Saw Right through It." Yahoo! Finance. Accessed September 1, 2024, https://finance

.yahoo.com/news/victoria-secret-hypersexualized-iconic-millennial
-110000464.html.

39. Maheshwari, Sapna, and Vanessa Friedman. "Victoria's Secret Swaps Angels for 'What Women Want.' Will They Buy It?" *The New York Times,* June 16, 2021. https://www.nytimes.com/2021/06/16/business /victorias-secret-collective-megan-rapinoe.html.

40. Body, Jamie. "Victoria's Secret Is Getting Slammed." *Newsweek,* October 23, 2023. https://www.newsweek.com/victorias-secret -slammed-classic-victorias-secret-sexiness-return-1836805.

41. Jackson, Lauren Michele. "The Invention of 'the Male Gaze.'" *The New Yorker,* July 14, 2023. https://www.newyorker.com/books /second-read/the-invention-of-the-male-gaze.

42. Cleveland Clinic. "Weaponized Incompetence: What It Is and 4 Signs." August 19, 2024, https://health.clevelandclinic.org/weaponized -incompetence.

43. Malone, Alicia. *The Female Gaze: Essential Movies Made by Women.* San Francisco, CA: Mango, 2018.

44. Chapman, Gary D. *The Five Love Languages: The Secret to Love That Lasts.* Chicago: Northfield Publishing, 2015.

45. Gottman, John, and Nan Silver. *The Seven Principles for Making Marriage Work: A Practical Guide from the Country's Foremost Relationship Expert.* New York: Harmony Books, 1999.

46. Kelly, Aliza. "A Handy Guide to (Surviving) Your Saturn Return." The Cut, August 16, 2024. https://www.thecut.com/article /saturn-return-what-it-is-what-to-expect.html.

47. Seife, Charles. *Zero: The Biography of a Dangerous Idea.* New York: Penguin Books, 2000.

48. Ariely, Dan. *Predictably Irrational: The Hidden Forces That Shape Our Decisions.* New York: HarperCollins, 2008.

49. "Instagram's Favorite Matchmaker Helped 2,500 People Get Engaged with 1 Tip." Bustle, April 15, 2024. https://www.bustle.com /life/matchmaker-maria-avgitidis.

50. Nissen, Hans J. *The Early History of the Ancient Near East: 9000–2000 B.C.* Chicago: University of Chicago Press, 1989.

51. Fisher, Helen E. *Why We Love: The Nature and Chemistry of Romantic Love.* Clitheroe, Lancashire, UK: Joosr Ltd, 2016.

52. Haller, Karen. *The Little Book of Colour: How to Use the Psychology of Colour to Transform Your Life.* London: Penguin Life, 2019.

53. Ury, Logan. *How to Not Die Alone: The Surprising Science That Will Help You Find Love.* New York: Simon & Schuster, 2021.

54. Gallo, Carmine. *The Power of Foursquare: 7 Innovative Ways to*

Get Your Customers to Check in Wherever They Are. New York: McGraw-Hill, 2012.

55. Lin, Nan. *Social Capital: A Theory of Social Structure and Action.* Cambridge: Cambridge University Press, 2001.

56. Walsh, James D. "You Might Not Be Checking in on Foursquare, but Foursquare Is Checking in on You." Intelligencer, August 27, 2019. https://nymag.com/intelligencer/2019/08/ten-years-on-foursquare-is-now-checking-in-to-you.html.

57. Sharabi, Liesel. "Finding Love on a First Data: Matching Algorithms in Online Dating." *Harvard Data Science Review,* January 27, 2022. https://hdsr.mitpress.mit.edu/pub/i4eb4e8b/release/2.

58. Maria Avgitidis, host, Ask a Matchmaker, season 1, episode 1, "That Episode with the Online Dating Coach Erika Ettin."

59. Siegel, Daniel J. *Brainstorm: The Power and Purpose of the Teenage Brain.* New York: TarcherPerigee, 2015.

60. Steinberg, Laurence. *Age of Opportunity: Lessons from the New Science of Adolescence.* Boston: Mariner Books, Houghton Mifflin Harcourt, 2015.

61. Maria Avgitidis, host, Ask a Matchmaker, season 1, episode 1, "That Episode with the Online Dating Coach Erika Ettin."

62. Oldenburg, Ray. *The Great Good Place: Cafes, Coffee Shops, Bookstores, Bars, Hair Salons, and Other Hangouts at the Heart of a Community.* New York: Marlowe & Company, 1999.

63. "An Epidemic of Loneliness." The Week, January 6, 2019. https://theweek.com/articles/815518/epidemic-loneliness.

64. Uda, Rachel. "In Such a Connected World, Why Are We Lonelier than Ever?" Katie Couric Media, February 6, 2023. https://katiecouric.com/health/mental-health/why-are-americans-lonelier-pandemic-social-media/.

65. Weissbourd, Richard, and Chris Murphy. "We Have Put Individualism Ahead of the Common Good for Too Long." *Time,* April 11, 2023. https://time.com/6269091/individualism-ahead-of-the-common-good-for-too-long/.

66. Coontz, Stephanie. *The Way We Never Were: American Families and the Nostalgia Trap.* New York: Basic Books, 2016.

67. Weissbourd, Richard, and Chris Murphy. "We Have Put Individualism Ahead of the Common Good for Too Long." *Time,* April 11, 2023. https://time.com/6269091/individualism-ahead-of-the-common-good-for-too-long/.

68. Rusk, David, Anthony Downs, Caroline O. N. Moser, Victoria Yan Wendy Edelberg, Elaine Kamarck William A. Galston, and Simon

Hodson Tara Watson. "'Third Places' as Community Builders." Brookings, July 13, 2023. https://www.brookings.edu/articles/third-places-as-community-builders/.

69. "Teens Need Malls. Malls Need Crowds. Why Are They Pushing Kids Away?" *The Guardian*, December 5, 2023, https://www.theguardian.com/lifeandstyle/2023/dec/05/teens-need-malls-malls-need-crowds-why-are-they-pushing-kids-away.

70. Galloway, Scott. "Losing My Religion." No Mercy / No Malice, September 22, 2023. https://www.profgalloway.com/losing-my-religion/.

71. "Trapped: The Secret Ways Social Media Is Built to Be Addictive (and What You Can Do to Fight Back)." BBC. Accessed September 12, 2024, https://www.sciencefocus.com/future-technology/trapped-the-secret-ways-social-media-is-built-to-be-addictive-and-what-you-can-do-to-fight-back.

72. Avin, Chen, Hadassa Daltrophe, and Zvi Lotker. "On the Impossibility of Breaking the Echo Chamber Effect in Social Media Using Regulation." *Nature News*, January 11, 2024. https://www.nature.com/articles/s41598-023-50850-6.

73. "A New Global Gender Divide Is Emerging." *Financial Times*. Accessed September 12, 2024. https://www.ft.com/content/29fd9b5c-2f35-41bf-9d4c-994db4e12998.

74. Murthy, Vivek Hallegere. *Together: The Healing Power of Human Connection in a Sometimes Lonely World*. New York: Harper Collins Publishers, 2020.

75. Cacioppo, John T., and William Patrick. *Loneliness: Human Nature and the Need for Social Connection*. New York: W. W. Norton & Company, 2008.

76. Cleveland Clinic. "How Loneliness Can Impact Your Health." September 12, 2024. https://health.clevelandclinic.org/what-happens-in-your-body-when-youre-lonely.

77. Cleveland Clinic. "Stress Sickness: Stress and Your Immune System." June 27, 2024. https://health.clevelandclinic.org/what-happens-when-your-immune-system-gets-stressed-out.

78. Bretherton, Inge. "The Origins of Attachment Theory: John Bowlby and Mary Ainsworth." *Developmental Psychology* 28, no. 5 (1992): 759–775.

79. Levine, Amir, and Rachel Heller. *Attached: The New Science of Adult Attachment and How It Can Help You Find—and Keep—Love*. New York: TarcherPerigee, 2010.

80. Ainsworth, Mary D. S., Mary C. Blehar, Everett Waters, and

Sally Wall. *Patterns of Attachment: A Psychological Study of the Strange Situation*. Hillsdale, NJ: Lawrence Erlbaum Associates, 1978.

81. Hazan, Cindy, and Philip Shaver. "Romantic Love Conceptualized as an Attachment Process." *Journal of Personality and Social Psychology* 52, no. 3 (1987): 511–524.

82. Arriaga, X. B., and M. Kumashiro (2019). "Walking a Security Tightrope: Relationship-induced Changes in Attachment Security." *Current Opinion in Psychology*, 25, 121–126. https://doi.org/10.1016/j.copsyc.2018.04.016.

83. Girme, Y. U., C. R. Agnew, L. E. VanderDrift, S. M. Harvey, W. S. Rholes, and J. A. Simpson. "The Ebbs and Flows of Attachment: Within-Person Variation in Attachment Undermine Secure Individuals' Relationship Wellbeing across Time." *Journal of Personality and Social Psychology*, 114, no. 3 (2018): 397–421. https://doi.org/10.1037/pspi0000115.

84. Griffiths, Emmy. "Hypergamy: Everything You Need to Know About the Dating Phenomenon." *Cosmopolitan*, August 25, 2023. https://www.cosmopolitan.com/uk/love-sex/relationships/a45592448/hypergamy-definition/.

85. Almås, Ingvild, Alexander W. Cappelen, and Bertil Tungodden. "The Economics of Hypergamy." *Journal of Human Resources*, 58, no. 3 (2023): 741–773. https://muse.jhu.edu/article/862236.

86. Birger, Jon. *Dateonomics: How Dating Became a Lopsided Numbers Game*. New York: Workman Publishing, 2015.

87. Pew Research Center. "What's Behind the Growing Gap Between Men and Women in College Completion?" November 8, 2021. https://www.pewresearch.org/short-reads/2021/11/08/whats-behind-the-growing-gap-between-men-and-women-in-college-completion/.

88. Brown, Brené. *Daring Greatly: How the Courage to Be Vulnerable Transforms the Way We Live, Love, Parent, and Lead*. New York: Gotham Books, 2012.

89. Fisher, Helen. *Why We Love: The Nature and Chemistry of Romantic Love*. New York: Henry Holt and Company, 2004.

90. Fisher, Helen. *Anatomy of Love: A Natural History of Mating, Marriage, and Why We Stray*. Revised Edition. New York: W. W. Norton & Company, 2016.

91. Ackerman, Joshua M., Vladas Griskevicius, and Norman P. Li. "Let's Get Serious: Communicating Commitment in Romantic Relationships." *Journal of Personality and Social Psychology* 100, no. 6 (2011): 1079–1094. https://doi.org/10.1037/a0022412.

92. Southwick, Steven M., and Dennis S. Charney. *Resilience: The Science of Mastering Life's Greatest Challenges*, 2nd ed. Cambridge: Cambridge University Press, 2018.

93. Gottman, John, and Nan Silver. *The Seven Principles for Making Marriage Work: A Practical Guide from the Country's Foremost Relationship Expert*. New York: Harmony Books, 1999.

94. "Singapore." *Anthony Bourdain: Parts Unknown*. Season 1, episode 10. October 1, 2017.

95. Rudder, Christian. *Inside OkCupid: The Math of Online Dating*. TED-Ed, 2021. https://ed.ted.com/lessons/inside-okcupid-the-math -of-online-dating-christian-rudder.

96. Kennedy, J. B. *Space, Time and Einstein*. Montreal: McGill-Queen's University Press, 2003.

97. Gottman, John. *What Makes Love Last?: How to Build Trust and Avoid Betrayal*. New York: Simon & Schuster, 2013.

98. Lisitsa, Ellie. "The Four Horsemen: Contempt." The Gottman Institute. Accessed September 1, 2024. https://www.gottman.com/blog /the-four-horsemen-contempt/.

99. Lisitsa, Ellie. "The Four Horsemen: Defensiveness." The Gottman Institute. Accessed September 1, 2024. https://www.gottman.com /blog/the-four-horsemen-defensiveness/.

100. Chapin, Angelina. "Who TF Did I Marry? The Viral TikTok Series, Explained." *The Cut*, March 5, 2024. https://www.thecut .com/article/who-tf-did-i-marry-summary-reesa-teesa-legion.html.

101. Gottman, John, and Joan DeClaire. *The Relationship Cure: A 5 Step Guide to Strengthening Your Marriage, Family, and Friendships*. New York: Harmony Books, 2001.

102. Ury, Logan. "Want to Improve Your Relationship? Start Paying More Attention to Bids." The Gottman Institute. Accessed September 1, 2024, https://www.gottman.com/blog/want-to-improve-your -relationship-start-paying-more-attention-to-bids/.

103. Gottman, John, and Nan Silver. *What Makes Love Last?: How to Build Trust and Avoid Betrayal*. New York: Simon & Schuster, 2013.

104. "Leslie and Ben." *Parks and Recreation*. Season 5, episode 14. February 21, 2013.

ABOUT THE AUTHOR

Jolene Siana

MARIA AVGITIDIS is the CEO of Agape Match, an award-winning matchmaking service based out of New York City, and the host of the dating and relationship podcast *Ask a Matchmaker*. For over a decade, she has successfully combined four generations of family matchmaking tradition with modern relationship psychology and search techniques to ensure her professional clientele are introduced to their ultimate matches. As the founder of Agape Match, Maria combines strong intuition with matchmaking methodology to leverage each client's unique personality, style, and history. Countless clients can attest to this success, and their true-love stories are a testament to how Maria has transformed matchmaking, utilizing behavioral science and the unique know-how gained through her four-generation-matchmaking inheritance. Better known as Matchmaker Maria, she has many theories to help people navigate dating, such as her green theory featured on *CBS Mornings* or her Stanley Tucci theory featured in *The New York Times*. Her 12-Date Rule method has helped thousands of couples enter committed relationships. She lives in Central Jersey with her supportive and loving husband, two sweet kids, their very old dog, and her proud immigrant parents in a multigenerational home.